D0475162

# LETTERS TO
# CHILDREN

823 POT

Potter, Beatrix, 1866-1943.
Letters to children from
Beatrix Potter.

| DATE DUE | | | |
|---|---|---|---|
| | | | |
| | | | |
| | | | |
| | | | |
| | | | |
| | | | |
| | | | |
| | | | |
| | | | |
| | | | |
| | | | |
| | | | |

83598

**Siskiyou County
Office of Education Library**
609 South Gold Street
Yreka, CA 96097

## SOME OTHER BOOKS BY JUDY TAYLOR

Beatrix Potter: Artist, Storyteller and Countrywoman

That Naughty Rabbit: Beatrix Potter and Peter Rabbit

Beatrix Potter 1866–1943: The Artist and Her World *(with J.I. Whalley, A.S. Hobbs and E.M. Battrick)*

Beatrix Potter's Letters: A Selection

My First Year: A Beatrix Potter Baby Book

*National Trust Guides*

Beatrix Potter and Hill Top

Beatrix Potter and Hawkshead

T 83598

Mrs Tom Thumb
Mouse Hole

# LETTERS TO CHILDREN

## from

## *Beatrix Potter*

### Collected and introduced by

### JUDY TAYLOR

Mr Brown Esq
Owl Island

FOR
LONDON & PLACES
ABROAD
Next Collection
6.15 a.m.
Hours of Collection.
3.15 a.m.
9.     a.m.
J.     a.m.
4.     p.m.
8.     p.m.
12.    p.m.

# FREDERICK WARNE

SISKIYOU CO. OFFICE OF ED
LIBRARY
609 S. GOLD ST., YREKA, CA 96097

*ACKNOWLEDGEMENTS*

Many people have helped me in the preparation of this book and I should particularly like to thank: Helen Allen; Mary Atwool; Felicity Barker; John E. Benson; Biggleswade History Society (Ken Page); Winifred Boultbee; Dr Robert Burn; Cambridge Central Library (Cambridge Collection); Lucie Carr; Henry P. Coolidge; Sharon Dell; Susan Denyer; Pamela Dugdale; Celia Dunlop; Geraldine Evans; Francisca Fellowes; Dr Lindo Ferguson; Doris Frohnsdorff; Joan Frost; Anthony Gaddum; the late Peter Gaddum (author of *Henry Theodore Gaddum*, privately published 1973); John Gibson; Alan Gill; Gloucestershire County Library; Jackie Gumpert; Beatrix Hammarling; Betty S. Hart; John Heelis; Anne S. Hobbs; Peter Ireland; Libby Joy; Nancy Kingman; Lady Marian Langham; Barbara Macmorran; Bob Matthews; Maypole Heritage (Alan Bigg); Daphne Milligan; John Millington; the late Norah Moore; Jane Morse; Robin Rogerson; Janie Smith; Sotheby's (Michael Heseltine and Catherine Porter); Willow Taylor; Dr Peter Tuckey; June Vargo; John Wilson; Mary Young; and everyone at Frederick Warne.

JUDY TAYLOR

FREDERICK WARNE

Published by the Penguin Group
27 Wrights Lane, London W8 5TZ, England
Penguin Books USA Inc., 375 Hudson Street, New York, N.Y. 10014, USA
Penguin Books Australia Ltd, Ringwood, Victoria, Australia
Penguin Books Canada Ltd, 10 Alcorn Avenue, Toronto, Ontario, Canada M4V 3B2
Penguin Books (N.Z.) Ltd, 182–190 Wairau Road, Auckland 10, New Zealand

Penguin Books Ltd, Registered Offices: Harmondsworth, Middlesex, England

First published 1992
1 3 5 7 9 10 8 6 4 2

Notes and introductions © Judy Taylor 1992

Beatrix Potter's original illustrations © Frederick Warne & Co., 1901, 1902, 1903, 1904, 1905, 1906, 1907, 1908, 1909, 1910, 1911, 1912, 1913, 1917, 1918, 1922, 1925, 1928, 1929, 1930, 1944, 1955, 1971, 1983, 1985, 1987, 1989, 1992

New reproductions of Beatrix Potter's book illustrations copyright © Frederick Warne & Co., 1987

Copyright in all countries signatory to the Berne Convention

All rights reserved. Without limiting the rights under copyright reserved above, no part of this publication may be reproduced, stored in or introduced into a retrieval system, or transmitted, in any form or by any means (electronic, mechanical, photocopying, recording or otherwise), without the prior written permission of the copyright owner and the above publisher of this book.

British Library Cataloguing in Publication Data available

ISBN 0 7232 3777 8

Printed and bound in Great Britain by William Clowes Limited, Beccles and London

# CONTENTS

*Beatrix Potter, aged 12, with her young brother Bertram*

*From* The Tale of Peter Rabbit *(1902), Beatrix Potter's first book that started as a picture letter*

## INTRODUCTION

In the ten years or so in which I have been writing about Beatrix Potter I have often had said to me, sometimes by those who knew her, usually by those who did not: 'Of course, Beatrix Potter never really liked children.' It is a statement that is made too frequently to be ignored and it has always puzzled me. How could the creator of a series of books unsurpassed in their lasting appeal to generation after generation not like children? Could it be true?

What undoubtedly is true is that Beatrix Potter had little close contact with children for much of her life. Born in 1866 to wealthy middle-class parents in Victorian London, she was virtually an only child during her formative years, her brother Bertram being six years her junior. She was educated at home by a series of governesses and had no childhood friends from school. As a young woman, however, she found great pleasure in the growing family of her friend and last governess, Annie Moore, and in the two children of her cousin, Edith Gaddum. She was never able to spend much time with them, certainly not enough to get to know them well, but she sent letters to them when she was away or unable to visit. It was in the letters to these children that she began to write and illustrate her stories, to weave her magic spell.

As the Moores and the Gaddums grew older, Beatrix's publishers, the Warne brothers, brought new child friends into her life, a fresh audience for her tales. A few weeks after sending a picture letter to the young daughter of Fruing Warne, Beatrix wrote to the child's mother: 'I hope I shall write Winifred lots of letters, it is much more satisfactory to address a real live child; I often think that was the secret success of Peter Rabbit, it was written to a child – not made to order.' Although there were already seven of her little books in print, Beatrix needed that continuing contact with children to give her the inspiration for new stories.

Beatrix had no children of her own – she was forty-seven when she married William Heelis – but she dedicated fourteen of her books to children. Some are for those who inspired a particular story or for whom a present was due; others are dedicated in more general terms, as in *The Flopsy Bunnies*, 'For all little friends of Mr McGregor & Peter & Benjamin', and in *Timmy Tiptoes*, 'For many unknown little friends, including Monica'. The latter was a school-friend of Beatrix's cousin whom she had never met but whose 'name took my fancy'. *Benjamin Bunny* is dedicated to 'The children of Sawrey from old Mr Bunny', although ironically it was the children of Sawrey who would later see Beatrix in a somewhat different light to those who knew her only as the author of their favourite books.

Children wrote to Beatrix from all over the world, some enclosing their own drawings and stories, others sending her presents they had made. In a letter sent in reply to one from Andrew Fayle in Ireland, she said that she received letters 'from little girls and boys as far off as New Zealand and America and Russia', and in another to Louisa Ferguson in New Zealand, that she hung up in her parlour 'photographs of little girls that I have never seen'. From her letters that have survived the years it would seem that Beatrix always replied to her fans, and for regular correspondents she often enclosed a copy of her latest book. In 1911 she 'posted a [Peter Rabbit painting] book to a big family in Africa' and after her wedding in 1913 she sent pieces of her wedding cake 'to several girls who have written to me'. Why should she bother to write to these children if she didn't like them?

I first encountered Beatrix's letters to children when amassing the material from which to select *Beatrix Potter's Letters* (1989), and I included some of them in that book. It has always surprised me that so many of the recipients kept her letters long before she became famous and it is gratifying that the majority of later generations continued to treasure them, or at least to ensure their safe-keeping by giving or selling them to collectors and institutions already holding Potter material. Reading the letters to children again convinced me that publication of all of them

The Tale of Mrs. Tiggy-Winkle *(1905) was dedicated to a young friend, Lucie Carr, who is the heroine of the story*

*Beatrix with her brother and their governess*

would act as important evidence in the debate about Beatrix's attitude to children – and then I started wondering about the children to whom the letters were sent. Nearly fifty years have passed since Beatrix's death and the earliest of the letters were written as long as fifty years before that, but some of the later recipients must still be alive. Did they ever meet Beatrix and could they recall their feelings about the woman who would have been to them already an old lady? If they had not met her, what kind of child would have been moved to write a fan letter in the days before the invention of the modern school exercise 'Writing to your Favourite Author'? Tracking them down would be an intriguing journey of research and reminiscence.

Of the forty-two 'children' whose letters are in this collection I have spoken or corresponded with ten, three of whom were over ninety and four well into their eighties. I have been in touch with the close relatives of twenty-two more – and been refused interviews by only two. Widely scattered throughout this island and from Australia and New Zealand to the United States of America and Canada, everyone has responded to my questions with great courtesy and enthusiasm. Ancient photograph albums have been plundered, diaries consulted and memories jogged. Eleven of the children I have been unable to trace, though it has been possible to discover a little about them or to speculate on who they might have been.

The letters fall into three categories: Beatrix's picture letters written between March 1892 and August 1912; her miniature letters written between the early 1900s and her marriage in 1913; and her more conventional letters – with only the occasional drawing – written between 1906 and 1942, a year before her death.

At the time of the early picture letters Beatrix was in her late twenties and living with her parents and brother in Bolton Gardens, Kensington, in London. Each April, for two or three weeks, the whole family moved to a south coast sea resort while the spring cleaning was in hand at Bolton Gardens, and in the late summer they went on holiday for three months, renting a large house either in

*Beatrix, aged 28, at the time she was writing picture letters to young friends*

Scotland or, in later years, in the Lake District. The wide range of addresses on the picture letters reflects this regular pattern of the Potter family life.

The picture letters are full of immediate news, of expeditions and local gossip, and occasionally they impart unexpected snippets of information – that there were Bath chairs for hire in St Leonards on Sea in December 1898 and fleas in the Reading Room of the British Museum in March 1900. It is interesting to read some of these early letters in conjunction with the similarly dated entries in *The Journal of Beatrix Potter*, particularly the accounts of Ginnet's Circus in the letter to Eric Moore of 5 September 1895 and the Potter family holiday in Sawrey in those to Noel and Eric Moore of August 1896.

The miniature letters, each one of which when folded becomes its own envelope, sometimes with a tiny stamp drawn in red crayon, were nearly all notes written as if from one character in Beatrix's books to another. They mark a change of gear in her letter-writing to children, almost as if, conscious of her young friends getting older, she felt she should provide them with more than just news. A full appreciation of the miniature letters is enhanced by a knowledge of the books.

The more conventional letters were nearly all written in the last half of Beatrix's life when she was living in the Lake District. The address on most of them is brief, 'Sawrey, Ambleside', but occasionally there is the additional 'Hill Top Farm' and, more frequently, 'Castle Cottage'. It was as early as 1882, soon after the family's first holiday in the Lake District and when Beatrix was only sixteen, that she resolved to own part of that beautiful countryside one day, but it was not until she was nearly forty that she was able to do so. In 1905, with accumulated royalties and a small legacy, she bought Hill Top Farm in Near Sawrey. It was a working farm and she decided to keep it that way, asking the farm manager and his family to stay on and run it for her. She travelled up from London on the train to stay as

*Andrew Fayle received this miniature letter from 'Peter Rabbit' in about 1913*

*Beatrix Potter's unfinished sketch of Hill Top Farm as it was when she bought it in 1905*

*The Hill Top Farm manager's children, Ralph and Betsy Cannon, in* The Tale of Jemima Puddle-Duck *(1908)*

*Also from* Jemima Puddle-Duck*, a view of the Sawrey village inn,* The Tower Bank Arms

often as her duties to her parents would allow, but once again she was the only child at home, for Bertram had married in 1905 and was living in Scotland.

In 1913, against her parents' wishes, Beatrix married her Lake District solicitor, William Heelis, and moved to Near Sawrey for good. By then she also owned Castle Farm, just across the field from Hill Top, and the Heelises decided to enlarge the farmhouse and to make Castle Cottage their home. The house at Hill Top Farm remained furnished but it was never lived in again for any length of time. Beatrix kept many of her favourite pictures and books at Hill Top and she guarded the house jealously as her study and place of retreat.

By the late 1920s Beatrix was an extensive landowner and important farmer in the Lake District. Most of the families in Near Sawrey were her tenants and she was disapproving of their children's escapades, particularly when she was the victim of their fun. There was the traditional scrumping of her apples and romps in her hayfields, the games in her barns and the innocent trespassing on her property. The idea that she did not like children may well stem from this time.

One of the Sawrey children then was Willow Burns, now Willow Taylor, whose parents William and Margaret Burns kept *The Tower Bank Arms*, the village inn which nestles up against Hill Top. To Willow Beatrix Potter – or Mrs Heelis as she was always known – was a crotchety old lady who interrupted her play and found fault with her appearance. 'I doubt whether she ever knew any ball games or skipped, played hop-scotch or hide-and-seek when she was a child. She was not the sweet old grandmotherly type which a lot of people imagine her to be. I sometimes wonder whether she resented the fact that we were enjoying the kind of childhood she had longed for? We had the freedom of the woods, the fields, the rivers and the footpaths, the whole of nature for us to explore – a children's paradise. It isn't that Mrs Heelis disliked children, it is just that she didn't understand their ways.'

Beatrix Heelis was by now a farmer and sheepbreeder of

note, with little time or energy left for writing and drawing. She was a fierce defender of the countryside from developers and a staunch supporter of the National Trust, helping to prevent the splitting up of farms and large estates. She could often be found on the fells checking on her sheep or down in the fields at harvest time. During the First World War she took over the responsibility for the feeding of the calves, the pigs and the poultry and in the Second World War, although well into her seventies, she supervised all the work on her farms and woods. But she always seemed to find time to answer the letters that came to her from children, usually with accounts of her farming life and enchanting stories about her farm animals and pets.

We shall never know the real answer to the question of whether or not Beatrix Potter liked children but there is no doubt at all that she had a strong *rapport* with them through her writing. Her little books are read all over the world and have proved their lasting appeal, and for me these letters provide the additional incontrovertible evidence that Beatrix Potter did indeed like children very much.

JUDY TAYLOR

*A watercolour painting by Beatrix of a Christmas delivery to her uncle Fred Burton's house, Gwaynynog, in North Wales*

## PUBLISHER'S NOTE

In the transcriptions of the letters Beatrix Potter's own punctuation and spelling, which were always somewhat idiosyncratic, have been followed throughout. She also frequently varied the spelling of her correspondents' names. The varied spelling of the Lake District house names cannot be blamed on Beatrix Potter, however; it is an eccentricity of the district.

## NOEL, ERIC, MARJORIE, WINIFREDE, NORAH, JOAN, HILDA AND BEATRIX MOORE

The eight Moores were the children of Annie Carter, Beatrix Potter's last governess. In April 1883, three years before her marriage to Edwin Moore, Annie Carter was appointed companion and teacher of German to Beatrix, an appointment that came as a surprise and disappointment to her pupil who, at seventeen, had hoped that her education might be at an end.

Miss Carter was a revelation to Beatrix. Only three years older in age, she was a great deal older in experience. She had lived in Germany as a student and had already been earning her own living for some years before she was employed by Mrs Potter. Annie and Beatrix found that they enjoyed each other's company and they became friends. Miss Carter stayed with the Potters in their house in Bolton Gardens for two years before she left to prepare for her wedding, and when she had departed Beatrix wrote in her journal: 'I have liked my last governess best on the whole – Miss Carter had her faults, and was one of the youngest people I have ever seen, but she was very good-tempered and intelligent.'

Annie Blanche Carter and Edwin Harry Moore were married in 1886 and went to live in Bayswater in London, where their first child, Noel, was born on Christmas Eve 1887. Soon after Noel's birth the young family moved into 20 Baskerville Road, a newly-built house overlooking Wandsworth Common. It was the house in which Annie would spend the rest of her life, dying there just a week before her eighty-seventh birthday in 1950.

Edwin Moore was a self-taught civil engineer and his job took him away from home – sometimes for as long as six months, as it did when he was working on the Aswan Dam in Egypt. As a consequence much of the bringing up of their quickly-growing family fell to Annie, and it was no easy task. By the time Noel was four he already had a brother, Eric, and two sisters, Marjorie and Winifrede

*Annie Moore, Beatrix Potter's last governess, with her two youngest daughters, Beatrix and Hilda*

(Freda). Four more girls would complete the family of eight, Norah (Bardy), Joan, Hilda and Beatrix.

Annie and Edwin Moore were totally opposed in their political views, she a Primrose League Tory and a firm Church of England believer, he a dedicated Socialist who became a member of the Communist Party. Their differences led to monumental arguments and constant warring. Their youngest child, Beatrix, recalls those quarrels over eighty years later: 'We children used to kick each other under the table whenever Father started politicking. He blamed everything on the capitalist system – even the mice in the cellar. Mother had an "At Home" every Thursday, with tea and cakes on a cakestand, and if Father was at home he used to shout through the door, "You are all parasites."'

In spite of the quarrels, Edwin returned from his lengthy tours abroad with presents for his family, and one year he brought a grey parrot from Entebbe, Uganda. 'We had to take turns to clean out the cage and none of us liked doing it because the parrot always bit us. Father taught the bird quite a vocabulary, much to our Mother's fury. She was particularly cross when, calling one of us, the parrot would answer, "Coming!", and then no one would appear. It could say clearly the name of each member of the family and at night, when the cloth was put over its cage, it would clear its throat and solemnly bid us all goodnight. Father spent hours trying to teach it to sing *The Red Flag* but it could only manage the first two notes which were repeated monotonously over and over again.'

Annie Moore was very strict with her children, sending them to bed or shutting them in the box-room when they were disobedient. She took them to church on Sunday morning and evening and the children were sent to Sunday School in the afternoons as well, with Bible reading a feature of every day. The house was full of religious pictures, in pride of place a print of Holman Hunt's *The Light of the World* in front of which Beatrix had to kneel before her Confirmation.

But it was not all strictness and religious fervour. There

*Edwin Moore, Annie's husband, in about 1914*

*The eldest of the Moore daughters,
Marjorie*

was often fun and gaiety, with frequent parties, and the
encouragement of wild hide-and-seek games all over the
house. A regular visitor was Annie's old pupil and friend,
Beatrix Potter, who was driven over the Thames in her
own pony and trap or in her mother's larger, two-horse
closed carriage. With a straw bonnet tied under her chin and
carrying a basket containing a rabbit or a cage of lively
white mice, this shy and retiring woman was always a
welcome guest. The contrast between the noisy, bustling
south-London home and her own rather severe and staid
household both excited and intrigued her. Beatrix knew
each of Annie's children from birth and followed their
progress with interest and delight. When they were ill or
when she was away from London she sent them letters, full
of accounts of what she had been doing and seeing, and
usually illustrated by quick pen sketches. When there was
no news to report she sent them stories and it was Annie
Moore who later suggested to Beatrix that perhaps some of
her letters might make good books.

As each new book came out Beatrix sent Annie an early
copy, and when Beatrix married and went to farm in the
Lake District, leaving London for good, she never lost
touch with her old friend. She sent a Christmas card each
year with a dedication that varied from 'to Annie B. Moore
with love' in 1927 to 'from B. Heelis to ABM' in 1938.
Christmas was a time for generous celebration in the house
in Wandsworth Common and the *pièce de résistance* on the
dinner table was always a large turkey sent down from Hill
Top Farm by Beatrix.

Annie Moore played the piano well and all her children
had music lessons, much to the delight of the parrot who
interrupted with its own contribution. To augment the
modest family income, Annie Moore gave French and
German lessons and she later started a small school in the
house which her own younger children attended. In spite of
his political beliefs, and as so often happens with those
whose own schooling has been of the most basic, Edwin
Moore was determined that his children should be well
educated. With the help of his sisters, two of whom lived in

some comfort in Ipswich, he arranged for Noel and Eric to go to Westminster School. The girls were sent to Clapham High School for Girls, crossing the common on their bicycles with strict instructions – and in fear of punishment – not to loiter on the journey.

It was to Edwin's two sisters in Suffolk that the children were usually sent for the summer holidays, but one special year, in August 1912, Norah and Joan were invited to the Lake District by Beatrix Potter. Although by then she already owned two farms there, Hill Top and Castle Farm, Beatrix was not yet living in that beautiful part of England. She was there with her parents on the annual family summer holiday, staying in the large house they had rented for three months, Broad Leys, which stands on the eastern shore of Windermere in Bowness. From there Beatrix made the daily journey to her farms, taking the ferry across the lake and walking the remaining mile and a half up the hill to Sawrey. During their visit the two girls went with her to Hill Top taking the newly-hatched chicks she had brought up with her on the train from London (see the letter to Augusta Burn on page 159). It was a holiday that Norah and Joan never forgot, Norah still able to convey her excitement and wonder at it over seventy-five years later.

*Norah and Joan Moore with newly-hatched chicks, photographed by Beatrix's father Rupert Potter on 12 August 1912*

Noel, the first of Annie's children and her favourite, was spoiled by his mother and over-protected. In 1897, at the age of nine, he contracted polio which damaged one of his legs and left him with a limp for life. Much influenced by his mother's strong religious beliefs, Noel became an Anglo-Catholic priest when he left Westminster and he worked for many years with the children of the poor at a number of churches in the East End of London. He never married and when he retired in the early 1960s, he went to live near his brother in East Sussex, becoming Chaplain to St Mary's Convent in Buxted, a home for mentally handicapped girls run by an Anglican order of nuns. He was eighty-one when he died in June 1969.

Of Beatrix Potter's letters to the Moore children reproduced here, spanning a period of twelve years from 1892 to 1904, thirteen are known to be to Noel, the first

*Noel Moore (above) and Eric (opposite) in their Westminster School uniform*

sent when he was only four years old. The letter written to him from Scotland on 4 September 1893, recounting the story of a disobedient rabbit called Peter, has become one of the most quoted and famous letters ever written and it is Beatrix's only letter to Noel that is known to be in Britain, having been bought from a private owner by Pearson plc in 1991 and housed with the Beatrix Potter Collection at the Victoria and Albert Museum in London. The others are now in the United States of America, eleven in the Pierpont Morgan Library in New York and one in the Houghton Library at Harvard University. A number of other letters to Noel, sold at auction in 1947, remain untraced; among them is one described in the sale catalogue as 'being the origin of "Benjamin Bunny" with drawings on every page'.

Annie Moore's second child and her only other son was born just eleven months after Noel, in November 1888. Like his father Eric became a civil engineer, but unlike his father he had the advantage of formal training, and with an engineering degree he went in 1912 to work for the Egyptian Government on Nile Bank projects. His career was interrupted by the outbreak of war, for he was a Special Reserve and joined the Royal Engineers in August 1914. Fighting throughout the war, in France, Belgium and Italy, Eric was badly gassed. He was also twice mentioned in despatches and awarded the Military Cross and Bar. (It was just after the end of the war, on 26 November 1918, that the only surviving letter from Beatrix Potter to Annie Moore was written: 'Dear Mrs Moore, I was so glad to hear Eric is safe & all of you fairly thriving – except I am afraid about yourself. You are overworked, that is all about it . . .'.) When he came out of the army Eric returned to Egypt and then worked in France and the Sudan until, in 1933, he went home to England and bought a house in Suffolk for his wife and three children. On retiring from civil engineering ten years later, Eric became a fruit and poultry farmer in East Sussex. He died at the age of eighty-two in 1971.

Most of Beatrix Potter's letters to Eric have disappeared into private collections and only two of the originals, together with Beatrix's own copy of a third, are reproduced here. It is certain that there were many more, and one in particular is of special interest. On 5 September 1893, a day after she had written the Peter Rabbit letter to Noel, Beatrix wrote to Eric from Eastwood: 'My dear Eric, Once upon a time there was a frog called Mr. Jeremy Fisher, and he lived in a little house on the bank of a river . . . One morning Mr. Fisher looked out and saw drops of rain . . .'. The last time that letter was seen in public was in 1947 when it was sold in the same auction with so many of Noel's letters.

The first four of Annie and Edwin's six daughters were born within six-and-a-half years of each other. Being so close they shared everything, clothes, toys – and their interest in music.. They played quartets together, Marjorie the violin, Freda the piano, Norah the cello and Joan the viola. Their parents' quarrelling made the girls determined to leave home just as soon as their schooling was finished – and the outside world came as a considerable shock to them after their strict and sheltered upbringing. Marjorie took up nursing, trained as a naval nurse at Chatham and served on board a hospital ship. Freda taught the piano at two girls' schools in south-west London and in 1936, when she was in her mid-forties, she married a constructional engineer, William Allen. He had been a widower for a long time and had a daughter who was away at boarding school, so Freda continued with her piano teaching in London after her marriage.

Beatrix Potter once mentioned in a letter to her publisher that she hoped she would be able to send Freda or Norah 'to college some day' but her plan never materialized. Norah was a good cello player and, with lessons paid for by the aunts, she passed her London Royal Academy of Music examinations. She played for a short time with what she much later called 'rather low class orchestras in hotels and theatres' and after drifting through various jobs she thought seriously about becoming a nun. She eventually settled for teaching crafts at an isolated mission in the Transkei. Norah lived to ninety-six and spent the last years of her life in a nursing home in Kent.

Joan Moore became an almoner, working in a number of

*Portrait photographs of Marjorie Moore (above) and Winifrede (below)*

London hospitals, and when she retired she shared a home with Marjorie near their brothers in Buxted, in a house they named Hill Top Cottage. After Joan's death in 1973 Marjorie stayed on in the cottage for a while but then she joined Freda in London and later the two sisters spent several happy years together in a hotel in East Sussex, both living well into their nineties.

Marjorie's letters from Beatrix Potter were her very special treasures and to keep them safe she tied them in a bundle with a piece of yellow ribbon. Unlike her brothers' letters and those of her sister, Norah, none of Marjorie's known letters were the source for a book but they were full of news and are particularly informative about Beatrix's travels. There are no stories either in Freda's letters published here, but one of Beatrix's missing letters is to Freda and was described by the auction house as: 'The tale of a dog called Nip who lived at a grocer's shop – an unpublished tale.' And it was to Freda in 1901 that Beatrix gave the story of *The Tailor of Gloucester*. It was sent to her in a stiff-covered exercise book, with twelve watercolour illustrations and the letter on page 76. That stiff-covered exercise book and all of Beatrix's letters to Freda are now in the United States of America. Seven of the letters are in the Houghton Library in Harvard; the eighth, together with the manuscript of *The Tailor of Gloucester*, is in the Free Library of Philadelphia. The one letter to Norah that can be found tells the tale of Squirrel Nutkin and it was sent from Lingholm, the Potter holiday home on Derwentwater, near Keswick. The story was much revised by Beatrix before she was completely satisfied with it for publication, and when it was published in 1903 *Squirrel Nutkin* carried the dedication 'A Story for Norah'. There are no known letters to Joan.

Joan Moore was nearing her sixth birthday when the fifth of the Moore daughters, Hilda, was born in 1902 and the last child, Beatrix, followed seventeen months later. When Hilda grew up she married a doctor, Peter Thwaites, and they had three children. Hilda died of multiple sclerosis in her middle years. There is only one known picture letter from Beatrix Potter to Hilda and, although the original has disappeared, it was reproduced as the endpapers for *Beatrix Potter: A Bibliographical Check List* by Jane Quinby, a catalogue of Potter holdings in the United States of America in 1954. Although printed there, and here, in black-and-white, it is probably in colour, in the same style as the picture letter written seventeen days earlier to Lucie Carr, also from Lingholm (see page 109).

Beatrix Moore was very much the baby of the family. 'Noel was nearly sixteen when I was born so I never really knew him. Beatrix Potter was my godmother and she gave me a silver sugar bowl which I still have, but I don't remember her very clearly. I was, after all, only ten when she married William Heelis and went to live in the Lake District. But I do remember the frocks she bought for Hilda and me. Mine had beading on it and pink and blue ribbons.'

Beatrix was also the rebel of the Moore family, in sympathy with her father's political views which clashed so strongly with her mother's. To distance herself as far as possible from her mother's disapproval, she left home as soon as she could. Armed with her London Royal Academy of Music certificate she embarked on a series of jobs teaching the piano at girls' boarding schools. In 1926, at the age of twenty-three, she went to South Africa on a three-year contract as a music teacher. While she was there she started writing, and on her return to England Beatrix determined that she would become a journalist. In the course of her work she met and married Vilgot Hammarling, who was a well-known journalist and press attaché at the Swedish Embassy in London.

Beatrix Hammarling was a contributor to the first issue of *Picture Post* in October 1938 and she worked regularly for the magazine in the years to follow. After her husband's death Beatrix shared her life for many years with the war poet, Edgell Rickword. Now the sole survivor of the Moore children, she is still an active journalist.

Beatrix Potter sent no picture letters to her godchild. By the time the child was old enough to receive letters, Beatrix Potter was putting much of her energy into her 'little books', and when writing to children she had had a new

*Hilda Moore aged 19*

*An early portrait of Beatrix Moore*

*The hand-made post bag in which Beatrix sent her miniature letters to the Moores*

idea, sending them miniature letters as if written from one character in her books to another. Each letter was written on a narrow slip of paper that either folded into an envelope shape or fitted into its own miniature envelope, some with a stamp drawn in red crayon. The miniature letters to the Moores came in a small post bag, inscribed with the letters G.P.O. (General Post Office), which Beatrix had made herself.

A full appreciation of these miniature letters requires a detailed knowledge of the books and as Beatrix Moore would not have been old enough to understand them she had to be content with her godmother's dedication in *The Pie and the Patty-Pan* – 'For Joan, to read to Baby'.

Most of the original miniature letters to the Moore children have disappeared in the last ten years and only those sent to Hilda have been positively identified. There are, however, transcripts of some forty of the tiny letters which were included in *Yours Affectionately, Peter Rabbit*, published in 1983. As it is believed that many of them belonged to the Moores they are included here.

*The complete Moore family, in order of seniority*

March 11th 92 — Falmouth Hotel
Falmouth

My dear Noel,

Thank you for your very interesting letter, which you sent me a long time ago.

I have come a very long way in a puff-puff to a place in Cornwall, where it is very hot, and there are palm trees in the gardens & camellias & rhodendrons [sic] in flower which are very pretty.

We are living in a big house close to the sea, we go on the harbour in a steam boat and see ever so many big ships.

Yesterday we went across the water to a pretty little village where the fishermen live. I saw them catching crabs in a basket cage which they let down into the sea with some meat in it & then the crabs go in to eat the meat & cannot get out.

*Nearly forty years later Beatrix was to use harbour scenes from her West Country holidays as background for* The Tale of Little Pig Robinson *(1930)*

I shall be quite sorry to come away from this nice place but we have been here 10 days. Before we go home we are going for two days to Plymouth to see some bigger ships still, I shall come to see you and tell your Mamma all about it when I get home. I have got a lot of shells for you & Eric, (I suppose they would not swallow them)

This is a pussy I saw looking for fish.

These are two little dogs that live in the hotel, & two tame seagulls & a great many cocks & hens in the garden.

I am going today to a place called the Lizard so I have no time to draw any more pictures,

& I remain yours affectionately
Beatrix Potter

*From* The Tale of Little Pig Robinson *(1930)*

22

Sep 4th 93            Eastwood
                           Dunkeld

My dear Noel,

     I don't know what to write to you, so I shall tell you a story about four little rabbits whose names were – Flopsy, Mopsy, Cottontail and Peter

     They lived with their mother in a sand bank under the root of a big fir tree.

     'Now, my dears,' said old Mrs Bunny 'you may go into the field or down the lane, but don't go into Mr McGregor's garden.'

     Flopsy, Mopsy & Cottontail, who were good little rabbits went down the lane to gather blackberries, but Peter, who was very naughty ran straight away to Mr McGregor's garden and squeezed underneath the gate.

     First he ate some lettuce, and some broad beans, then some radishes, and then, feeling

*Flopsy, Mopsy and Cottontail gathering blackberries in the published version of* The Tale of Peter Rabbit *(1902)*

ran straight away to Mr McGregor's garden and squeezed underneath the gate.

First he ate some lettuce, and some broad beans, then some radishes, and then, feeling rather sick, he went to look for some parsley; but round of the end of a cucumber frame whom should he meet but Mr McGregor!

Mr McGregor was planting out young cabbages but he jumped up & ran after Peter waving a rake & calling out 'Stop thief'!

Peter was most dreadfully frightened & rushed all over the garden for he had forgotten the way back to the gate. He lost one of his shoes among the cabbages

rather sick, he went to look for some parsley; but round the end of a cucumber frame whom should he meet but Mr McGregor!

Mr McGregor was planting out young cabbages but he jumped up & ran after Peter waving a rake & calling out 'Stop thief'!

Peter was most dreadfully frightened & rushed all over the garden, for he had forgotten the way back to the gate. He lost one of his shoes among the cabbages and the other shoe amongst the potatoes. After losing them he ran on four legs & went faster, so that I think he would have got away altogether, if he had not unfortunately run into a gooseberry net and got caught fast by the large buttons on his jacket. It was a blue jacket with brass buttons, quite new.

Mr McGregor came up with a basket which he intended to pop on the top of Peter, but Peter wriggled out just in time, leaving his jacket behind, and this time he found the gate, slipped underneath and ran home safely.

Mr McGregor hung up the little jacket & shoes for a scarecrow, to frighten the blackbirds.

Peter was ill during the evening, in consequence of overeating himself. His mother put him to bed and gave him a dose of camomile tea, but Flopsy, Mopsy and Cottontail had bread and milk and blackberries for supper.

I am coming back to London next Thursday, so I hope I shall see you soon, and the new baby [Norah, born on 13 July]

I remain, dear Noel, yours affectionately

Beatrix Potter

and the other shoe amongst the potatoes. After losing them he ran on four legs & went faster, so that I think he wou—

Mr McGregor came up with a basket which he intended to pop on the top of Peter, but Peter wriggled out just in time, leaving his jacket behind,

have got away altogether; but unfortunately ran into a gooseberry net... caught by the... and this time he found the gate, slipped underneath and ran

Mr McGregor hung up the little jacket & shoes for a scarecrow, to frighten the black birds.

but Flopsy, Mopsy, and Cottontail had bread and milk and blackberries for supper. I am coming back to London next Thursday, so I hope I shall see you soon, and the new baby I remain, dear Noel, yours affectionately Beatrix Potter

Peter was ill during the evening, in consequence of over-eating himself. His mother put him to bed and gave him a dose of camomile tea,

*From* The Tale of Little Pig Robinson *(1930)*

March 28. 94        Pendennis Hotel
                                     Falmouth

My dear Eric

. .there are a great many ships here some very large ones. There is one from Norway, and a French one unloading at the quay. Some of the sailors have little dogs, and cocks and hens on the ships. I have read about the owl & the pussy cat, who went to sea in a peagreen boat, but I never saw anything of that kind till today.

I was looking at a ship called the Pearl of Falmouth which was being mended at the bottom because it had rubbed on a rock, when I heard something grunt!

I went up a bank where I could see onto the deck & there was a white pig with a curly tail walking about. It is a ship that goes to Newfoundland & the sailors always take a pig I daresay it enjoys the voyage, but when the sailors get hungry they eat it. If that pig had any sense it would slip down into the boat at the end of the ship & row away.

This is the captain & the boatswain & the ship's cook pursuing the pig. The cook is waving a knife and fork. He wants to make the pig into sausages!

This is the pig rowing away from the sailors, it is squealing because it sees the knife & fork. This is the pig living on Robinson Crusoe's Island. He is still rather afraid of the cook & is looking for the ship through a telescope. This is the same pig after he has lived ten years upon the island, he has grown very very fat and the cook has never found him.

I went up a bank where I could see onto the deck & there was a white pig with a curly tail walking about. It is a ship that goes to Newfoundland & the sailors always take a pig pig O daresay it enjoys the voyage, but when the men get hungry they eat it. sailors get hungry they eat it. pig had any sense it would slip down into the boat at the end of the ship & row away. This is the captain & the boatswain & the ships cook pursuing the pig. The cook is waving a knife & fork. He wants

to make the pig into sausages!

If theirs, it is
because it
knife & fork.
is the pig
on Robinson
soe's Island.
he is still
rather afraid of the cook & is looking for the ship through a telescope.
This is the same pig after he has lived ten years upon the island; he has grown very very fat and the cook has never found him.

Feb. 4th 95                    2, Bolton Gardens,
                               S.W.

My dear Noel,

It is a long time since I have been to see you, but it is too cold to drive with my pony. I shall be very glad when the warm weather comes. I wonder if you have been making a snow-man in the garden? or feeding the sparrows, we have a great many every morning.

My rabbit Peter is so lazy, he lies before the fire in a box, with a little rug. His claws grew too long, quite uncomfortable, so I tried to cut them with scissors but they were so hard that I had to use the big gardens scissors He sat quite still and allowed me to do his little front paws but when I cut the other hind foot claws he was tickled, & kicked, very naughty. If he were a wild rabbit digging holes they would be worn down & would not need cutting.

Here are some rabbits throwing snow balls.

I wonder if your pussycat has learned to catch mice yet. I think it would rather lap milk, it is too fine to work like a common cat.

These mice are getting away down a hole.

I wonder if those dolls have any hair still & whether they have eaten all those nice sausages.

I remain with love yrs aff
Beatrix Potter

My rabbit Peter is so lazy, he lies before the fire in a box, with a little rug. His claws grew too long, quite uncomfortable, so I tried to cut them with scissors.

but they were so hard that I had to use the big gardens scissors He sat quite still and allowed

hind foot claws

he was tickled, + kicked, very naughty. If he were a wild rabbit digging holes they would be worn down + would not need cutting.

Here are some rabbits throwing snow balls.

I wonder if your pussy cat has learned to catch mice yet. I think it would rather lap milk; it is too fine to work like a common cat.

These mice are getting away down a hole. I wonder if those dolls have any hair still + whether they have eaten all those nice sausages. I remain with love yrs aff Beatrix Potter

*From the cover of* Appley Dapply's Nursery Rhymes
*(1917) – see also the sketch in the letter on page 64*

March 8th 95

2, Bolton Gardens,
London, S.W.

My dear Noel,

I am so sorry to hear through your Aunt Rosie that you are ill, you must be like this little mouse, and this is the doctor Mr Mole, and Nurse Mouse with a tea-cup. I hope the little mouse will soon be able to sit up in a chair by the fire.

I went to the zoo on Wednesday & saw the new giraffe. It is a young one, very pretty, and the keeper says it will grow a good deal taller.

I saw the box that it came in, the keeper says it had quite a stiff neck because the box was not large enough. They brought it by train from Southampton and they could not have a larger box because of getting through the tunnels. I also saw a new monky [sic], called Jenny, it had black hair & a face like a very ugly old woman. A man gave it a pair of gloves which it put on, and it took a bunch of keys & tried to unlock its cage door.

I gave the elephant a lot of buns out of a bag but I did not give any to the ostriches because people are not allowed to feed them, since a naughty boy gave them old gloves & made them ill. I saw a black bear rolling on its back. I did not know that the old wolf was so good tempered.

I remain yrs aff
Beatrix Potter

I hope the little mouse will soon be able to sit up in a chair by the fire.

I went to the Zoo on Wednesday, saw the new giraffe. It is a young one, very pretty, and the keeper says it will grow a good deal

had quite a stiff neck because the box was not large enough. They brought it by train from ....hampton and they could not have .... box because of getting through .... I also saw a new .... Jenny, it had black

.... that it .... eper says it ....

.... it put on, and it took .... of heeps & tried .... lock its cage door.

I gave the elephant a lot of buns out of a bag but I did not give any to the ostriches because people are not allowed to feed them since a naughty boy gave them old gloves & made them ill.

I saw a black bear rolling on its back.

I did not know that the old wolf was so good tempered. I remain yours aff

Beatrix Potter

MA2999 (2)

June 4th 95.    2, Bolton Gardens,
South Kensington. S.W

My dear Noël,

We came home from Wales this afternoon. I should have written to you from there but I was so busy taking photographs with Cousin Alice. We took some inside the house [Gwaynynog, Denbigh, the home of her uncle, Fred Burton], there are very handsome chimney pieces, some parts of the house are as old as 1571.

She has a very pretty pony called Pearl, it is larger than mine and she rides it. One day the coachman put it in the gig, it ran very nicely on the flat road but did not like going up hill with a heavy load.

We drove to a nasty dirty Welsh village & when we asked the way, there was only one woman who could speak English. There is a fine castle at Denbigh & very pretty hills & woods, but I think the Welsh people are disagre[e]able & I should not care to live there. My Uncle's game keeper walks about with a big stick looking for poachers.

There is a man in the town who has 3 donkys [sic] dragging a coal cart, but they do not look strong enough. Alice has a little dog called 'Toby', and a big dog called 'Rough'.

I hope your leg is getting better; I should like to see you before I go away again on Saturday, but I have a good deal to do, so I am not sure if I shall find time.

I remain with love yrs aff
Beatrix Potter

parts of the house are as old as 1571.
She has a very pretty pony called Pearl, it is larger than mine and she rides it. One day the coachman put it in the gig, it ran very nicely on the flat road but did not like going up hill with a heavy load.

We drove to a nasty dirty Welsh village & when we asked the way, there was only one woman who could speak There is a ... at ... very ... woods, but I think ... ple are disagreable ... should not care to live there. My Uncle's game keeper ... poachers.

There is a man in the town who has 3 donkys dragging a coal cart, but they do not look strong enough. Alice has a little dog called "Toby", and a big dog called "Rough".

I hope your leg is getting better; I should like to see you before I go away again on Saturday, but I have a good deal to do, so I am not sure if I shall find time. I remain with love yrs aff. Beatrix Potter.

MA 2009 (5)

33

Sept 3rd 95         Holehird,
Windermere.

My dear Noël,

I was so glad to get your nice little letter and to hear that you can walk about again. I hope you are having finer weather, it has been so wet here.

This is a tent near Skelwith bridge in a flood. I think they are stupid things, there have been 3 in a field near Ambleside, very much annoyed with an old sow and two young pigs. We have a very good dry house but I think we shall come home in three weeks unless the rain stops.

This is the ferry boat across Windermere, the horses are very good but one day there were 2 Italians with a donky [sic] with an organ, they tied an apron over its head but I never saw a donky so frightened. We went with an organ, they tied an apron over its head but I never saw a donkey so frightened. We went across to see Cousin Edith who lives at the other side of the lake, her little boy has 2 old pigeons & 3 young ones, they live over the stable, he wanted me to go up the ladder. He has 2 tortoises & he had a jackdaw but it hopped away.

making pictures with windows and Molly like I make for you. My rabbit lives in the garden & has grown so fat, I take him for a walk with a collar for fear he should run away. My brother catches fish when it rains & paints a picture on fine days. This is a hen stealing corn out of a nose bag. This is a puppy we found in the middle of a wood, its mother lives in the next cottage, we think she kept it in a hole. I remain yrs aff Beatrix Potter

across to see Cousin Edith [Gaddum, see page 94] who lives at the other side of the lake, her little boy [Walter] has 2 old pigeons & 3 young ones, they live over the stable, he wanted me to go up the ladder. He has 2 tortoises & he had a jackdaw but it hopped away.

I have been making pictures with windows for him and Molly [his sister] like I make for you.

My rabbit lives in the garden & has grown so fat, I take him for a walk with a collar for fear he should run away.

My brother [Bertram] catches fish when it rains & paints a picture on fine days. This is a hen stealing corn out of a nose bag. This is a puppy we found in the middle of a wood, its mother lives in the next cottage, we think she kept it in a hole.

I remain yrs aff
Beatrix Potter

[This is Beatrix's copy of her original letter]

Sept 5.95                    [Holehird]

My dear Eric

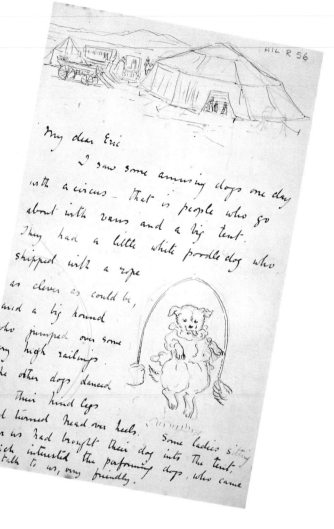

I saw some amusing dogs one day with a circus – that is people who go about with vans and a big tent. They had a little white poodle dog who skipped with a rope as clever as could be, and a big hound who jumped over some very high railings. The other dogs danced on their hind legs and turned head over heels. Some ladies sitting near us had brought their dog into the tent, which interested the performing dogs, who came to talk to us, very friendly.

The last time when I saw the circus Mr Ginnet possessed a red bull which he rode, but I fancy he has made it into beef; it was beginning to show temper then. He has now 6 horses; a fat piebald, 2 cream coloured, and a very old old performing grey mare.

I never saw a horse dance better but I wondered if it would ever be able to get up again when it curtseyed

The others were 2 ponies; one called Joey was very shy. When the clown told it to jump it jumped, but when the other man spoke to it, it pretended to bite him.

Half the school children in Ambleside were there, and several little boys tried to ride but the ponies went down on their knees & tumbled them off right & left. The grass was too soft to hurt them. In fact it was so damp & soft that when madame got off her horse, she put on goloshes over her satin slippers. It was a very odd circus.

*The circus as it appeared in* The Fairy Caravan *(1930)*

The last time when I saw
the circus Mr Ginnet
possessed a red bull
which he rode, but I
fancy he has made it into
beef, it was beginning
to show temper then —
He has now 6 horses,
a fat piebald, 2 cream cloured,
and a very old old
performing grey mare.

saw a horse dance better but I
if it would
to get

When the clown told it to jump it jumped
but when the other man spoke to it,
it pretended to
bite him.
Half the school children in Ambleside were
there, and several little boys tried to
ride, but the
ponies went
down on their
knees & tumbled them. "B right." left.
the grass was too soft to hurt them. In
fact it was so damp, soft that when
madame got off her horse, she put on
Goloshes over her satin slippers.
a very odd circus.

Sept 5. 95

The others were 2
ponies; one called
Joey was very shy.

It was

April 6th 96                    2 Bolton Gardens

My dear Noël,

Thank you for your nice letter. I should like to see you riding the big dog, here is a picture of Tom Thumb on a mouse.

We are going to Swanage next Monday; I am sure you must have enjoyed Felixstow[e], I dare say you had a [spade] and a [bucket]. I expect to find some shells.

I went to the zoo and it rained. The seals seemed to like the rain, but most of the animals were in their little houses. The big elephant is dead. What a pity! They went to Mr Rhind a chemist for some medicine, but it died. It is going to be put in the museum. There is a new lion at the zoo, which is so savage, it made a great noise.

I have got some pretty hyacinths in my garden. The sparrows are naughty, they pull off the flowers. There are two nests, just under the gutter at the top of our house. We see them flying up with grass to make the nest. We do not like it because the little birds fall out onto our door-steps.

I hope that you and Eric will have a very good time,

and with love I remain yrs aff
Beatrix Potter

*Above and below: The 'friendly sparrows' from* The Tale of Peter Rabbit *(1902)*

Monday; I am sure you must have enjoyed Felixstow, I dare say you had a [spade] and a [bucket]. I expect to find some shells [shells]. I went to the Zoo and it rained. The seals seemed to like the rain, but most of the animals were in their little houses. The big elephant is dead. What a pity! Th...

to Mr Rhind a chemist for some medecine, but it died. It is going to be put in the museum. There is a new lion at the Zoo, which is so savage, it [makes] a great noise. I have got some pretty hyacinths in my garden.

The sparrows are naughty, they pull off the flowers. There are two nests, just under the gutter at the top of our house. We see them flying up with grass to make the nest. We do not like it because the little birds fall out onto our door-steps. I hope that you and Eric have a very good time, and with [love I remain] yrs. aff. Beatrix Potter.

Aug 7th 96

Lakefield,
Sawrey,
Ambleside.

My dear Noël,

I hope that you are all very well. We are having a very good time here. It is such a pretty place, and we have a boat on Esthwaite Lake. There are tall rushes at the edge of the lake and beds of water lilies.

I sometimes sit quite still in the boat & watch the water hens. They are black with red bills and make a noise just like kissing, when they are hiding in the reeds. They walk on the lily leaves, nodding their heads and peeping underneath for water snails. There are wild ducks too, but they are not so tame. One evening I went in the boat when it was nearly dark and saw a flock of lapwings asleep, standing on one leg in the water. What a funny way to go to bed! Perhaps they are afraid of foxes, the hens are.

There are some cocks & hens on the hill, who sleep right at the top of a hawthorn bush, the branches are quite covered with chickens. Those at the farm go up a stone wall into a loft. The farmer has a beautiful fat pig. He is a funny old man, he feeds the calves every morning, he rattles the spoon on the tin pail, to tell them breakfast is ready but they won't always come, then there is a noise like a German band.

I remain yrs aff
Beatrix Potter

*Esthwaite Water may well have been the setting for* The Tale of Mr. Jeremy Fisher *(1906)*

on Esthwaite Lake. There are tall rushes at the edge of the lake and beds of water lilies. underneath for water snails. There are wild ducks too, but they are not so tame. One evening I went in the boat when it was nearly dark

I some times sit quite still in the boat & watch the water hens. They are black with red bills and make a noise just like kissing, when they are hiding in the reeds. They walk on the lily leaves, nodding their heads and peeping

and saw a flock of lapwings asleep, standing on one leg in the water. What a funny way to go to bed! Perhaps they are afraid of foxes. The hens

sleep right at the top of a haw-thorn bush, the branches are quite covered with chickens. Those at the farm go up a stone wall into a loft. The farmer

There are hens on the hill, who

has a beautiful fat pig. He is a funny old man, he feeds the calves every morning, he rattles the spoon on the tin pail, to tell them breakfast is ready, but they won't always come, then there is a noise like a German band. I remain yrs. aff. Beatrix Potter.

Aug 8th 96.

Lakefield,
Sawrey,
Ambleside.

My dear Eric,

My little cousin Molly Gaddum has got a squirrel who has 2 baby squirrels in a hay nest. You cannot think how pretty. They are not much bigger than mice yet. They live in a box in the hay loft & one day Molly opened the lid and Mrs Squirrel jumped out. They had such a business to catch her. Jim [Walter] her brother has 2 jackdaws which sit all day on a stick in a corner, I think they are not very interesting, he wishes to give me one. He has also got a hedgehog & some gold fish.

There are plenty of hedgehogs here in the fields, they come out in the evening. So do the rabbits, there are two black ones in a field near the house.

Our coachman brought his cat in a basket. It mewed dreadfully amongst the luggage, but I think it is enjoying itself. It sings songs with the gardener's cat, which is grey, & the farm cat, which is white with a black tail. There is a very pretty yellow colley dog, it is so clever with the sheep, it drives them right & left, which ever way it is told and never bites them. Sometimes it comes in at our dining room window & shakes hands.

We have got a tame owl he eats mice, he sits with a tail hanging out of his mouth.

I remain yours aff
Beatrix Potter

*Old Brown the owl, from* The Tale of Squirrel Nutkin *(1903)*

Feb 27th 97.     2 Bolton Gardens.

My dear Noël,

Thank you for your nice little letter, I am so sorry to hear what a bad time you have been having, you must get better now. I should have come to see you this week if I had not been prevented. I am sure your Mamma is quite tired of cooking and medecine [sic] bottles; tell her it was a little hood we wanted, I will come for it some day soon. Here is the rest of the Owl and the Pussy cat [a letter to Noel of 13

February 1897, with the earlier verses by Edward Lear, was sold at auction in 1947 and has not been traced].

I remain dear Noël yours affectionately
Beatrix Potter

They sailed away
for a year and a day,
To the Land where the
Bong Tree grows

*Above and below:* The Owl and the
Pussy Cat and the Land of the Bong
Tree *feature at the end of* The Tale of
Little Pig Robinson *(1930)*

And there in a wood
A piggy-wig stood
With a ring at the end
his nose, his nose.
With a ring at the end of

"Dear Pig are you willing
To sell for one shilling your ring?"
Said the piggy- "I will."
So they sailed away
And were married next day-
By the Turkey who lives on
the Hill.

45

March 4th 97          2, Bolton Gardens,
                      S.W.

My dear Noël

Here is another picture of the owl and the pussy cat, after they were married. It is funny to see a bird with hands, but how could he play the guitar without them!

I must tell you about the wind in our garden on Wednesday night. It was so rough I went out after dark, all wrapped up with goloshes on, and brought in my rabbit in a basket. Next morning the hutch was blown right over.

I remains yours aff
Beatrix Potter

*[handwritten letter with animal sketches at top: a horse, foals labelled BESS, DARLING, LOBBIN, June 14 97, cows labelled JOAN, APRIL]*

My dear Freda,

I think I must write you a letter too. What a nice time you are having, going to so many tea parties!

*[sketch of mice at a tea party]*

*Twenty-one years later the mouse tea party became a mouse dinner party in* The Tale of Johnny Town-Mouse *(1918)*

*[handwritten continuation of letter]*

I wonder if there are going to be any decorations at Wandsworth on Jubilee Day. I shall not go to see the procession; it is too hot. I shall stop at home and have a large flag out of the window. At the last Jubilee there was a wind, and our flag kept rolling up.

June 14th 97                    [Gwaynynog?]

My dear Freda,

I think I must write you a letter too. What a nice time you are having, going to so many tea parties! I wonder if there are going to be any decorations at Wandsworth on Jubilee Day [20 June, Diamond Jubilee of Queen Victoria's accession to the throne]. I shall not go to see the procession; it is too hot.

I shall stop at home and have a large flag out of the window. At the last [Golden] Jubilee there was a wind, and our flag kept rolling up. We had to reach out of the window with a broom to unroll it. We are going to have nightlights on the window sills, red, blue, and white.

My rabbit is so hot he does not know what to do with himself. He has such thick fur, I think he would be more comfortable if he had a little coat which would take off. I shall send this to Wandsworth. I daresay it will be sent on to Ipswich, if you have not come home.

I remain yours affectionately
Beatrix Potter

The little foal belongs to my uncle, it is so tame.

*Beatrix put Peter into a 'little coat' in* The Tale of Peter Rabbit *(1902)*

Aug 26th 97

Lingholm,
Keswick,
Cumberland.

My dear Noël,

We have got a trap for catching
minnows, which is amusing. It is made of
perforated zinc. I did not believe it would
answer, but my brother tied a bit of string
to it, put some bread inside and watched.
The minnows came all round snuffing and
at last one old fish found the way in at the
end, and all the others followed. I should
think there were 50 or 60 inside when it was
pulled out of the water. We use them for
bait for larger fish, trout and perch. The
fishing is not very good in the lake; the
groom, who drives my pony, catches more
than anybody. He is always at it. One day
the otter hounds came round the lake to

*A detail from Beatrix's watercolour
illustration 'Fishes come bite', made for
an unpublished nursery rhyme book in
1905*

hunt, they did not find an otter and we have never seen one as they only come out at night. I went out in our boat & watched the dogs. The men wade about with long poles.

There is a lady who lives on an island on the lake who told me some curious things about animals swimming. She had a cat which she did not want, so she gave it to someone in Keswick, but a week afterwards it came back into her house dripping wet!

Also when her nuts are ripe, squirrels appear on the island, but she has not seen them coming. There is an American story that squirrels go down the rivers on little rafts, using their tails for sails, but I think the Keswick squirrels must swim

I must write to Eric next time I hope you are quite well again.

I remain dear Noël yrs aff –
Beatrix Potter

*The squirrels crossing Derwentwater on rafts in* The Tale of Squirrel Nutkin *(1903)*

Nov 3rd 97          Harescombe Grange.

My dear Frida,

I must tell you a funny thing about the guinea-hens here. You know what they are like, I daresay, grey speckled birds with very small silly heads. One day Parton, the coachman, saw them in the field, running backwards and forwards, bobbing their heads up & down & cackling. (They say Pot Rack! Pot Rack! Pot Rackety Rack!) They were watching something white, which was waving about in the long grass. Parton could not tell what it was either, so he went close up to it, & up jumped a fox! It had been lying on its back waving its tail.

I heard of another fox when I was at Woodcote [the house in Surrey of her uncle, Sir Henry Roscoe], which had gone to the gamekeeper's & killed 4 hens & then went to sleep in the pig stye with the pig. The gamekeeper was so cross, he said the people who had the foxhounds had let loose some tame foxes, & they would not stay in the woods. He ran for a gun but Mr Fox woke up.

              yrs aff
              Beatrix Potter

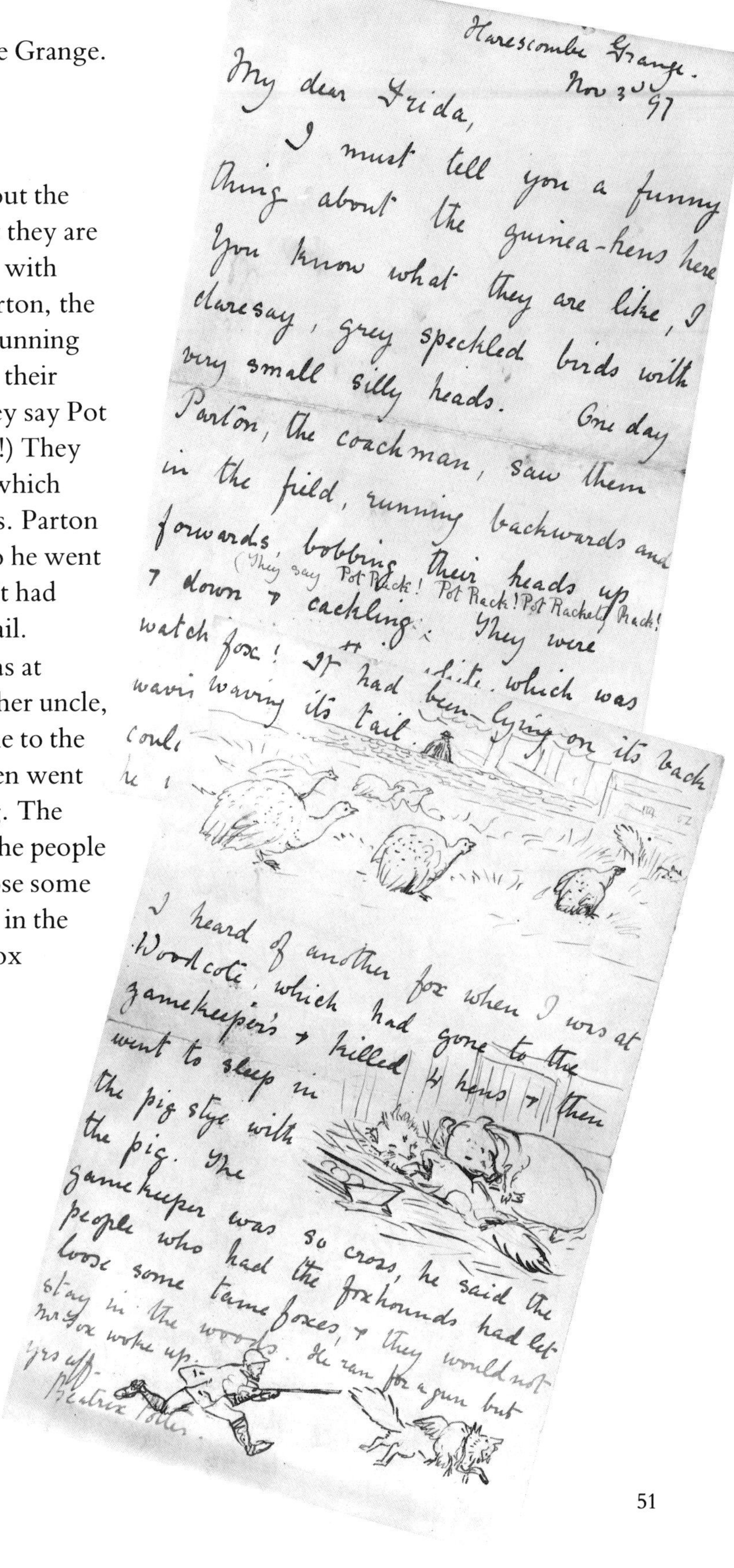

51

Ap. 17th 98.             Cottymeade.
                         Sidmouth.

My dear Noel,

Thank you very much for your nice little letter, and your Mother's too. I was so glad to hear you had both come away for a holiday. We are going home on Tuesday, after a good time here. We have lots of friends, and live in a house just outside the town, where it is all fields & lanes. There are such funny little thatched cottages, with sparrows nests in the thatch, and a pussy-cat sitting in every doorway. Indeed the cottages are so little, I think they must have been meant for cats and dogs!

My brother sleeps in a cottage belonging to a dog called "Stumpy", such a fine solemn brown-and-white dog. He sits on a little mat on the grass plot, and when I go in he gives me a large white paw but he doesn't wag his tail. He is such a polite grave gentleman but so proud! I meet him out shopping in the morning, he looks at me sideways but he never speaks!

Miss Hayward keeps the house, but it really does belong to Stumpy, it is quite a pretty story.

Once upon a time there was an old clergyman, who had no family, and Stumpy was his dog, and Miss Hayward was his servant, and so when he died he left his money to Stumpy, ten shillings a week for the rest of his life!

My brother
sleeps in
a
cottage
belonging
to a dog
called "Stumpy", such a

solemn b...

s

g. Miss Hayward
he     keeps the
but   house, but
He   it really does belong to Stumpy.
         it is quite a pretty story.
         Once upon
         a time

there was an old clergyman who
had no family, and Stumpy was

but so
proud!
I met him
out shopping in the morning, he looks at
one sideways but he never speaks!

when he died
left
money
...py.

Hayward

life! for the rest of
I am sure I hope Stumpy.

53

I am sure I hope Stumpy will live a very long time, It is so convenient for him and Miss Hayward, and "Friday", and "Percy" the cat, to live all together on Stumpy's ten shillings!

I hope you will find a great many nests, and get quite strong before you go home again,

and I remain with love, yours aff
Beatrix Potter

July 30th 98    Lingholm,
Keswick,
Cumberland.

My dear Frida,

I am writing to you instead of Eric because I think you saw my tame snail, and he did not see it. I will write to him and Marjory [sic] next time. I had to dig up my snail's nest when I left home. I found there were 79 large eggs! It was such a queer nest in the ground and the snail had covered it up with soil. The eggs were white just like the eggs you had for breakfast, they would be just the right size for little mice! I brought them here in a little box; the old snail did not take any more trouble about them after she had covered up the hole. Yesterday morning, after 4 weeks, the eggs began to hatch, 9 came out, and 4 more today. They are such pretty little snails with quite hard shells, but almost like glass, I expect they will soon go darker, they are beginning to eat.

My brother has got a jackdaw, a very sly bird. Directly we let him loose he gets into the fire place and brings out rubbish which has been thrown in the fender I think he must have lived in a chimny [sic], it will be very awkward when the fire is lighted.

We are all quite well and there has not been quite so much rain as there usually is here, but I shall be glad to get home again, I don't like going away for such a long time.

I remain yrs affectionately
Beatrix Potter

July 30th 98

LINGHOLM,
KESWICK,
CUMBERLAND.

My dear Frida,
    I am writing to you
instead of Eric because I think
you saw my tame snail, and
he did not see it. I will
write to him and Marjory
next time.        I had to
di... up my snail's nest
    she had covered up the hole.
Yesterday morning, after 4 weeks,
the eggs began to hatch,
9 came out, and 4 more

They are such pretty little ...
with quite hard shells, but alm...
like glass, I expect they will
soon go darker, they are
beginning to eat.
    My brother has got
a jack daw, a
very sly bird.

It was                such a queer
nest in                    the ground
and the snail had covered it up
with soil. The eggs were white
just like the
eggs you
had for breakfast,
they would be just
right size for little mice!
'rought them here in little
the old snail
more +

Directly we let him loose he gets like
into the fire place and brings
out rubbish which has been
thrown in the fender
I think he must
have lived in a
chimny, it will be very awkward
when the fire is lighted. We are
all quite well and there has not
been quite so much rain as there
usually is here, but I shall be glad
to get home again, I don't like
going away for such a long time
remain yrs affectionately
Beatrix Potter.

55

Aug 23rd 98        Waverley hotel
                       Dumfries

My dear Marjory,

I was so much pleased to get all your nice little letters, I intended to have written to you sooner but I have been travelling about so much I have always been too sleepy. You will have to look on the map for the places. My brother and I left Keswick on Tuesday 16th came through Carlisle to Dumfries, then to Kirkcudbright then to Stanraer & Belfast, back to Stanraer to Ayr & Dumfries. We shall go home tomorrow or Saturday. I have seen so much I shall have to pick out things to tell you about. One day we were on the train at Castle Douglas and there was a great sheep fair. Three old farmers got into the railway carriage with a big brown & white colley. One said "I never take a ticket for him, he will go under seat!" and sure enough the dog hid himself in a minute, without being told to do so. Directly we had started he came out & sat up. The carriage door was locked, so when the old man wanted to get out at his station he got out of the window You would have laughed to see how nicely the dog jumped after him. Another farmer has just gone past this house driving six pigs, so I suppose there is a fair today in Dumfries. When we were out we met one driving a big flock of lambs; two of them were so tired they could not go on, so the poor little things were left lying in a corner with their legs tied. The farmer would pick them up as he went home.

I have just been laughing till I cried, there is a very solemn American gentleman with his wife and daughter staying in the hotel, & he has just sat down on a chair which came to pieces quite flat. Everybody screamed with laughter, but he never said nothing. I don't think any Englishman could have been so dignified.

I was very much amused at your Mamma saying she felt like a rag; I have felt like one too! like a very dirty pocket handkerchief, they don't give one much water for washing in Scotch hotels.

I remain dear Marjory, yr aff Aunt

Beatrix Potter

I will draw some better pictures next time.

Dec 23rd 98          Eversfield Hotel
                        St Leonards on Sea

My dear Noël,

    What a shocking thing! I have not got you any Christmas cards! I remembered them this afternoon when I was in a bath chair but there was such a crowd at the shops I thought we might run over somebody. I daresay you would rather have a letter. There are a number of chairs always waiting opposite the hotel, the men pounce upon any one who comes out, but I insist upon having one with 2 wheels in front. The man this afternoon was very talkative about ships & fishing.

    We see numbers of ships, quite a procession, always a long way off & keeping along the same track. They come round Dungeness & then keep straight across outside a lightship called the Royal Sovereign. The lightship is 11 miles off but we can see the revolving light on clear nights. The man told me it broke loose in a storm one winter, breaking two cables, but a tug boat caught it & took it back as near the right place as it could, it is called the Diamond Sands. After the ships pass that they go outside the Isle of Wight. We saw a very large one, North German Lloyd, on Sunday; we could see the passengers walking about on the decks through our big telescope.

    He also told me about the Hastings fishing boats they are very pretty, painted bright colours & have all got brown sails. They are smaller than usual & do not go very far out, 20 miles, because they have so much difficulty in getting home against the wind. The men sell quantities of fish in the streets, I never saw such a mixture, all sorts of colours. My chairman told me he had caught conger eels 20 feet long, which made me laugh, for they are savage! He said they were so difficult to kill they have to put a string through the gills & tie them to the boat to prevent them from jumping out again, which I can quite believe. He says all the herrings & mackerel here are very small because the water is shallow & the old big fish all go off round Dungeness into the North Sea, where it is deep.

                                   yrs aff
                                Beatrix Potter

There are a number of chairs always waiting opposite the hotel, the men pounce upon any one who comes out, but I insist upon having one with 2 wheels in front. The man this afternoon was very talkative about ships & fishing

We see numbers of ships, quite a procession, always a long way & keeping along the same track. They come round Dungeness, then keep straight on in a light ship. The light ship cap...

The man told me it broke loose in a storm one winter, breaking two cables, but a tug boat caught it & took it back as near the right place as it could, it is called the diamond Sands. After the ships pass that they go outside the Isle of Wight. We saw a very large one, North German Lloyd, on Sunday; we could see the passengers walking about on the decks through our big telescope. He... told me about the Hastings...

...pretty, painted bright ...all brown sails. They ...usual & do not ...iles, because

They have so much difficulty in getting home against the wind. The men sell quantities of fish in the streets, I never saw such a mixture, all sorts of colours. My chairman told me he had caught conger eels 20 feet long, which made me laugh, for they are savage!

He said they were so difficult to kill they have to put a string through the gills & tie them to the boat, when I can quite believe. He says all the herrings & mackerel here are very small because the water is shallow & the old big fish all go off round Dungeness into the north sea where it is deep.

yrs aff. Beatrix Potter.

Jan 13th 99.             16 Robertson Terrace
                        Hastings

My dear Marjorie,

The last time I wrote to the boys I was at Hastings. I went home on Dec. 28th but I did not like the cold weather in London so I came back here, with a servant. I am feeling much better and I shall go home next Monday. There are some other people in the lodgings who have such a funny cat, a Manx cat, from the Isle of Man, where they have no tails. It runs about in a curious way, I think it has longer legs than an ordinary cat. It peeps into my room but I cannot catch it, but I always know when it is there because it wears a bell.

Monday.    There are some other people in the lodgings who have such a funny cat, a Manx cat, from the Isle of Man, where they have no tails. It runs about in a curious way, I think it has longer legs than an ordinary cat. It peeps into my room but I — it, but —

There are some little goats carriages on the Parade, they would be just the right size for Baby; one of the goats is very pretty, I saw him eating his dinner one day out of a nose bag, just like a horse's nose bag, only very small. He has a long beard, but it was tucked inside —  There are

a great many carriages, one fat old gentleman always amuses me, he has the very smallest grey ponies in little blue & red coats —

My pony must be having a lazy time, I shall come and see you some day when it is fine —

yrs. aff — Beatrix Potter —

There are some little goat carriages on the Parade, they would be just the right size for Baby [Joan was two and a half]; one of the goats is very pretty, I saw him eating his dinner one day out of a nose bag, just like a horse's nose bag, only very small. He has a long beard, but it was tucked inside. There are a great many carriages, one fat old gentleman always amuses me, he has the very smallest grey ponies in little blue & red coats.

My pony must be having a lazy time. I shall come and see you some day when it is fine.

yrs aff
Beatrix Potter

Jan 13th 99.    16 Robertson Terrace
Hastings

My dear Frida,

It is very wet today but there is something to look at, just opposite the house. The sea has knocked over 20 yards of iron railing and thrown great big coping stones onto the road. It happened in the night, but I saw very fine waves yesterday. I stood on the end of the terrace and looked down on a lower street where the water was rushing down the gutter. People were putting boards over the windows but it flooded a boot shop in the night. I'm afraid I cannot draw it but I tried to take some photographs of the little boys rushing up the lamp posts & railings. There was a large crowd & whenever anyone tried to get round the corner of the terrace they made such a noise, one old gentleman was wet all over, and some girls came round when it was a little quieter & found themselves in a pond. There were baskets & things floating about, and a very nice brown terrier dog, barking & rushing about. A stupid boy

61

threw a stone into the waves & it jumped off the wall before anyone could stop it. I thought it would be drowned but the next big waves threw it out again into the road. It walked off looking quite offended but I think it was rather frightened. The sea has smashed a large gas lamp at the pier, I hope nothing worse. The Hastings boats all came home in a great hurry before the gale. I hope you are all very well,

yrs aff<br>Beatrix Potter

January 26th 1900    Derwent Cottage
Winchelsea

My dear Marjory,

I shall write to you and Frida [sic], for I suppose the boys have gone away to school by this time; I wonder if they have got boxes like we used to have

I wonder if I have spelt your name right this time! If I have not, you will say I ought to go to school too, and learn out of a big spelling book.

I expect when I see you again, you and Frida will have grown so big I shall not know you! I believe I haven't seen you since last July, it is quite shocking. It is all because of my poor old pony being dead; when I want to drive to Wandsworth in the big carriage, my Mamma wants to drive the other way; and when your Mamma wanted to call at Bolton Gardens at Christmas, I could not ask her to come because we had influenza in the house. I hope you did not have a visit from him, he is a disagreeable old person! I have been very well, but my brother and Cox [the butler] had it rather badly.

I daresay Bardy [Norah Moore] is big enough now to want a letter, so I must not put any more nonsense into this letter, or I shall have none left for her. Good bye dear Marjory,

from yrs aff<br>Beatrix Potter

January 26ᵗʰ 1900
Derwent Cottage
Winchelsea.

My dear Marjory,
I shall write to you and
Frida, for I suppose the
boys have gone away to school
by this time; I wonder
if they have got boxes like
we used to have
I wonder if I have spelt
name right this time!

from him.
he is a dis-
"agreeable old
person!
I have been very well, but my
brother and Cox had it rather
badly. I daresay Bardy
is big enough now to want a
letter, so I must not put any
more nonsense into this letter, or
I shall have none left for her.
Good bye dear Marjory, from
yrs aff. Beatrix Potter.

If I have not, you will
say I ought to go to school
too, and learn
out of a big
spelling book.
I expect when I see you again,
you and Frida will have grown
so big I shall
not know you!
I believe I
haven't seen you since last
year, it is quite
to drive to Wandsworth in the
big carriage; my Mamma
wants to drive
the other
way;
and when your Mamma
wanted to call at Bolton
Gardens at Christmas, I
could not ask her to come,
because we had influenza in
the house. I hope you
did not have a visit

Jan 26th 1900          Derwent Cottage
                       Winchelsea

My dear Frida,

    I am staying in such a funny old cottage; it is like the little mouse–houses I have often drawn in pictures.

    I am sure – (when I am half asleep) – that it is a mouse-house, for Mrs Cooke, the landlady, and her family go to bed up a sort of ladder stair-case, and I can hear them scuffling about upon the rafters just above my head! The ceiling of my bed-room is so low I can touch it with my hand, and there is a little lattice window just the right size for mice to peep out of. Then there are cupboards in the walls, that little people could hide in, and steps up and down into the rooms, and doors in every corner; very draughty! I wish it would stop raining and be bright and fine; I don't think my brother & I will stop more than a week if the weather does not mend. We came here last Wednesday. I have been for 2 long walks, it is pretty country, & on nearly every hill there is a windmill, spinning round in the wind and rain.

I am dear Frida yrs affectionately
Beatrix Potter

*The cupboard in the wall which
Beatrix drew for* Appley Dapply's
Nursery Rhymes *(1917)*

March 13th 1900     2, Bolton Gardens,
                    London, S.W.

My dear Marjory,

   You will begin to be afraid I have run away with the letters altogether! I will keep them a little longer because I want to make a list of them, but I don't think they will be made into a book this time because the publisher wants poetry. The publisher is a gentleman who prints books, and he wants a bigger book than he has got enough money to pay for! and Miss Potter has arguments with him. He was taken ill on Sunday and his sisters and his cousins and his aunts had arguments, I wonder if that book will ever be printed! I think Miss Potter will go off to another publisher soon! She would rather make 2 or 3 little books costing 1/– each, than one big book costing 6/– because she thinks little rabbits cannot afford to spend 6 shillings on one book, and would never buy it.

*From the manuscript version of* The Tale of Peter Rabbit, *offered to several publishers before being taken by Frederick Warne*

   I went to the Reading Room at the British Museum this morning to see a delightful old book full of rhymes I shall draw pictures of some of them whether they are printed or not. The Reading Room is an *enormous* big room, quite round, with galleries round the sides the walls covered with books, and hundreds of chairs and desks on the floor. There were not many people, but some of them were very funny to look at! And there are some people who live there always but Miss Potter didn't see them, although they are said to be the largest people of their sort in London! Next time Miss Potter goes to the British Museum she will take some Keating's powder! It is very odd there should be fleas in books!

a bigger book, each, than one big book costing than he has 6/. because got enough she thinks money to pay for! and miss little rabbits Potter has arguments with him. cannot afford to spend 6 shillings He was taken ill on Sunday and on one book, and would never his sisters and his cousins and buy it. I went to the his Aunts had arguments; I Reading Room at the British wonder if that book will ever be Museum this morning to see a printed! I think Miss Potter delightful old book full of rhymes. will go off to another publisher soon! I shall draw pictures of some She would rather whether they are printed make 2 or 3 little books costing 1/

enormous big room, quite round. with galleries round the sides the walls covered with books, and hundreds of chairs and desks on the floor. There were not many people but some of them were very funny to look at! And there are some people who live there always but Miss Potter didn't see them, although they are said to be the largest people of their sort in London! Next time miss Potter goes to the British Museum she will take some heating powder! It is very old there should be holes in books!

*'Three Blind Mice', one of the old rhymes Beatrix illustrated for* Cecily Parsley's Nursery Rhymes *(1922)*

April 24th 00          2, Croft Terrace, Tenby

My dear Marjory,

It is quite time for me to write to you, I generally send a letter from the sea-side at Easter and I am going home on Thursday 26th. It has been so hot lately, the only cool place is on the water in a boat. I go out every morning and I generally tell the boat man to row close under the cliffs so that I can watch the birds. The rocks are a tremendous height, as high as a church, and quite straight from top to bottom in many places, but sometimes there are little ledges half way up with wild cabbages growing on them, & at the top where there is soil there is a row of rabbit-holes. What a very funny place for cabbages & rabbits right up in the air! My boat man says he has sometimes picked up poor dead rabbits that have tumbled off; but as long as they don't go too near the edge – or if they have a little railing – it is a very nice safe place, for nobody can possibly get near them, & their little cabbage gardens. They have wall flowers too, just like the garden wall flowers only they are all yellow. Another thing that is very convenient is the coal. I can see it like black lines between the cracks in the cliffs, and little bits of it fall down onto the sand, so if Mrs Bunny picks some cabbage leaves for dinner she can light a little fire and boil the pot.

yrs aff
Beatrix Potter

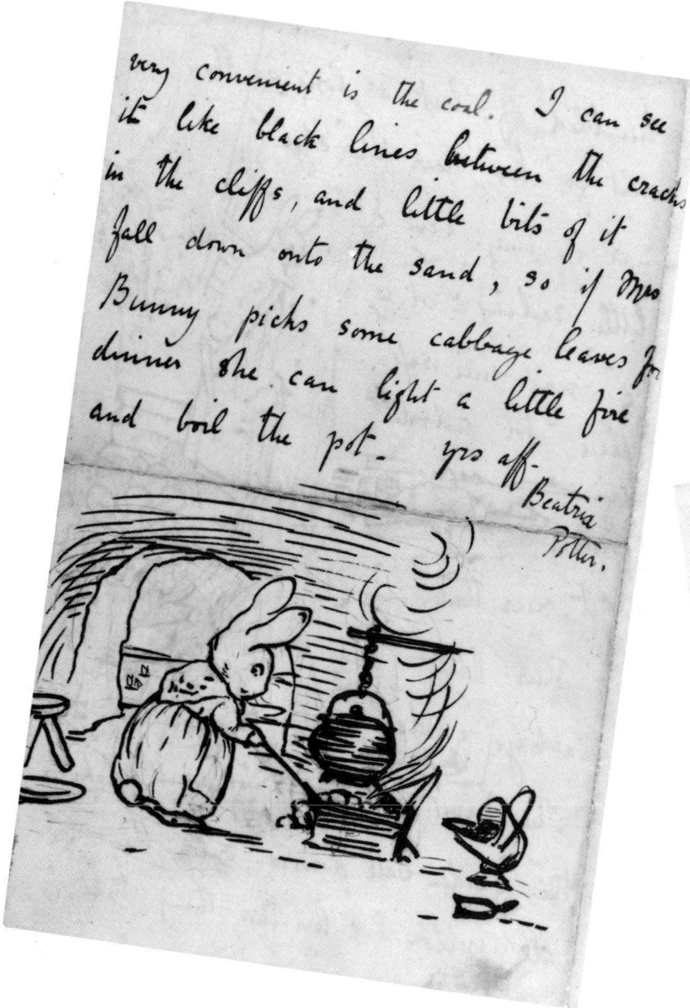

April 24th 00                    Tenby

My dear Frida,

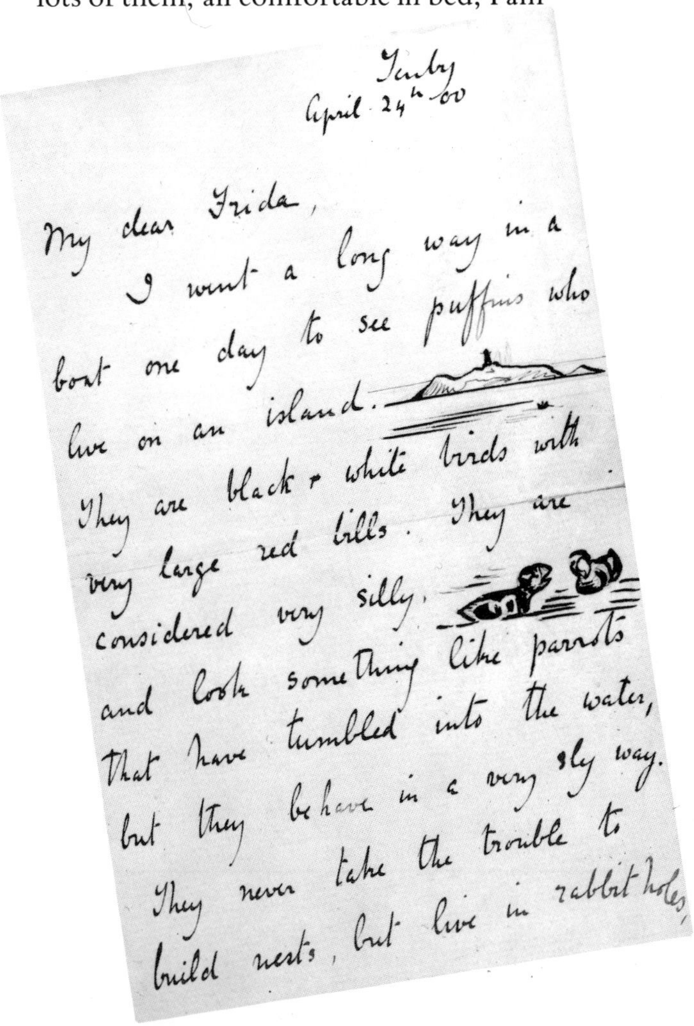

I went a long way in a boat one day to see puffins who live on an island. They are black & white birds with very large red bills. They are considered very silly, and look something like parrots that have tumbled into the water, but they behave in a very sly way. They never take the trouble to build nests, but live in rabbit holes. They look for a nice hole and drive the rabbits out. They do not live here in the winter but arrived about a fortnight since, it must be most annoying to the rabbits to see them landing. There are little rabbits by this time, lots of them, all comfortable in bed, I am sure they don't give up their holes without a fight! I don't believe either rabbits or puffins are able to hurt much, but the puffins always win and take possession of the best holes. I don't know what becomes of the rabbits; perhaps they go and live with the jackdaws, who are much more polite, they walk about bobbing their heads as if they were bowing. I notice the rabbits & jackdaws live close together quite nicely. The jackdaws go into holes in the rock exactly like little square doors.

I am very sleepy with going on the sea in the wind.

> With love to all of you from yrs aff
> Beatrix Potter

Miss Potter is sitting upon her book at present & considering! The publisher cannot tell what has become of it.

Sept 25th 01                      Lingholme,
Keswick

My dear Norah,

    There are such numbers of squirrels in the woods here. They are all very busy just now gathering nuts, which they hide away in little holes, where they can find them again, in the winter.

    An old lady who lives on the island says she thinks they come over the lake when her nuts are ripe; but I wonder how they can get across the water? Perhaps they make little rafts!

    One day I saw a most comical little squirrel; his tail was only an inch long, but he was so impertinent, he chattered and clattered and threw down acorns onto my head. I believe that his name was Nutkin and that he had a brother called Twinkleberry, and this is the story of how he lost his tail.

There is a big island in the middle of the lake, covered with woods, and in the middle of it stands a hollow oak-tree which is the house of an owl, called Old Brown. One autumn when the nuts were ripe, Nutkin and Twinkleberry, and all the other little squirrels came down to the edge of the lake and paddled across over the water to Owl Island to gather nuts. Each squirrel had a little sack with him, and a large oar, and spread out his tail for a sail They also carried with them an offering of 3 fat mice for Old Brown, which they placed upon a stone opposite his door. Then Twinkleberry and the other squirrels each made a low bow, and said politely – "Old Mr Brown, will you favour us with permission to gather nuts upon your island?"

But Nutkin, who was excessively impertinent in his manners, jumped up & down, and shouted –

"Old Mr B! riddle-me-ree?
Higgledy piggledy
    Here we lie,
Pick'd and pluck'd,
    And put in a pie:
My first is snapping, snarling, growling
My second's industrious, romping, prowling
    Higgledy, piggledy,
    Here we lie,
    Pick'd and pluck'd
    And put in a pie!"

Now this riddle is as old as the hills. Mr Brown paid no attention whatever to Nutkin.

The squirrels filled their bags and sailed away home in the evening.

The next morning they all came back again to Owl Island, and Twinkleberry and the others brought a fine fat mole, and laid it on the stone in front of Old Brown's door, and said – "Mr Brown will you favour us with your gracious permission to gather some more nuts?" But Nutkin, who had no respect, danced up & down, and sang –

"Old Mr B! riddle-me-ree?
    As soft as silk,
    As white as milk,
As bitter as gall, a thick wall,
And a green coat covers me all!"

The squirrels filled their bags and sailed away home in the evening.

The next morning they all came back again to Owl Island; and Twinkleberry and the others brought a fine fat mole, and laid it on the stone in front of Old Brown's door, and said –

"Mr Brown will your favour us with your gracious permission to gather some more nuts?" But of 7 fat minnows. [a present]

But Nutkin who had no manners danced up & down, and sang –

danced up and down and sang as rudely as ever —

comb of [wax] sweet that they licked their [lips] when they put it down upon the stone.

But Nutkin danced about, as saucy

Mr Brown made no reply to the impertinent Nutkin.

On the 3rd day the squirrels came back again and brought a present of 7 fat minnows.

But Nutkin who had no manners danced up & down, and sang –

"Old Mr B! riddle-me-ree?
As I came through the garden gap,
Who should I meet but Dick Red-cap,
A stick in his hand, a stone in his throat
If you'll tell me this riddle
I'll give you a groat!"

Which was very absurd of Nutkin, because he did not possess 4 pence; even if Mr Brown *had* taken the trouble to answer.

The fourth day the squirrels came with a present of 6 large beetles for old Brown. But Nutkin danced up and down and sang as rudely as ever –

"Old Mr B! riddle-me-ree?
Flour of England, fruit of Spain,
Met together in a shower of rain;
Put in a bag tied round with a string,
If you'll tell me this riddle,
I'll give you a ring!"

which was rediculous [sic] of Nutkin, because he hadn't got any ring to give to old Brown.

The fifth day the squirrels came again and brought a present of a combe [sic] of wild honey. It was so sweet that they licked their fingers when they put it down upon the stone.

But Nutkin danced about, as saucy as ever and sang –

"Old Mr B! riddle-me-ree?
As I went over Tipple Tine
I met a flock of bonny swine;
  Some green-lapp'd
  Some green-back'd,
They were the very bonniest swine,
That e'er went over Tipple Tine!
Hum-a-bum, bum, buz-z-z-z-

Old Brown turned up his nose in disgust at the impertinence of Nutkin. But he ate up the honey.

The sixth day, which was Saturday, the squirrels came for the last time. They brought a parting present for Old Brown, consisting of a pie with 4 & 20 blackbirds.

But I am sorry to say that Nutkin was more saucy and excited than ever.

He jumped up and down and sang –

"Old Mr B! riddle-me-ree?
Humpty Dumpty lies in the beck
With a white counterpane round his neck.
All the king's horses, and all the king's men,
Can't put Humpty Dumpty
  together again!"

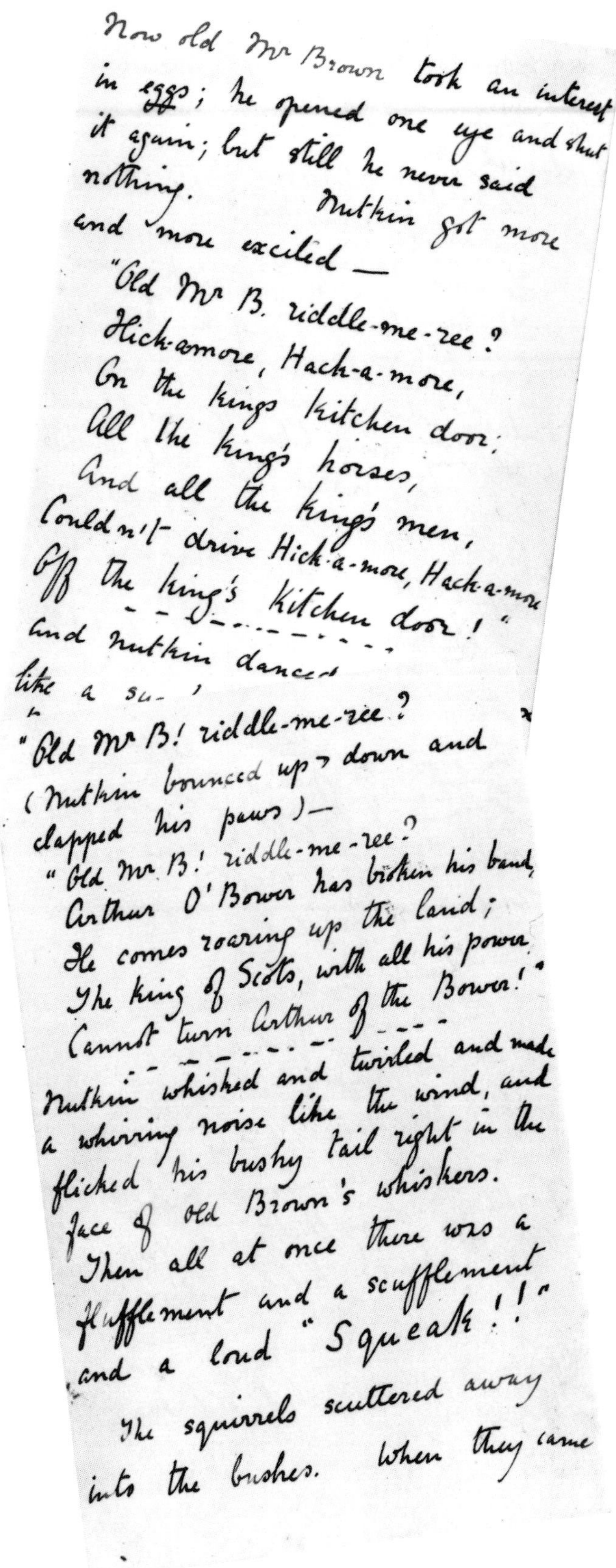

Now old Mr Brown took an interest in *eggs*; he opened one eye and shut it again; but still he never said nothing. Nutkin got more and more excited –

"Old Mr B. riddle-me-ree?
Hick-a-more, Hack-a-more,
On the kings kitchen door.
All the king's horses
And all the king's men,
Couldn't drive Hick-a-more, Hack-a-more
Off the king's kitchen door!"

And Nutkin danced up and down like a sun-beam; but old Mr Brown never said nothing.

Then Nutkin began again –

"Old Mr B! riddle-me-ree?

(Nutkin bounced up & down and clapped his paws) –

"Old Mr B! riddle-me-ree?
Arthur O'Bower has broken his band,
He comes roaring up the land;
The king of Scots, with all his power
Cannot turn Arthur of the Bower!"

Nutkin whisked and twirled and made a whirring noise like the wind, and flicked his bushy tail right in the face of old Brown's whiskers.

Then all at once there was a flufflement and a scufflement and a loud "Squeak!!"

The squirrels scuttered away into the bushes. When they came back and peeped

Now old Mr Brown took an interest in eggs; he opened one eye and shut it again; but still he never said nothing. Nutkin got more and more excited —
"Old Mr B. riddle-me-ree?
Hick-a-more, Hack-a-more,
On the kings kitchen door;
All the king's horses,
And all the king's men,
Couldn't drive Hick-a-more, Hack-a-more
Off the king's kitchen door!"
And Nutkin danced
like a su-
"Old Mr B! riddle-me-ree?
(Nutkin bounced up & down and clapped his paws) —
"Old Mr B! riddle-me-ree?
Arthur O'Bower has broken his band,
He comes roaring up the land;
The king of Scots, with all his power
Cannot turn Arthur of the Bower!"
Nutkin whisked and twirled and made a whirring noise like the wind, and flicked his bushy tail right in the face of old Brown's whiskers.
Then all at once there was a flufflement and a scufflement and a loud "Squeak!!"
The squirrels scuttered away into the bushes. When they came

cautiously round the tree – there was Old Brown sitting on his door step, quite still, with his eyes closed: as if nothing had happened.

But Nutkin was in his waist-coat pocket!!!

That is the end of the story. Old Brown carried Nutkin into his house, and held him up by the tail, intending to skin him; but Nutkin pulled so hard that his tail broke in two, and he dashed up the stair-case, and escaped out of the attic window.

And to this day, if you meet Nutkin up a tree, and ask him a riddle, he will throw sticks at you, and chatter his teeth, and scold, and shout – "Cuck cuck cuck cuck cur-r-r-r"!

> Yours aff
> Beatrix Potter

*From* The Tailor of Gloucester *(1903)*

The following letter accompanied the manuscript of *The Tailor of Gloucester* which was written out in a stiff-covered exercise book and illustrated with twelve watercolours.

Christmas 1901.

My dear Freda,

Because you are fond of fairy-tales and have been ill, I have made you a story all for yourself – a new one that nobody has read before.

And the queerest thing about it – is that I heard it in Gloucestershire, and it is true! at least about the tailor, the waistcoat, and the 'No more twist'.

There ought to be more pictures towards the end, and they would have been the best ones; only Miss Potter was tired of it! Which was lazy of Miss Potter.

> yrs aff
> H.B.P.

*back and peeped cautiously round the tree – there was Old Brown sitting on his door step, quite still, with his eyes closed: as if nothing had happened.*

*But Nutkin was in his waistcoat pocket!!!*

July 6th 02                    Laund House
                               Bolton Abbey

My dear Freda,

I have kept your picture book [*The Tailor of Gloucester*] a long time and I have not done with it yet. I had to copy out the pictures rather larger and it took me a long time, but you will get it back some day.

I hope soon I shall have the new edition of the little rabbit book [*Peter Rabbit*] with coloured pictures – I have had the pictures to look at and they were very pretty, but not made up into a proper book yet.

I have been such a fine long walk this morning right up onto the top of a hill, where there was heather and lots of grouse. We could see a very long way, hills & hills one behind another & white roads going up & down from one valley to the next. There is a beautiful old church called Bolton Abbey about a mile off, most of it is in ruins, but there is a little piece in the middle where they have service.

The river winds round about it and at the end of the lawn below the abbey there are stepping stones, like this, such a width, I did not try to cross. I thought I should fall in. What a mess I have made with the ink! there is too much in the pot, and everyone is talking at once. I wonder how I am going to get to the station with my box, it is such a way!

I hope your Mamma is quite well, give her my love.

                               Your aff. friend,
                               Beatrix Potter

Oct 6th 02                     Eeswyke,
                               Sawrey,
                               Lancashire.

My dear Freda,

I had such nice letters from you and Marjory [sic] just after I came here, and I have been intending to answer them all summer, but I have left it till the last day! We are coming home on Wednesday. We have all got colds in our noses at present to end up with. I hope I shall be able to drive over to see your Mamma with the new pony; but I shall not keep him long if he does not improve his manners when he gets to London. One of his little games – when he is lazy and does not want to go – is to sail away round a corner & up a wrong road.

Then I pull & scold, & then the groom takes the reins & pulls, & at last we stop, & then the groom gets out & turns him round and punches him very hard in the ribs! Other times he stands still at the bottom of a hill & won't go at all. When he does occasionally go, he is a very good pony indeed & nice looking.

Your mouse-book [*The Tailor of Gloucester*] is not printed yet; but the coloured edition of Peter Rabbit is ready, & I think it is to be in the shops this week; if there are any book shops about Wandsworth you must look whether it is in the windows. The publisher has sold more copies than he printed (6000) so he is going to print another edition at once.

We have had a very cold summer, the last few weeks have been the pleasantest we have had; although it is sharp & frosty there is less wind & more sunshine than in August. My brother has been shooting pheasants & rabbits, lots of rabbits; the gardener puts a ferret into the hole & then the rabbit rushes out; he got 11 today. I have a little rabbit which I tamed, it jumps over my hands for bits of biscuit, but it is so frightened of everyone else I cannot show off its tricks to people. My brother was bitten with a snake a fortnight ago, he had a bad arm but it is all right again now. We have caught a good many pike in the lake, we fish with a thing they call a "wagtail"! It is a very ugly imitation fish made of bits of leather. I must do some more packing, so good night, & love to all of you.

from yrs aff–
Beatrix Potter

Sept 10th 04

Lingholme
Keswick
Cumberland

My dear Hilda

This is a picture of the piebald mouse her name is "Thingummy-jig!" And these are the 4 little mouseys – "Whatzername!" Thingummy bob! Whiteface and Spot!

I gave away all the 4 little mice and got a brown mouse called 'Pippin', who lives with Thingummy-jig. Generally they are very good friends, but sometimes there is a dreadful fight; they squeak very loud, and the piebald mouse raps her tail on the table, making quite a loud tapping when she is very angry.

I do not think Pippin will be able to wag *her* tail about – she has had an inch bitten off the end! I found the piece.

I was very much shocked; but Pippin does not seem to care, she walks about with her short tail straight up in the air.

I do not think that it was the piebald mouse who bit off Pippin's tail; I think it was a brown mouse called Applely [sic] Dapply.

I hope that you are all quite well; I wonder if you have any apples in your garden.

yrs aff
Beatrix Potter

[For Marjorie Moore, undated, an
adaptation of the traditional rhyme]

I saw a ship a-sailing
A-sailing on the sea;
And Oh! it was all laden
With pretty things for thee!

There were comfits in the cabin
And apples in the hold;
The sails were made of silk
And the masts were made of gold.

And 4 and 20 sailors
That stood upon the decks
Were four and twenty white mice
With chains about their necks

The captain was a guinea-pig —
The pilot was a rat —

the Captain

The ship

The passengers embarking

And the passengers were rabbits
Who ran about, pit pat!

All of which will have to be carefully drawn,
but I think the words are lovely. Just imagine
the white mice letting down the bags of comfits
into the hold!

## *UNDATED COPIES OF EXTRACTS FROM*
## *LETTERS TO THE MOORE CHILDREN*

When Annie Moore suggested to Beatrix that some of her letters to the children might be turned into books Beatrix borrowed them back to make copies. She copied out both the words and the pictures, occasionally changing a word or phrase as she went along. With the exception of the letter to Eric of 5 September 1895, those so far reproduced here are the originals, not copies. However, it has not been possible to trace all the Moore letters and the following are Beatrix's copies of snippets from 'lost' letters found among her possessions at Castle Cottage after her death. With the copies was a note in her hand, 'These are not the original letters. I borrowed them from the Moores and copied them roughly. It was unfortunate that I did not copy the dates on the original letters.' She was not to know that many of the originals would still be treasured possessions a hundred years after she first wrote them.

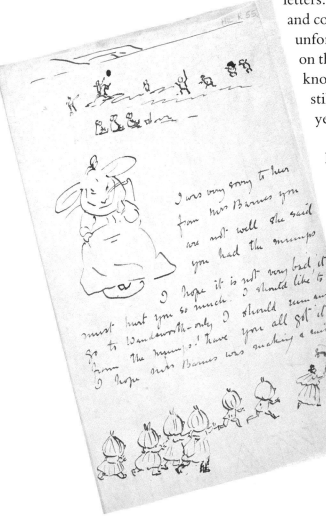

I was very sorry to hear from Mrs Barnes you are not well she said you had the mumps. I hope it is not very bad, it must hurt you so much. I should like to go to Wandsworth – only I should run away from the mumps! Have you all got it? I hope Mrs Barnes was making a mistake.

I was very much interested to watch some fishermen with a long net. 2 of them stood on the beach holding one end of the net, & another man went out with a boat throwing the rest out like this. Then the man in the boat came back & they all pulled. The net stuck fast, I thought what a big fish! but it was an old kettle.

When the net was all dragged out on the beach there were two little flat fish & the kettle & more than 100 little smelts, such pretty little silver fish, I daresay you have seen them in the shops & at breakfast. There was a pussy cat sitting in the sun on a doorstep & directly the men began to put the fish into a basket she ran down some steps & begged for one. A little boy threw a fish to her & she ran home with it in her mouth. I have made this picture of pussy coming down to the beach for her fish with a basket, only she was not really dressed up you know, but I think she was a very wise cat.

The fishermen are such funny old fellows one old man got into the omnibus with a string of very smelly fish. He said "Every fish in the sea had got a blue eye except one! The oyster's got a blue eye: the scollops got 32 blue eyes!! You don't know what fish hasn't got a blue eye?" He asked everybody in the omnibus which fish hadn't got a blue eye & then told us it was the whiting. I don't know if it was a joke but I thought he was very funny.

She is such a pretty animal, when she is sitting down; when she stands up you can see she has lost a paw. She is not much bigger than Fritz, & has a tail like his only it is [?]; she has a beautiful sleek coat & such a nasty smell! I tried to draw her picture but it makes her feel shy, & she hides underneath the kennel & peeps out at me, but if I take a bit of meat she runs out. Mr Cooke says I mustn't touch her as she would bite.

I saw a baby eland, just 4 weeks old, with little short horns & large ears, it was lying down in some soft straw & a mouse was running about but it took no notice. The mother eland was eating hay.

I think you would like to hear about my rabbit. I brought him from London in a basket. I think he likes this place because there is so much green stuff for him to eat, but there is no wall round the garden so I have to lead him with a string. When he is sleepy he digs up the sand & lies down. Yesterday I took him round the garden, when I heard something rustling among the cabbages & a little wild rabbit came out to talk to my Mr Bunny. It sat upon its hind legs & made a little grunting noise, but Mr Bunny was eating so fast he took no notice till it came close to him round a cabbage

There is a funny sight here in the field, a very fussy old hen with 7 ducklings. She has such a sad time with them; when it rains they rush about in great spirits catching worms & slugs, while she stands on one leg

& sneezes. In the evening when the chickens have gone to bed the little ducks stop out late & she follows them about everywhere. I think she is a very good hen. I saw a crow fly across the field & she bristled up her feathers & all the little ducks ran behind her. There was such a loss one day! 26 chickens killed by a ferret! The gardener set a rabbit trap next night & caught it when it came back for more. Ferrets are tame animals belonging to gamekeepers but no one in the neighbourhood will say he has lost one; for Mr Pring says they were prize chickens worth £3 & Mr Ferret had no money in his pocket, nothing but chickens!
I went to Thirlspot to see an old farmer "Humph humph, tobesure tobesure!

We have been here for a week it is so hot that I have to walk about with an umbrella. We went on the steamer called Roseland this morning, across the harbour. We went very close to a queer looking ship & then the steamer stopped. The other ship called the Alma had broken its mast & torn its sail so that it could not get along. They tied it to the Roseland with a thick rope & dragged it home. After that we went in a little row boat with a fisherman. We gave him a photograph of his cottage & he was so pleased that he fetched us some very large oysters which we have eaten for tea. He told us they were so big because they were 10 years old. He put the little oysters into a sort of little garden under the water called an oyster bed & now that they are grown up he gets them out when the tide goes down but he cannot reach the biggest except when the tide goes down.

[To Hilda Moore]

Mr Brown
Owl Island

Sir,

I should esteem it a favour if you would let me have back my tail, as I miss it very much. I would pay postage.

yrs truly
Squirrel Nutkin.

Mr Old Brown Esq
Owl Island.

Dear Sir

I should be extremely obliged if you could kindly send back a tail which you have had for some time. It is fluffy brown with a white tip.

I wrote to you before about it, but perhaps I did not address the letter properly.

I will pay the postage.
yrs respectifully [sic]
Sq. Nutkin

Old Mr Brown Esq
Owl Island.

Dear Sir

I should be exceedingly obliged if you will let me have back my tail. I will gladly pay 3 bags of nuts for it, if you will please post it back to me, I have written to you twice Mr Brown. I think I did not give my address, it is Derwent Bay Wood.

yrs respectifully [sic]
Sq. Nutkin.

O. Brown Esq MP
Owl Island.

Dear Sir

I write on behalf of my brother Nutkin to beg that as a great favour you would send him back his tail. He never makes – or asks – riddles now, and he is truly sorry that he was so rude.

Trusting that you continue to enjoy good health.

I remain yr obedient servant
Twinkleberry Squirrel

Sir Isaac Newton
The Well

Mr Alderman
Ptolemy Tortoise

*Request the pleasure of*

Sir Isaac Newton's
*Company at Dinner*
on Dec. 25th
(to meet our friend Fisher)

R.S.V.P.

---

Mr Alderman Ptolemy
Tortoise
The Melon Pit.

Dear Mr Alderman,
I shall have much
pleasure in dining with you
on Dec 25th. It is a surprise
as I thought that you were
asleep.
Perhaps the present
disagreeable frost has not
yet penetrated into the
genial atmosphere of the
Melon Pit.
Our friend Fisher was
taking mud baths at the
bottom of the pond when
last I heard of him.
Faithfully yrs
I. Newton.

---

Mr. Jeremy Fisher.
Pond House.

Mr. Alderman
Ptolemy Tortoise

*Request the pleasure of*

Mr. Jeremy Fisher's
*Company at Dinner*
on Dec. 25th
(there will be a snail)

R.S.V.P.

Mr. Alderman Ptolemy
Tortoise
Melon Pit,
South Border.

Mr. Jeremy Fisher accepts
with pleasure Alderman P.
Tortoise's kind invitation to
dinner for Dec. 25.

Miss Lucinda Doll
Doll's House.

Honoured Madam

Would you forgive my asking whether you can spare a feather bed? The feathers are all coming out of the one we stole from your house.

If you can spare another, me & my wife would be truly grateful.

yr obedient
humble servant
Thomas Thumb

P.S. Me & my wife are grateful to you for employing her as char-woman. I hope that she continues to give satisfaction.

P.P.S. Me and my wife would be grateful for any old clothes, we have 9 of a family at present.

Mr T. Thumb
Mouse Hole

Miss Lucinda Doll has received Tom Thumbs appeal, but she regrets to inform Tom Thumb that she has never had another feather bed for *herself*.

She also regrets to say that Hunca Munca forgot to dust the mantelpiece on Wednesday.

Miss Lucinda Doll
Doll's House.

Honoured Madam

I am sorry to hear that my wife forgot to dust the mantelpiece. I have whipped her. Me & my wife would be very grateful for another kettle, the last one is full of holes. Me & my wife do not think that it was made of tin at all.

We have nine of a family at present & they require hot water.

I remain honoured madam

yr obedient servant
Thomas Thumb

Miss Lucinda Doll
Doll's House.

Honoured Madam,
I thank you kindly for your letter informing me that Tom Kitten is coming to sweep the kitchen chimney at 6. I will arrive punctually at 7.

Thanking you for past favours.

yr obedient servant
Hunca Munca.

Mrs Thomas Thumb
Mouse Hole

Miss Lucinda Doll will require Hunca Munca to come for the whole day on Saturday.

Jane Dollcook has had an accident.

She has broken the soup tureen and both her wooden legs.

Mrs Duchess
Belle Green.

My dear Duchess,
    If you are at home and not engaged will you come to tea tomorrow? but if you are away I shall put this in the post and invite cousin Tabitha Twitchit. There will be a red herring, & muffins & crumpets.
    The patty pans are all locked up. Do come.
                    yr aff friend
                        Ribby.

Mrs. Tabitha Twitchit
Hill Top Farm.

Dear Cousin Tabitha,
    If you can leave your family with safety I shall be much pleased if you will take tea with me this afternoon. There will be muffins and crumpets and a red herring.
    I have just been to call upon my friend Duchess, she is away from home.
                yr. aff cousin,
                    Ribby

Mrs. Ribstone Pippin
Lakefield Cottage.

Dear Cousin Ribby,
    I shall be pleased to take tea with you. I am glad that Duchess is away from home, I do not care for dogs. My son Thomas is well, but he grows out of all his clothes, and I have other troubles
                    yr aff cousin
                    Tabitha Twitchit.

Mrs. Ribstone Pippin
Lakefield Cottage.

My dear Ribby,

   I am so sorry I was out, it would have given me so much pleasure to accept your kind invitation. I had gone to a dog show. I enjoyed it very much but I am a little disappointed that I did not take a prize and I missed the red herring.

yr. aff. friend,<br>Duchess

Mrs. Tiggy Winkle
Cat Bells.

Dear Madam,

   Though unwilling to hurt the feelings of another widow, I really cannot any longer put up with *starch* in my pocket handkerchiefs. I am sending this one back to you, to be washed again. Unless the washing improves next week I shall (reluctantly) feel obliged to change my laundry.

yrs. truly,<br>Josephine Rabbit

Mrs Rabbit
Sand Bank
Under Fir-tree

If you please'm,

   Indeed I appologize [sic] sincerely for the starchiness & hope you will forgive me if you please mum, indeed it is Tom Titmouse and the rest of them; they do want their collar that *starchy* if you please mum my mind do get mixed up. If you please I will wash the clothes without charge for a fortnight if you will give another trial to your obedient servant & washer-woman

Tiggy Winkle.

Mrs. Tiggy Winkle
Cat Bells.

Dear Mrs. Tiggy Winkle,

   I am much pleased with the getting up of the children's muslin frocks. Your explanation about the starch is perfectly satisfactory & I have no intention of changing my laundry at present. Nobody washes flannels like Mrs. Tiggy Winkle.

   With kind regards,

yrs. truly,<br>Josephine Rabbit

[The transcriptions of all the following letters appeared in *Yours Affectionately, Peter Rabbit*, published in 1983, but the whereabouts of the original letters are now unknown.]

The Right Honourable
   Old Brown Esq.,
Owl Island.

Sir,

   I write respectfully to beg that you will sell me back my tail, I am so uncomfortable without it, and I have heard of a tailor who would sew it on again. I would pay three bags of nuts for it. Please Sir, Mr. Brown, send it back by post & oblige.
            yrs. respectfully,
               Sq. Nutkin

Dr. Maggotty,
The Dispensary.

Dear Dr. Maggotty,
   Having seen an advertisement (nailed on the smithy door) of your blue beans to cure chilblains, I write to ask whether you think a boxful would make my tail grow? I tried to buy it back from the gentleman who pulled it off, but he has not answered my letters. It spoils my appearance. Are the beans very strong?
            yrs. truly,
               Sq. Nutkin

Sq. Nutkin Esq.,
Derwent Bay Wood.

Sir,

   I have much pleasure in forwarding a box of blue beans as requested. Kindly acknowledge receipt & send 30 peppercorns as payment.
            yrs.
      Matthew Maggotty, M.D

Dr. Maggotty Esq., M.D.
The Dispensary.

Sir,

   I am obliged for the box of blue beans. I have not tried them yet. I have been wondering is there any fear they might make me grow a *blue* tail? It would spoil my appearance.
            yrs. truly,
               Sq. Nutkin

*Right: Dr Maggotty making his mixture in* The Tale of The Pie and The Patty-Pan *(1905)*

Sq. Nutkin Esq.,
Derwent Bay Wood.

Sir,

   I do not think that there is the slightest risk of my beans causing you to grow a blue tail. The price per box is 30 peppercorns.
            yrs. truly,
               M. Maggotty, M.D

Dr. Maggotty.

Sir,

   I am sending back the box of blue beans, I think they have a very funny smell & so does my brother Twinkleberry.
            yrs truly,
               Sq. Nutkin

Mr. McGregor,
Gardener's Cottage.

Dear Sir,

   I write to ask whether your spring cabbages are ready? Kindly reply by return & oblige.

yrs truly,
Peter Rabbit

Master P. Rabbit,
Under Fir Tree.

Sir,

   I rite by desir of my Husband Mr. McGregor who is in Bedd with a Cauld to say if you Comes heer agane we will inform the Polisse.

Jane McGregor

P.S. I have bort a new py-Dish, itt is vary Large.

Master Benjamin Bunny,
The Warren.

Dear Cousin Benjamin,
   I have had a very ill written letter from Mrs. McGregor she says Mr. M. is in bed with a cold will

you meet me at the corner of the wood near their garden at 6 this evening? In haste.

yr. aff. cousin,
Peter Rabbit

To Samuel Rat,
High Barn.

Sir,

   I hereby give you one day's notice to quit my barn & stables and byre, with your wife, children, grand children & great grand children to the latest generation.

signed: William Potatoes,
farmer

witness: Gilbert Cat
& John Stoat-Ferret

Farmer Potatoes,
The Priddings.

Sir,

   I have opened a letter addressed to one Samuel Rat. If Samuel Rat means me, I inform you I shall *not go*, and you can't turn us out.

yrs. etc.
Samuel Whiskers

*Above left: Mrs McGregor in the privately published edition of* The Tale of Peter Rabbit *(1901)*

Mr. Obediah Rat,
Barley Mill.

Dear Friend Obediah,
   Expect us – bag and baggage – at 9 o'clock in the morning. Am sorry to come upon you suddenly; but my landlord William Potatoes has given me one day's notice to quit. I am of opinion that it is not legal & I could sit till Candlemas because the notice is not addressed to my proper sur-name. *I* would stand up to William Potatoes, but my wife will not face John Stoat-Ferret, so we have decided on a midnight flitting as it is full-moon. I think there are 96 of us, but am not certain. Had it been the May-day term we could have gone to the Field Drains, but it is out of the question at this season.
   Trusting that the meal bags are full.

yr. obliged friend,
Samuel Whiskers

*Above: From* The Tale of Samuel Whiskers *(1908)*

(Private)
Master Tom Kitten,
Hill Top Farm.

Sally Henny Penny
at Home
at the Barn Door
Dec. 24th
Indian Corn and Dancing
Master T. Kitten,
Miss Moppet
&
Miss Mittens Kitten.

Miss Sally Henny Penny,
Barn Door.

Dear Henny,
   Me and Moppet and
Mittens will all come, if our
Ma doesn't catch us.
                    T. Kitten

The Puddle-Duck Family,
Farm Yard.

Sally Henny Penny
at Home
at the Barn Door
Dec. 24th
Indian Corn and Dancing
Mr. Drake Puddle-Duck
&
Mrs. Jemima
&
Mrs. Rebeccah

Miss Sally Henny Penny,
Barn Door.

   Mr. Drake Puddle-Duck
and Mrs. Jemima accept
with much pleasure, but
Mrs. Rebeccah is laid up
with a sore throat.

Mrs. Ribstone Pippin,
Lakefield Cottage.

Dear Mrs. Ribby,
   Can you lend me a red
flannel petticoat to wear as a
comforter. I have laid up
with a sore throat and I do
not wish to call in Dr.
Maggotty. It is 12 inches
long, a mustard leaf is no
use.
          yr. sincere friend,
          Rebeccah Puddleduck

Mrs. Rebeccah
   Puddleduck,
Farm Yard.

Dear Beccy,
   I am sorry to hear of your
sore throat, but what can
you expect if you will stand
on your head in a pond? I
will bring the flannel
petticoat & some more head
drops directly.
          yr. sincere friend,
                    Ribby

Miss Jenny Wren,
The Nest,
Beech Hedge.

Dear Miss Jenny,
   Will you accept a little
cask of currant wine from
your trusted friend Cock
Robin! The carrier will
leave it at the garden gate.

Cock Robin Esq.,
The Holly Bush.

Dear Cock Robin,

I thank you kindly for the little cask of currant wine. I have worked a new little scarlet waistcoat for you. Will you dine with me on Christmas day on the parlour window sill?

yr. aff. friend,
Jenny Wren

Jack Sparrow,
The Eaves.

Dear Jack Sparrow,

I have overheard that Jenny Wren & Cock Robin are going to eat their Christmas dinner on the parlour window sill. Lets all go and gobble up the crumbs. Bring Dick Chaffinch and I'll tell the Starlings.

yr. friend in mischief,
Tom Titmouse

Mess^rs Ginger & Pickles—Grocers—in account with Miss Lucinda Doll, Doll's House

4 thimblefuls of brown sugar
  @ 2d        = 1    farthing
6 thimblefuls of white ditto
  @ 2d        = 1½ farthing
3 tastes stilton Cheese
  @ 1/3 per lb.   say ¹⁄₁₀ farthing
                2⁹⁄₁₀ farthings
                2½d (about)
with Mess^rs G & P^s comp^ts & thanks.

Miss Lucinda Doll has received Mess^rs Pickle & Ginger's account, about which there is some mistake. She has lived for some months upon German plaster provisions & saw dust, and had given no order for the groceries mentioned in the bill.

Miss Lucinda Doll,
Doll's House

Mess^rs Ginger & Pickles beg to apologize to Miss Lucinda Doll for their mistake. The goods were selected (& taken away from the shop) to the order of Miss Doll. But Mess^rs Ginger & Pickles' young man had his doubts at the time. The messenger will not be served again.

*Left and right: Beatrix introduced many of the characters from her earlier books in* The Tale of Ginger and Pickles *(1909), including the two dolls Lucinda and Jane*

## *WALTER (JIM) AND MARGERY (MOLLY) GADDUM*

*Walter and Molly Gaddum*

Walter and Margery Gaddum were the children of Beatrix Potter's cousin, Edith, and her husband, William. Beatrix and Edith were, unusually, double cousins, their fathers being Potter brothers and their mothers Leech sisters.

William Gaddum's grandfather was of mixed French, Austrian and German blood and he had brought his Swiss wife to Manchester from Trieste in 1826 to found a textile business there. Their daughter Sophie also married a first cousin, an Austrian and also a Gaddum, so when their son William Henry (Willie) was born in Manchester in 1856 his was a multi-cultured and strong Gaddum lineage.

Edith Potter came from Manchester, too, her grandfather Edmund having founded the world's largest firm of calico printers in nearby Dinting. And it was in Manchester, in the then fashionable area of Victoria Park, that the newly-married Willie and Edith Gaddum settled in 1886. Their first child, Walter Frederick, known to the family as Jim, was born two years later and his sister, Elizabeth Margery (Molly), in 1892.

Willie and Edith had been introduced to the Lake District when they were children and as they both knew and loved the area they took a house there, Sawrey Knotts, on the western shore of Windermere. It was from this house that the Gaddum family visited Beatrix Potter (whom they called Cousin B) in September 1895, when she was staying with her parents at Holehird, high on the opposite side of the lake. Beatrix noted in her journal: 'Edith came with the children after lunch. They were charmed with Peter Piper [Beatrix's pet rabbit] who condescended to jump.'

Four years older than his sister, young Walter Gaddum spent a solitary childhood in Victoria Park. He was a mischievous boy, relieving his boredom by playing pranks on unsuspecting strangers. His favourite trick was to wrap up a piece of coal, place it on the footpath and watch from behind the garden wall as the parcel was opened by a

curious passer-by. And the pranks did not stop when
Walter was away from Manchester. Cousin Beatrix,
staying in Sawrey in 1896, recorded in her journal for 28
July: 'Edith's little Molly to tea. Master Jim in disgrace,
having gone against orders with the gardener to the running
of a fallow deer escaped from Curwen's island. That boy is
a tyke.'

About Walter's four-year-old sister Beatrix wrote,
'Molly is a queer little person, grown since last year, but
unnaturally delicate-looking'. Delicate-looking or not,
Molly kept pace with Walter and shared with him his love
of animals. Beatrix visited the Gaddums at Sawrey Knotts
on 8 August 1896 and recorded in her journal:

> Went up into the loft to see Mrs Frisky [a squirrel],
> who had been loose the previous night, let out by Miss
> Molly, and caught with much difficulty with a candle
> among the hay. I should think it is very unusual for
> squirrels to breed in confinement. The lady in question
> could not help herself, having been caught in a cage-
> trap four days before the event.

That same day Beatrix sent her picture letter about Mrs
Frisky to seven-year-old Eric Moore [see page 42].

As well as the picture letters Beatrix sent toy pictures to a
number of her young friends. These 'movables',
fashionable distractions for children at that time, were
usually on stiff card and often had double-sided pictures in
which part of the image could be moved or changed by
lifting a flap, pulling a string or turning a wheel. At least six
of the toy pictures Beatrix made for Walter, dated by her
between 1889 and 1891, have survived in good, workable
condition. They include one of two guinea pigs in a hutch
with a lifting lid and, on the grass beside it, a tortoise that
grazes. Another is of a greengrocer's shop, a barrel and a
basket outside with lids that lift to reveal a display of apples
– and a rabbit. (See pages 97 and 105.)

By the late 1890s the Gaddum family firm had built up a
large import and export business with India and was

*Molly Gaddum*

prospering. As a result Willie found himself able to realize one of his lifetime ambitions, to build a house in the Lake District which the family would make their permanent home. He bought a large area of land halfway between Windermere and Ambleside, some thirty-two acres, that lay between the road and the lake. On old maps the land was marked as 'Brock Hole' or 'Badger Sett' and thus Brockhole was the name that Willie chose for his elegant home. He appointed the young Daniel Gibson as his architect for the house and commissioned Gibson's friend and celebrated landscape architect, Thomas Mawson, to lay out the magnificent gardens.

It was two years before the building and landscaping were finished so the Gaddum children were twelve and eight when the family moved into Brockhole in 1900. Walter had been at school at Eton for a year but during the holidays he was able to take full advantage of the new house's unrivalled position on the lake to share in one of his father's favourite sports, sailing. The move into Brockhole coincided with the start of a decline in the fortunes of the Gaddum family business and by 1917 the company had to be wound up altogether, leaving Walter's father free to enjoy his life in Windermere without interruption.

The Gaddums had been delighted when, in 1913, Beatrix Potter had married William Heelis and come to live in Sawrey across the lake. Edith and Beatrix corresponded frequently throughout the 1920s, exchanging the information they had each uncovered in tracing the Potter family history, and Willie was for some time the trustee for Beatrix's mother who lived nearby. Edith died in 1937, and Willie married again the following year, Agnes Vey, a widow living on the adjoining property. Willie died in 1945.

From Eton Walter progressed to Trinity College, Cambridge, where he took part in another favourite sport, beagling, with the Trinity Foot Beagles. In 1914 he had joined the Westmorland and Cumberland Yeomanry, fighting with them throughout the war and being badly wounded in the throat. At the very end of the war, in September 1918, Captain Walter Gaddum married Benita

*Molly gives a helping hand*

Fisher from Distington Hall near Whitehaven in
Cumberland and they set up house together near Kendal.

Walter took little interest in work or in earning his living
and, although he was never a rich young man, he lived the
life of a country gentleman. He resumed his passion for
hare-hunting and helped to restore the Windermere
Harriers which had been disbanded during the war,
becoming Joint Master with Bruce Logan until the latter's
retirement three years later. Walter was Master and owner
of the Windermere Harriers for thirty-three years and was
eventually senior Master of Hounds in the country. His
hunting activities did not best please his cousin, Beatrix,
who wrote to him when his hounds once followed a hare
into the garden of Troutbeck Park Farm when she was
there, 'If you had more sense, you would keep your nasty
dogs away from here.' But Beatrix always remained fond of
Walter and she remembered him generously in her will. In
the year of her death, 1943, Walter was High Sheriff of
Westmorland and he became a Deputy Lieutenant of the
county in 1946. When he died in 1956 Walter was buried in
Troutbeck 'in the shadow of the fells over which he had
often hunted hounds'.

Molly Gaddum had married before her brother – in 1912
at the age of only twenty. Her husband was fifteen years her
senior and called John (Jack) Payne and they went to live
near Manchester. While Jack fought in the war, Molly

*Walter with his mother, Edith Gaddum*

*Below: One of the toy pictures Beatrix
made for Walter. As well as the hinged
flap to the hutch, a string at the back
enables the tortoise to graze*

97

returned to Brockhole, but when the fighting was over the Paynes settled in Shropshire where, in 1919, they had a son whom they christened John Walter. When her husband died in 1951, Molly stayed for the rest of her life in Shropshire, living with her son and his family.

Brockhole had been sold after Willie Gaddum's death in 1945 and for twenty years it became a convalescent home for Merseyside Hospitals. In 1966 the estate was bought by the Lake District National Park Planning Board and was opened in 1969 as the first National Park Visitor Centre. Every year thousands of people visit Brockhole. As well as learning a great deal about the Lake District there, they can also enjoy the glories of the Gaddum family house and gardens.

*The Tale of Mr. Jeremy Fisher (1909) also ends with a meal of roast grasshopper 'with lady-bird sauce'*

Oct 11th 95

My dear Molly

These are some pictures of a frog who went fishing and had a bite, but the fish jumped out of the boat before he could put it into his basket. He was very sorry because he has asked one of the tortoises to come to dinner so they wanted a nice dish of minnows. He goes out again with a butterfly net, to find something else. You see in the last picture they are going to eat a roast grasshopper. It looks rather like a chicken on the plate, but I don't think it will be so good as those at Sawrey. With thanks for your Mother's letter, and much love,

I remain your aff.
Cousin B

*Oct 11ᵗʰ 95.*

My dear Molly
These are some pictures of a frog who went fishing and had a bite, but the fish jumped out of the boat before he could put it into his basket. He was very sorry because he has asked one of the tortoises to come to dinner so they wanted a nice dish of minnows. He goes out again with a butterfly net, to find something else. You see in the last picture they are going to eat a roast grasshopper. It looks rather like a chicken on the plate, but I don't think it will be so good as those at Sawrey. With thanks for your Mother's letter, and much love, I remain your aff. Cousin B.

March 6th 97

My dear Walter

Thank you for your nice letter, but I am sorry to hear about poor Frisky. Another squirrel I knew died lately. It was a grey American squirrel and lived 8 or 9 years. The lady who had it says red squirrels do not live so well in cages as the grey ones.

Peter Rabbit is very well and fat, generally asleep before the fire. On Tuesday night there was a tremendous wind and I went out after dark and brought him into the house. Next morning the hutch was blown right over; if he had been inside he would have been hurt, for the blue saucer was all in bits.

I have not heard much about Jack [a jackdaw] lately but the owl is said to be a great nuisance. Bertram has got them with him in Scotland and the owl hoots all night. If he has a dead mouse he bites its head off and then shouts as loud as he can.

An old woman gave Bertram a present of 5 dozen eggs, rather too many to eat, he sent them to us.

I have been drawing funguses very hard, I think some day they will be put in a book but it will be a dull one to read We have had one little fungus like red holly berries, it had only been found once before in Scotland. I am glad you have got a nice dog, ours had the cramp very badly in the cold weather; he falls down when he is walking. We have got 4 canaries, I hope they will lay some eggs.

A friend of mine has got a savage dormouse, it bites something like the prick of a pin. It lost half its tail by accident, it seems to have spoiled its temper.

I remain yr aff Cousin
Beatrix Potter

Peter Rabbit is very well and fat, generally asleep before the fire. On Tuesday night there was a tremendous wind and I went out after dark and brought him into the house. Next morning the hutch was blown right over; if he had been inside he would have been hurt, for the blue saucer was all in bits.

I have not heard much about Jack lately but the owl is said to be a great nuisance. Bertram has got them with him in Scotland and the owl hoots all night. If he has a dead mouse bites it's head off and shouts as loud as he can. old woman gave Bertram a [...] of 5 dozen eggs, rather too [...] in a book but it will be a [...] one to read. We have had one [...] has little fungus like red holly berries. [...] it had only been found once before in Scotland. I am glad you have got a nice dog, ours had the cramp very badly in the cold weather; he falls down when he is walking. We have got 4 canaries. I hope they will lay some eggs. A friend of mine has got a savage dormouse, it bites something like the prick of a pin. It lost half its tail by accident, it seems to have spoiled its temper. I remain yr aff Cousin

Beatrix Potter.

*Left: Walter Gaddum in his Eton boater*
*Below: Beatrix's watercolour of Peter Rabbit asleep before the fire, August 1899*

March 6, 97

My dear Molly,

I have drawn you some pictures of the owl and the pussycat. It is very odd to see an owl with hands, but how could he play on the guitar without them?

I remain your affectionate cousin,

B

March 6th 97

My dear Molly
I have drawn you some pictures of the owl and the pussy-cat.
It is very odd to see an owl with hands, but how could he play on the guitar without them? I remain your affectionate cousin B.



The owl and the Pussy-cat went to sea
In a beautiful pea green boat,
They took some honey and plenty of money
Wrapped up in a £5 note.

The Owl looked up to the stars above
And sang to a small guitar,
"Oh dear sweet pussy,' Oh pussy my love
What a beautiful pussy you are!
You are!
What a beautiful Pussy you are!"

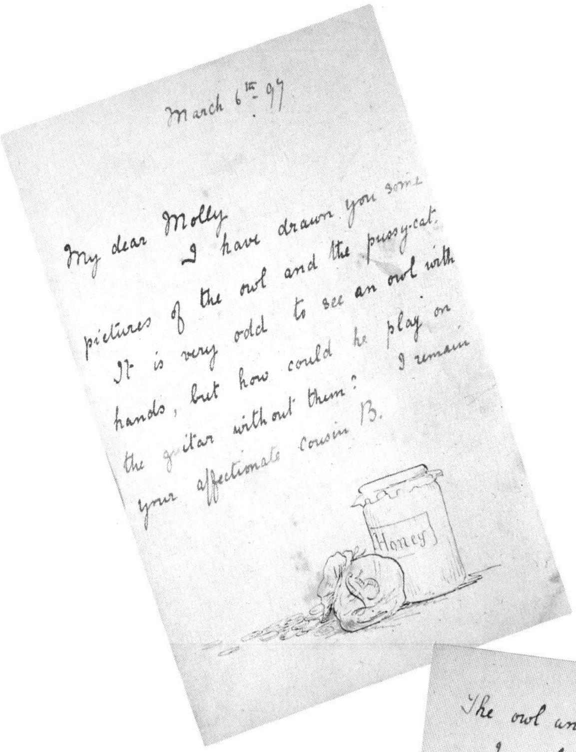

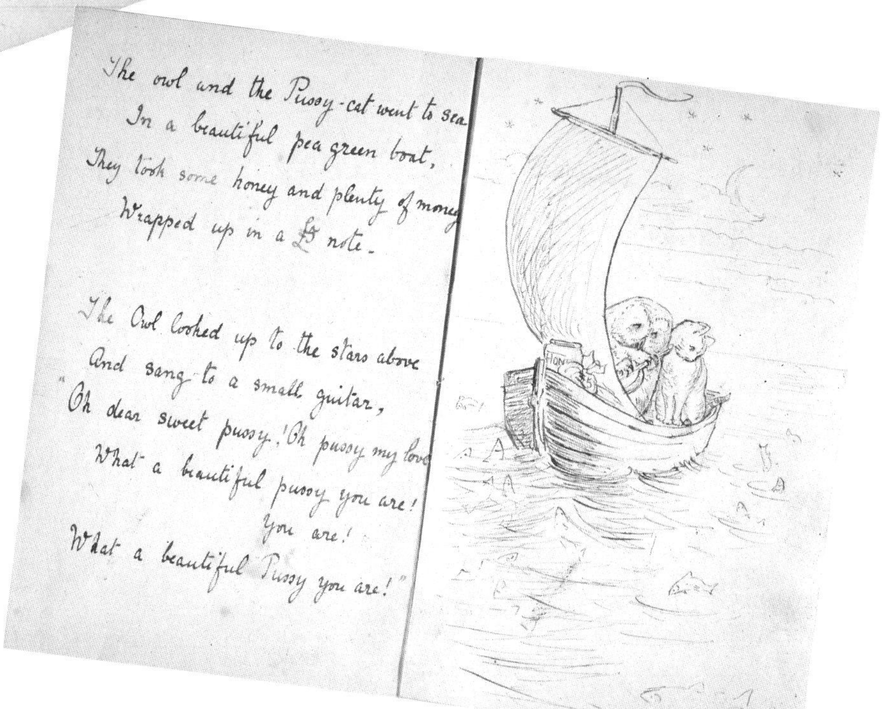

They sailed away.
for a year and a day
To the land where the Bong tree
grows.

And there in a wood
a piggy wig stood,
With a ring at the end of his nose
his nose!
at the end of his nose.

"Dear pig are you willing
to sell for one shilling
your ring?"
Said the piggy
"I will"

So they sailed away,
and were married next day.
By the Turkey who lives on the hill.

It is fine today I have been to look at the broken windows, the stones are all over the roads near the sea.

Jan 14th 99                  16 Robertson Terrace
                             Hastings

My dear Walter,

I had intended to write to you last summer but I was very lazy. I thought you would like to hear about a hawk which your Cousin Bertram got from the postman at Lingholm. It was a young sparrowhawk, it caught itself in some wire netting on a railing but was not hurt. We kept it on a

block of wood on the floor, with leather straps on its legs, and in 10 days it was tame enough to get onto his hand for food. I don't know whether he would have succeeded in taming it sufficiently to fly out of doors, but we were much disappointed that it died, it never seemed to have enough appetite. It was a very pretty bird, with very thin long legs. I was quite afraid the straps would hurt it, but it is said to be the proper way to fasten them. We wrote to a falconer in Holland for a hood & bells. He sent a beautifully made hood, scarlate [sic] & green cloth. Bertram tried to buy another hawk when he was in London, & was very much inclined to get a gos-hawk, nearly as big as a turkey cock but it was too expensive. Then he bought a foreign one, called a Barbary falcon. I have not seen it, but I should say it is so tame that it is quite silly. It climbs up his clothes & sits on his head, steals off his plate, & has broken two teacups & burnt one of its wings with warming itself on the fender. I hope it will not want to sit on my head! I must keep my rabbit out of sight. My rabbit is very well, but the poor dog Binkie died last November.

I suppose you are at home for the holidays, I heard that you liked being at school [Eton].

> I remain yr aff cousin
> Beatrix Potter

*Below: In this toy picture Beatrix made for Walter, the lids of the barrel and basket are hinged*

## *LUCIE AND KATHLEEN CARR*

Lucie and Kathleen Carr lived at the vicarage in the spectacular Newlands valley, near Keswick, to the west of Cat Bells and High Crags, for their father was the vicar of the small white church that stands at the head of the valley.

In 1901 the Carrs were introduced to the Potters by an old friend of both families, the vicar of Crosthwaite, Canon Hardwicke Rawnsley. It was summer and Mr and Mrs Potter, their son and daughter were staying at Lingholm, on the shore of Derwentwater, for the seventh consecutive year. Beatrix was much intrigued by the Carrs and she even made up a poem on hearing how they had acquired their cat. There are seventeen verses but only room for three here.

*Lucie Carr's father, the Vicar of Newlands (left), with Rupert Potter*

The wanderings of a small black cat
   inspire my simple tale,
It met a worthy clergyman
   at dusk near Portinscale.

On serious thoughts his mind was bent,
   of cats he took small heed,
So when that pussy followed him
   he walked with greater speed . . .

It followed him, it followed him,
   through ditches, gates and stiles;
And when the parson ran – it ran.
   It ran three weary miles! . . .

Some thirty years after that first meeting with the Carrs Beatrix told an American friend about Mrs Carr: 'She was a large lack a daisical rather handsome lady with a quantity of yellow hair, in a 'bun' which was always coming down. When I first recollect her she was still suffecently [sic] a bride to go out to dinner in her wedding gown, with a long train, shedding hairpins as she went. The[re] was something both pleasing & comical'.

The Carrs' first child, a son, had died at only three months, and in 1901 their daughter Lucie was just a year old, her sister Kathleen not yet born. Beatrix Potter loved the baby and the following Christmas the Carr family received a copy of the privately printed *Peter Rabbit* inscribed, 'For Lucie with love from H.B.P., Christmas 1901 – I should like to put Lucie into a little book.'

The Potters were once again at Lingholm for the summer of 1904. Beatrix had finished *Benjamin Bunny* and *The Tale of Two Bad Mice* and was starting to think about the illustrations for her new book. She had already chosen the story, one she planned soon after meeting the Carrs for the first time; it featured Beatrix's pet hedgehog, Mrs Tiggy, and 'a little girl called Lucie, who lived at a farm called Little-town'. One August afternoon that year the Carrs had been to Lingholm for tea, in those days a somewhat formal occasion for which even young children wore their best clothes, and when the family arrived home they were dismayed to discover that four-year-old Lucie's gloves had been left behind. The postman delivered the gloves to Newlands the following day, accompanied by a letter for Lucie (see page 109). It is one of only two known Beatrix Potter picture letters where the illustrations are in colour. (The other coloured picture letter, sent to Hilda Moore two weeks later (see page 78), is also about the piebald mouse and her family, but as the original of this letter has disappeared into a private collection it is sadly only possible to reproduce it in black and white.)

Beatrix also wrote a short verse about the finding of Lucie's gloves. It was included in the 1905 manuscript of *Appley Dapply's Nursery Rhymes*, but omitted when the book was finally published in 1917. The verse was later quoted in the letter Beatrix sent to those children who had collected stamps for the Invalid Children's Aid Association (see page 207).

'The letter about my gloves was the only picture letter I ever had,' recalls Lucie Carr over eighty years later, 'but Beatrix Potter wrote quite a number of those tiny letters to both K and me over the years. She sent them to us posted in

*A preparatory sketch of Lucie outside the door in the hillside for* The Tale of Mrs. Tiggy-Winkle *(1905)*

*Above: The small tin letter boxes in which Beatrix 'posted' her miniature letters to the Carr children*

*Below: Lucie and Kathleen Carr*

miniature red letter boxes. As we played postmen with them for hours, it is wonderful that any of them have survived.' The miniature letters are not dated but as Kathleen Carr was born in 1902 and the characters featured in the letters come from Potter books published between 1903 and 1905, it is fairly safe to assume that they were written in the early 1900s. Lucie Carr also remembers that Beatrix gave them a little writing box. 'It was made of strong card with a slope, containing within a tiny ink-pot and miniature stationery. I am afraid it is long since gone.'

*The Tale of Mrs. Tiggy-Winkle*, featuring Lucie and Mrs Tiggy, was published in good time for the Christmas market of 1905. It was dedicated to 'The Real Little Lucie of Newlands' and in the copy the author sent to Newlands she wrote, 'For little Lucie with much love from Beatrix Potter and from dear "Mrs Tiggy Winkle" September 24th. 05.' Beatrix had had trouble drawing the figure of Lucie for the book and she was unhappy with the result, writing to her publisher: 'I wish I had drawn the child better; I feel sure I could get into the way of it, only it is too much of a hurry.' The 'real' Lucie commented later, 'I never modelled for Beatrix Potter but I expect she asked my parents' permission to put me in the book. You don't realize what an honour it is at the time – which is perhaps just as well or we would never have been allowed to play with the book!'

At Christmas in 1910 Mrs Carr sent a photograph to the Potters in London, for which Beatrix thanked her: 'We were delighted with the photograph of the children. It is so like them and so very nicely "got up". It is very creditable to the photographer to have printed it like that. I like Lucie best and my mother likes Kathleen, they are both very good indeed.'

Two years later the Carrs left Newlands and moved to Waterstock, near Oxford. 'We never saw Beatrix Potter again after we left the Lake District,' recalls Lucie Carr, 'and now I only remember her very vaguely. I was so very young at the time.'

The gloves are too big for the
piebald mouse, so she has

put them in an envelope!
and she is going to send
them back to Lucie.

This is the pie-bald mouse,
trying on Lucie's gloves!

When the pie-bald mouse
goes to a party in her best
clothes – she wears gloves with
only one button!

[To Lucie Carr]

Aug. 24. 04                    Lingholme
                               Keswick
                               Cumberland

This is the pie-bald mouse, trying on
Lucie's gloves!

The gloves are too big for the piebald
mouse, so she has put them in an envelope!
And she is going to send them back to
Lucie.

When the pie-bald mouse goes to a party
in her best clothes – she wears gloves with
only one button!

109

[To Lucie Carr]

Mr Old Brown
Owl Island

Dear Sir,

I should esteem it a favour if you will let me have back my tail, as I miss it very much. I would pay postage.

yrs truly
Squirrel Nutkin
An answer will oblige

Mr Old Brown Esq
Owl Island

Dear Sir,

I should be exceedingly obliged if you could kindly send back a tail which you have had for some time. It is fluffy brown with a white tip.

I wrote before but I am afraid I did not direct my letter right.

I will pay postage.
yrs respectifully [sic]
Sqr. Nutkin.

Rt Hon O. Brown Esq M.P.
Owl Island.

Dear Sir,

I write on behalf of my brother Nutkin to beg that as a great favour you would send him back his tail, for which he will gladly pay three bags of nuts. He never asks riddles now and he is truly sorry that he was so rude.

Trusting that you continue to enjoy good health.

I remain yrs obediently
Twinkleberry Squirrel.

Master Squirrel Nutkin
Derwent Bay Wood

Mr Brown writes to say that he cannot reply to letters as he is asleep.

Mr Brown cannot return the tail.

He ate it some time ago; it nearly choked him.

Mr Brown requests Nutkin not to write again, as his repeated letters are a nuisance.

Mrs Tom Thumb
Mouse Hole

Miss Lucinda Doll will be obliged if Hunca Munca will come half an hour earlier than usual on Thursday morning, as Tom Kitten is expected to sweep the kitchen chimny [sic] at 6 'o'clock.

Miss Lucinda wishes Hunca Munca to come not later than 5.45 am.

Mrs Tom Thumb
Mouse Hole

Miss Lucinda Doll requires Hunca Munca to come for the whole day on Tuesday.

Jane Dollcook has had an accident, she has broken the soup tureen and both her wooden legs.

Mrs Rabbit
Sand Bank
under Fir-tree

If you please 'm,
Indeed I apologize for the *starch* & hope you will forgive me. Indeed it is Tom Titmouse if you please 'm, he does want his collars that *starchy* my mind does get full of pins! If you please I will wash the clothes for a fortnight for nothing if you will give another trial to your obedient washerwoman
Tiggy Winkle.

Miss K. Carr
Newlands.

My dear Kathleen
We are all going home to London on Wednesday, and Miss Potter is rather sorry. And I am rather sorry too, because I have had lots to eat here; but I have not been allowed to run about the garden, for fear of getting lost. I travel in a little wooden box.
Your affectionate rabbit
Joseph!

111

[To Lucie Carr]

My dear Duchess,

If you are at home and not engaged will you come to tea tomorrow? but if you are away I shall put this in the post and invite cousin Tabitha Twitchit. There will be a red herring & muffins & crumpets. The patty pans are all locked up. Do come

yr aff friend
Ribby

Mrs Tabitha Twitchit
Hill Top Farm.

Dear Cousin Tabitha,

If you can leave your family with safety I shall be much pleased if you will take tea with me this afternoon. There will be muffins and crumpets and a red herring.

I have just been to call upon my friend Duchess, she is away from home.

yr aff cousin
Ribby.

Mrs Ribstone Pippin
Lakefield Cottage.

Dear Cousin Ribby,

I shall be pleased to take tea with you. I am glad that Duchess is away from home. I have a poor opinion of dogs.

My son Thomas is well, but he grows out of all his clothes; and I have other troubles.

yr aff. cousin
Tabitha Twitchitt [sic].

Mrs Ribstone Pippin
Lakefield Cottage.

My dear Ribby

I am so sorry I was out, it would have given me so much pleasure to accept your kind invitation I had gone to a dog show. I enjoyed it very much, but I am a little disappointed that I did not take a prize; and I missed the red herring.

yr aff friend
Duchess.

*Right: Duchess takes tea with Ribby in*
The Tale of The Pie and The Patty-Pan *(1905)*

My dear Duchess,
If you are at home and not engaged
will you come to tea tomorrow? but if you
are away I shall put this in the post and
invite cousin Tabitha Twitchit. There will
be a red herring! muffins & crumpets.
The patty pans are all looked up—
yr aff friend Ribby—

Dear Cousin Ribby,
Glad that Duchess is away from home. I have a poor
opinion of dogs. My son Thomas is well, but he
grows out of all his clothes; and I have other
troubles—
yr aff cousin
Tabitha Twitchitt.

Dear Cousin Tabitha,
If you can leave your family with
safety I shall be much pleased if you will take tea
with me this afternoon. There will be muffins and
crumpets and a red herring.
I have just been to call upon my friend Duchess,
she is away from home.
yr aff cousin
Ribby.

My dear Ribby
I am so sorry I was out, it would have
given me so much pleasure to accept your kind invitation
I had gone to a dog show. I enjoyed it very much, but
I am a little disappointed that I did not take a
prize; and I missed the red herring.
yr aff friend
Duchess.

113

## LOUIE AND WINIFRED WARNE

Louie and Winifred Warne were cousins. Louie was the daughter of the oldest of the three publishing Warne brothers, Harold, and Winifred was the daughter of the middle brother, Fruing.

Harold, Fruing and Norman Warne had taken control of the family publishing firm following the retirement of their father, Frederick Warne, in 1895. Harold was the managing director and chief editor, Fruing looked after the sales and Norman was mainly concerned with overseeing the production and design of the books.

It was Harold Warne, on the advice of his best-selling author-artist, Leslie Brooke, who accepted Beatrix Potter's first book for children, *The Tale of Peter Rabbit*, for publication in 1902. The immediate success of that book led to the publication of two more by her the following year, two the year after and so on, until Beatrix Potter became the company's most prolific and profitable author. She was a regular caller at the offices in Bedford Court to discuss the production of her books with Norman or an editorial point with Harold, and her friendship with the Warnes grew quickly. She visited the family home in Bedford Square where Norman lived with his now widowed mother and his unmarried sister, Millie, and was often a guest at their frequent celebrations there.

*Winifred Warne with her baby sister Eveline in September 1903*

Most of the Warne family congregated at Bedford Square for a party. It was too far for the oldest daughter, Edith Stephens, to bring her two children, Frederick and Jennie, from Devon but Harold and his wife, Alice, came with Louie and Nellie (Eleanor) from Primrose Hill in north London, and Fruing and Mary brought their two girls, Winifred and Eveline (and later their son, Norman), from Surbiton, south of London. 'The parties were for the children,' recalls Winifred. 'The grown-ups played games with us but we were never noisy and rowdy together, as some people have said. On one particular occasion Uncle Norman dressed up as Father Christmas and my cousin, Louie, who was a bold child, recognized him and went up and kissed him. The servants and nurses, who were watching from an alcove, all remarked on her "very forward behaviour".'

The children liked Beatrix Potter, even though they were sometimes a little in awe of this somewhat reserved and severely-dressed lady. They were also delighted with the letters she sent at Christmas and for birthdays. Four-year-old Winifred was particularly pleased when she discovered that *The Tale of Two Bad Mice* had been dedicated to her: 'For W.M.L.W. the little girl who had the doll's house'. Beatrix had used as the model for the book the doll's house made with such care by Norman Warne for his favourite niece, Winifred Mary Langrish Warne.

By the summer of 1905 'Uncle Norman' and Beatrix Potter were engaged to be married, after a formal courtship much of which was conducted in the offices of Frederick Warne. Winifred remembered family discussions about it many years later. 'They were never alone together. When Beatrix went to the office she was always chaperoned and when she went to Bedford Square some other member of the family would be there, too, though Millie was more of a help than a hindrance.'

Sadly, the marriage did not take place, for Norman died of pernicious anaemia on 25 August 1905, 'after a brief illness at the early age of 37', as printed in the family announcement. In her grief Beatrix turned for distraction to her newly-acquired Lake District farm, Hill Top, and to her books.

In response to a request from six-year-old Louie for a story about a really naughty rabbit – Louie thought that Peter was much too good – Beatrix sent Harold Warne in early 1906 *The Story of a Fierce Bad Rabbit*, a simpler tale than her earlier books, intended for younger children. The very few words and the fourteen pictures were set out in a folding panorama, the style in which the story was published later that year. Beatrix gave the original manuscript to Louie and her father had it bound up for her in exactly the same way as the published books.

In March 1906 Louie's younger sister, Nellie, received a

*Winifred with the doll's house which Beatrix used as a model for* The Tale of Two Bad Mice *(1904)*

115

similarly produced story, *The Sly Old Cat*. Harold had that bound up, too, but before it could be published production of the panoramic books had been stopped, following protests from bookshops that the format was inhibiting customers who wanted to examine the books before buying them. *The Sly Old Cat* had to wait sixty-five years for publication, long after the death of both the author and the story's recipient.

The Warne children had a bumper crop of Potter stories in 1906 and it was Winifred's turn that Christmas. *The Roly-Poly Pudding* (retitled *The Tale of Samuel Whiskers* in 1926) arrived at the Warne office in a stiff-covered exercise book bearing Winifred's name and address. It took Beatrix longer than she expected to finish the artwork for this tale of the rats who lived at Hill Top and the book was not ready for publication until October 1908, but shortly afterwards Winifred was brought up-to-date with news of Mr Samuel Whiskers in the picture letter sent to her from Beatrix's holiday address in Sidmouth (see page 126).

Many of the letters that arrived at the office for Harold Warne from Beatrix at that time included love to the children and good wishes for their recovery from whooping cough or chicken pox or a bad cold. The progress of their education was followed closely and Beatrix sent congratulations when they had done well or she encouraged them to further effort. And the children had their own picture letters and their miniature letters, though Beatrix sometimes had doubts about the latter's suitability. Writing to Harold Warne on 23 December 1907 she commented, 'You will find some curious correspondence in Louie's post office. I am not sure whether it is rather over the heads of the children.'

In November 1908 Beatrix sent a new story to Harold with the comment, 'I am sending this to Primrose Hill in case you want to try it on the children. It seems to me to be more like The Tailor – older and sentimental.' *The Tale of the Faithful Dove* had no pictures and was written out in a paper-covered exercise book inscribed 'Hastings Feb 14th' and with a note: 'I used Winchelsea and *Rye* as background.

*Drawings from* The Tale of Samuel Whiskers *(1908) written for Winifred Warne as* The Roly-Poly Pudding

This story was written for the Warne children.' There is no record of what the children thought of it but *The Faithful Dove* lay in the Warne office until 1918 when Fruing discovered it and tried to persuade Beatrix to illustrate it for publication. But by then Beatrix had lost interest in the story and it remained unpublished until 1956, thirteen years after the author's death.

The last of the little books written especially for a Warne child was posted to Harold on 22 December 1908. 'I send Louie's Christmas book to you to read first! Best wishes to all for a Merry Christmas.' The story and pictures for *Ginger and Pickles* were laid out in the now familiar exercise book, this time inscribed, 'With love to Louie from Aunt Beatrix Christmas 1908'. When the book was nearing publication, in August of the following year, Beatrix asked for the dedication to be to 'old Mr John Taylor . . .', adding to Harold, 'It ought to be Louie's book, but she can look forward'.

As it turned out poor Louie had missed her chance for a dedication altogether. The next book, *Mrs Tittlemouse*, went to Nellie Warne, and when Beatrix came to dedicate *Timmy Tiptoes* in July 1911 she commented to Louie's father, 'I think Louie is rather ill used in not having had her name on a book; but she has got too big for these little books now.'

The Warne children saw less and less of Aunt Beatrix in the ensuing years and after her marriage in 1913 they hardly saw her at all. Harold Warne, however, was in his usual almost daily contact with his friend and most important author through the office. The onset of war seemed hardly to affect the continuing sales of the books but Frederick Warne was in serious financial trouble and, in an effort to ward off the foreclosing of the company's debtors, the family had to raise money quickly. Fruing and Mary sold their house in Surbiton and took Winifred and the two younger children to a house near Richmond Park, about which Beatrix wrote comfortingly to Fruing, 'When she [Mary] gets over the wrench of leaving a pretty home – there will be less housekeeping in a smaller house.'

*From* The Tale of Ginger and Pickles *(1909), written as a present for Louie Warne*

*Winifred and her little sister Eveline in 1905*

117

*Above and opposite: Two gentlemen about town. Johnny Town-Mouse and the Amiable Guinea-pig are characters from the two books Beatrix produced to help the Warne company through a financial crisis*

Harold, who had been responsible for the company's troubles, no longer had any connection with the family firm and there was now only one remaining Warne brother there. Fruing's two years of hard work to save the family business were succeeding. He persuaded Beatrix to do two new books, *Appley Dapply's Nursery Rhymes* and *The Tale of Johnny Town-Mouse*, and he revived the programme of merchandise based on all the books. He also obtained Beatrix's agreement to the acceptance of part of her overdue royalties in the form of shares in a new company, Frederick Warne & Company, registered in 1919. The following year Fruing Warne was elected managing director; it was a happy day for his children as Winifred recounts. 'We had gone to bed before Daddy came back from the meeting, and knowing that we would be up at the crack of dawn Mother arranged to put a notice on the wardrobe on the landing telling us how it went. When we came down there it was: "Daddy made Managing Director. £500 a year." It was wonderful.'

Winifred was turning out to be an accomplished artist and in the early 1920s her father published four small books, each one 'an original fairy story by Skimble Skamble, illustrated by Winifred M. Warne' with a number of black-and-white line drawings and four colour plates. When sent a copy by Fruing Beatrix commented, 'I am very glad to see that you have got a young illustrator coming on who has good taste and common sense to follow the old-fashioned road. These pictures give me far more pleasure than the modern bizarre style.'

Soon after the publication of her books Winifred left home and London and went to live near Liverpool, and there she met James Boultbee to whom she was soon engaged to be married. Her Aunt Millie was quick to inform Beatrix of the situation, and she wrote to Winifred's father, 'Millie told me some news! I remember your Winifred like a little quiet white mouse! I can scarcely believe she is grown up, I wish her every happiness.' The wedding took place on 8 May 1924 and the couple lived first in Toxteth, Liverpool, and then in Cheadle, near

Manchester, where James was the curate. In 1928 he was appointed vicar of St Luke's in Wolverhampton and in 1938 they moved to a church in Birkenhead. Fourteen years later James was vicar in Tolleshunt Major in Essex. Winifred and James had two children, a girl and a boy.

Louie Warne taught the piano before her marriage in 1929 to a stock jobber, Geoffrey Berkeley. The couple lived in north London and had three children, two girls and a boy. When Louie's father, Harold, died in 1939 Louie wrote to tell Beatrix, adding that her own children were now in turn enjoying Beatrix's little books. As well as sending her sympathy Beatrix replied: 'How well I remember you both and your parents – on hot Sunday afternoons in the garden behind the house on Primrose Hill. And your Father & Mother, & Nurse – it seems a lifetime ago. I am glad the little books are giving pleasure to another generation – they go on and on.' Louie Warne died in 1957 at the age of fifty-seven.

*Louie Warne with her sister Nellie*

Gwaynynog nr Denbigh.
Sept 6th 05

My dear Winifred,
Would you like a letter from the "Peter. Rabbit Lady?" I want to tell you all about my 2 bunnies, I have got them with me here.
They are called Josey and Mopsy; Josey is a dear rabbit, she is so tame; although she is only a common wild one, who lived in a rabbit hole under a hedge.
A boy caught her when she was quite a baby, she could sit in my hand. She is 3 years old now.

The other rabbit Mopsy is quite young, but it is frightened and silly; I am not quite sure whether I shall keep it; perhaps I shall take it into the wood and let it run away down a rabbit hole.
We picked such lots of mushrooms yesterday, my cousin and I and the gardener.
We looked out after breakfast and we saw a naughty old man with a basket, & a little girl with a black shawl quite full of mushrooms. So we ran out in a great hurry to get some before they were

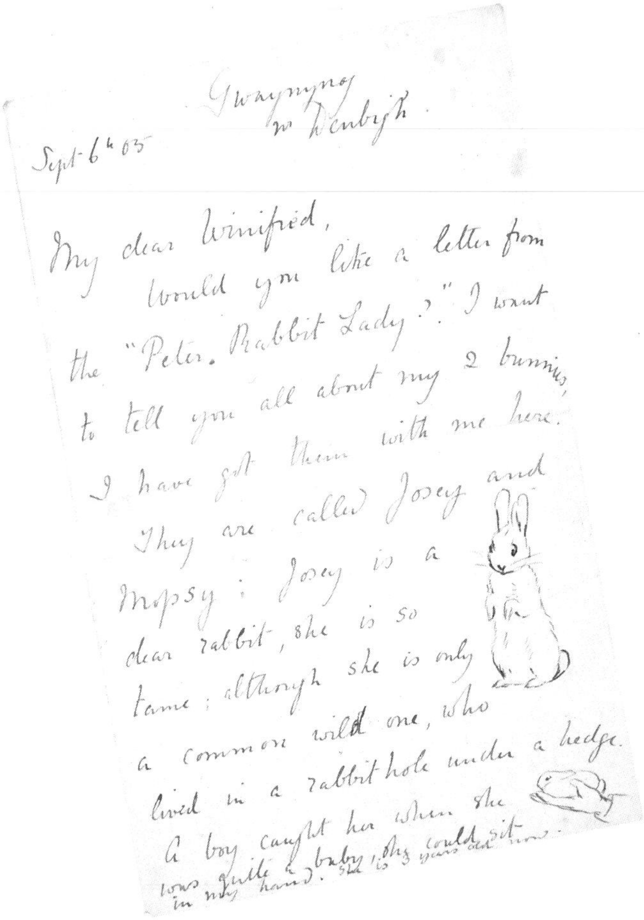

Sept 6th 05

Gwaynynog
Nr Denbigh

My dear Winifred,

Would you like a letter from the "Peter Rabbit Lady?" I want to tell you all about my 2 bunnies, I have got them with me here.

They are called Josey and Mopsy; Josey is a dear rabbit, she is so tame; although she is only a common wild one, who lived in a rabbit hole under a hedge. A boy caught her when she was quite a baby, she could sit in my hand. She is 3 years old now.

The other rabbit Mopsy is quite young, but it is frightened and silly; I am not quite sure whether I shall keep it; perhaps I shall take it into the wood and let it run away down a rabbit hole.

We picked such lots of mushrooms yesterday, my cousin and I and the gardener.

We looked out after breakfast and we saw a naughty old man with a basket, & a little girl with a black shawl *quite full* of mushrooms. So we ran out in a great hurry to get some before they were all stolen.

I am going to put a picture of mushrooms in a book. I have got my hedgehog here

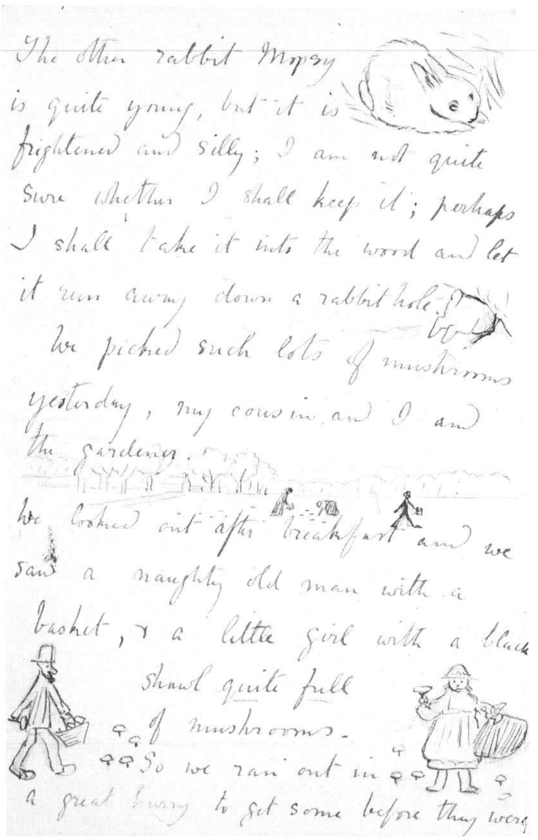

with me too; she enjoys going by train, she is always very hungry when she is on a journey. I carry her in a little basket and the bunnies in a small wooden box, I don't take any tickets for them.

My hedgehog Mrs Tiggy-winkle is a great traveller, I don't know how many journeys she hasn't done.

The next journey will be quite a short one, I think I am going to the sea-side on Saturday.

I wonder if I shall find any crabs and shells and shrimps. Mrs Tiggy-winkle won't eat shrimps; I think it is very silly of her, she will eat worms and beetles, and I am sure that shrimps would be much nicer. I think you must ask Mrs Tiggy-winkle to tea when she comes back to London later on, she will drink milk like anything, out of a doll's tea-cup!

With a great many kisses, from your loving friend
Beatrix Potter

Dec 15. 05

Dear Winifred,

This is all that is to be seen of Mrs Tiggy today! She went to sleep on Wednesday night and I don't expect her to wake up till Sunday. Did you ever hear any thing so lazy? She sleeps for 4 days at a time!

When I touch her she snores very loud, and curls herself up tighter.

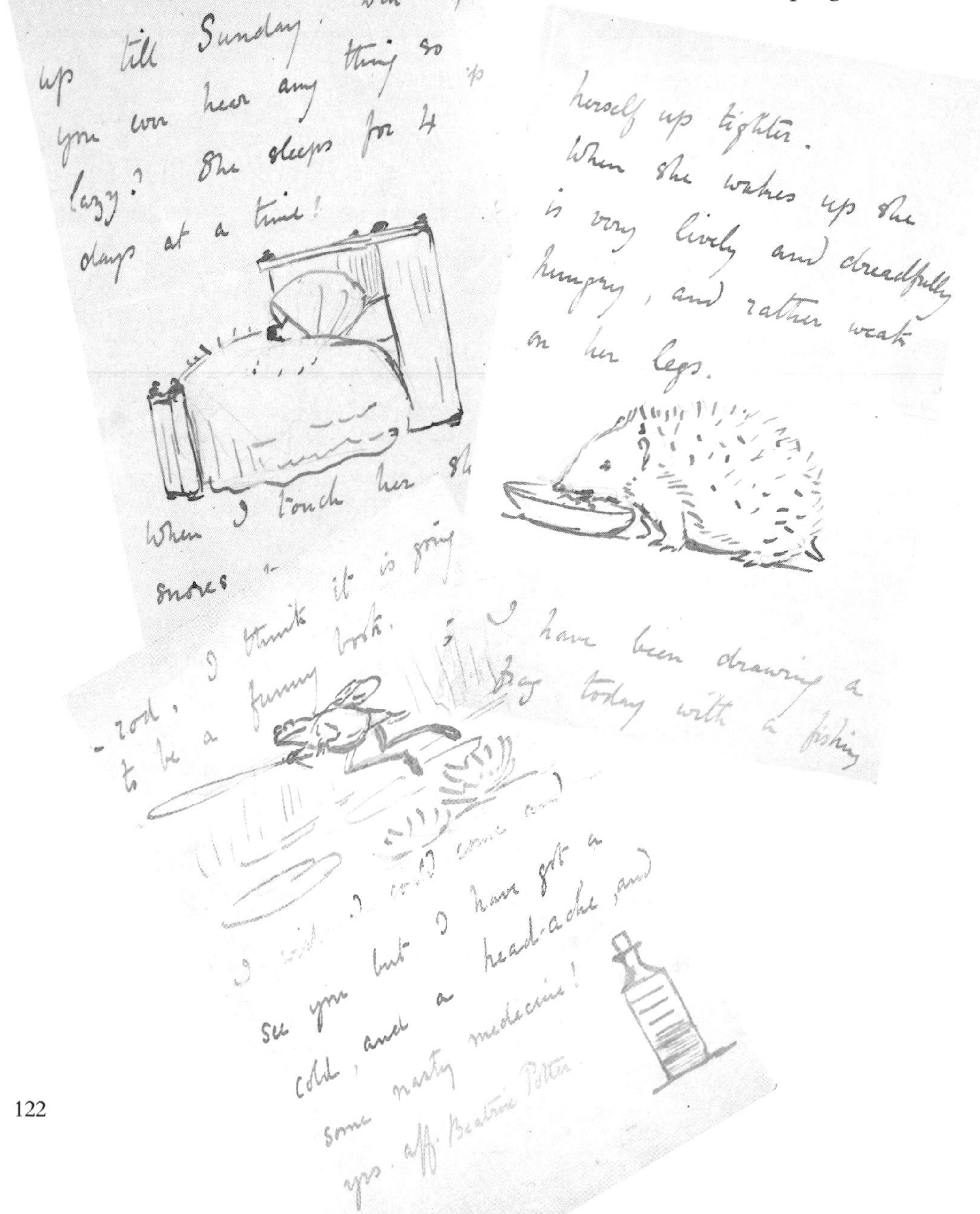

When she wakes up she is very lively and dreadfully hungry, and rather weak on her legs.

I have been drawing a frog today with a fishing-rod, I think it is going to be a funny book [*Mr. Jeremy Fisher*].

I wish I could come and see you but I have got a cold, and a head-ache, and some nasty medecine [sic]!

yrs. aff.
Beatrix Potter

*The 'frog with a fishing rod' as he appears in* The Tale of Mr. Jeremy Fisher *(1906)*

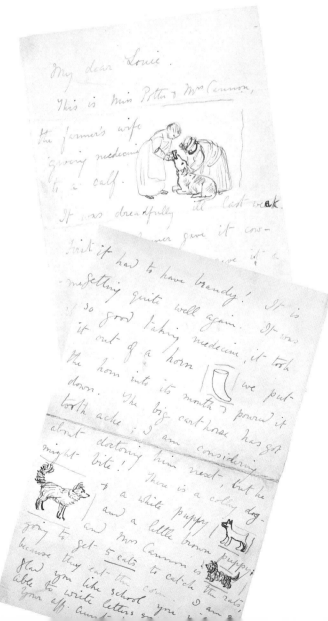

[July 6 07]                    [Ambleside]

My dear Louie

This is Miss Potter & Mrs Cannon, the farmer's wife [at Hill Top] giving medecine [sic] to a calf. It was dreadfully ill last week. First the farmer gave it cow-medecine, then we gave it a whole bottle of chalk mixture, then I bought half a pound of arrowroot & it had it for gruel. Then it was so very ill it had to have brandy! It is getting quite well again. It was so good taking medecine, it took it out of a horn we put the horn into its mouth & poured it down. The big cart horse has got tooth ache; I am considering about doctoring him next, but he might bite! There is a colley dog & a white puppy and a little brown puppy; and Mrs Cannon is going to get *5 cats* to catch the rats, because they eat the corn.

I am so glad you like school you will be able to write letters soon

Your aff.
Aunt B

123

July 8th 07          Hill Top Farm
                        Sawrey

My dear little Louie,

I was so pleased with your letter, you are a grand scholar! I must be very careful with my spelling when I write to you.

I have got two lovely pigs, one is a little bigger than the other, she is very fat and black with a very turned up nose and the fattest cheeks I ever saw; she likes being tickled under the chin, she is a very friendly pig. I call her Aunt Susan. I call the smaller pig Dorcas; she is not so tame , she runs round & round the pig-stye and if I catch her by the ear she squaels [sic]. But Aunt Susan is so tame I have to kick her when she wants to nibble my galoshes. They have both got rings in their noses to prevent them from digging holes in the field, but at present they are shut up in their little house because the field is so wet. It rains every day – whatever shall we do for hay! There is a little bit cut and it is sopping wet.

When I lie in bed I can see a hill of green grass opposite the window about as high as Primrose Hill, and when the sheep walk across there is a crooked pane of glass that makes them like this and the hens are all wrong too; it is a very funny house. It would be a beautiful house for playing hide & seek, I think there are 13 wall cupbards [sic]; some of them are quite big rooms, quite dark.

There are 6 cows, they have got funny names, the best cow is called "Kitchen", I watched her being milked tonight, such a big bucketful. There is another cow called "White stockings" because she has white legs, and another called "Garnett"; and calves called Rose, & Norah & Blossom.

       I remain yours affectionately
                  Beatrix Potter

2 Bolton Gardens
Nov 14 07

My dear Louie,
I was much pleased to receive your very neat letter, which I ought to have replied to sooner; but my spare time is occupied in playing that dreadful game! I am disappointed to find that you cannot play it properly either! I thought you would

go to the Lord Mayor.
but I saw lots of people there, in the underground railway. And I was thinking about Kings and Queens.
Just at the time that you were looking at the procession, I was showing my cousin an old oak tree at Hatfield, where Princess ~~Queen~~ Elizabeth was sitting when they came to tell her that Queen Mary was dead.

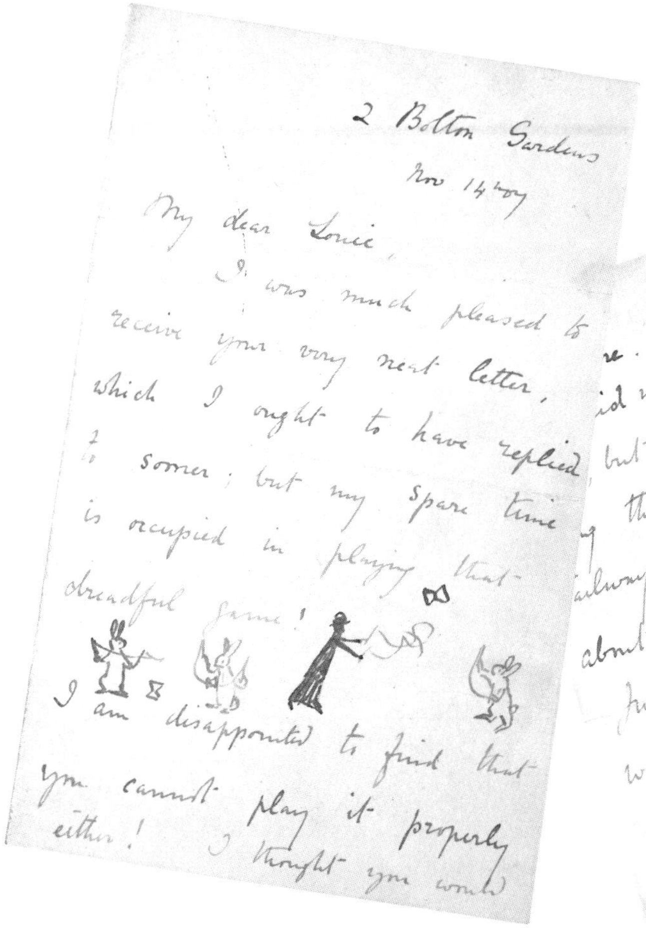

Nov 14th 07 2 Bolton Gardens

My dear Louie

I was much pleased to receive your very neat letter, which I ought to have replied to sooner; but my spare time is occupied in playing that dreadful game [diabolo]! I am disappointed to find that you cannot play it properly either! I thought you would teach me.

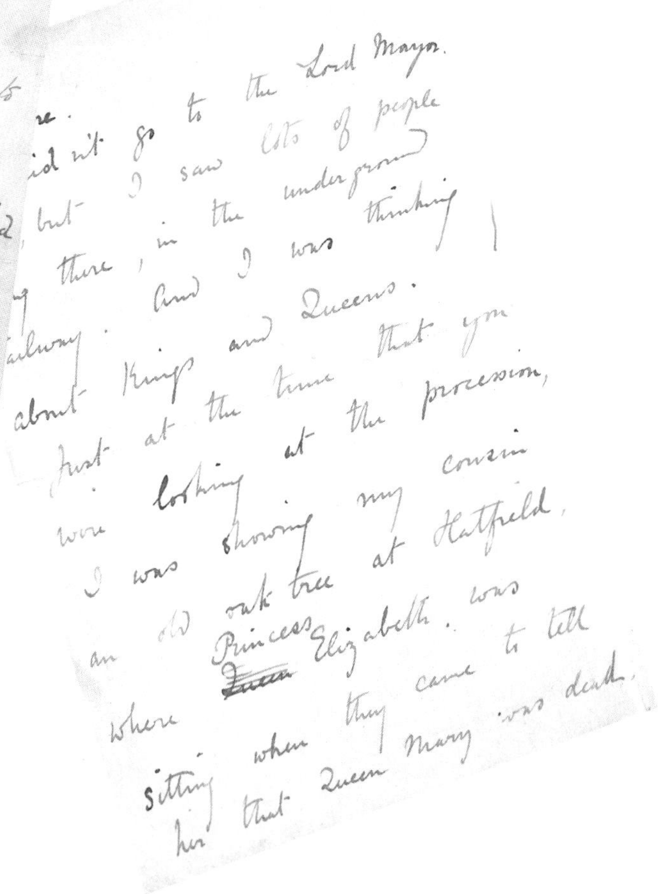

I didn't go to the Lord Mayor's Show, but I saw lots of people going there, in the underground railway. And I was thinking about Kings and Queens.

Just at the time that you were looking at the procession, I was showing my cousin an old oak tree at Hatfield where Princess Elizabeth was sitting when they came to tell her that Queen Mary was dead and she was Queen Elizabeth. She wore a ruff and had a big nose; she could not sit under the tree today because there is nothing left except the trunk with no branches! There is a railing round it to keep it safe. I went to Hatfield to see a woman who used to be my Grandmother's servant. She lives in a little

red house at the edge of Hatfield Park, her father is a gamekeeper.

I never saw such lots of rabbits! Will you give one of these postcards to Nellie. I must come and see you next time.

With much love yrs aff.
Beatrix Potter

Dec 29 08                                        Meadhurst
                                                 Sidmouth

Dear Winifred,

I said last Christmas I was afraid I should see a great deal more of Mr Samuel Whiskers; but I am glad to tell you he is still living at Farmer Potatoes'. He only comes now and then up to Hill Top Farm. He never came near the place for months, because we had a wonderful clever black cat, called Smutty. She was such a good rat-catcher! But alas poor Smutty went for a walk one night and she did not come home again, I am afraid she met a bad man with a gun, early in the morning. We have 3 of her children & some grandchildren, swarms of cats! I say they are to be all kept for a little while, till we see which is the cleverest. There is one little gray kitten that is very sharp, it stands up & fluffs itself out and scratches great big Kep [Beatrix's collie]! No sooner had Smutty disappeared than there began to be swarms of mice! And one evening there was a visit from Mr Whiskers! I was sitting very quiet before the fire in the library reading a book, and I heard someone pitter patter along the passage, & then someone scratched at the outside of the library door. I thought it was the puppy or the kitten so I took no notice. But next morning we discovered that Mr Whiskers had been in the house! We could not find him anywhere, so we think he had got in – and out again – by squeezing under a door. He had stolen the very oddest thing! There is a sort of large cupboard or closet where I do my photographing, it is papered inside with rather a pretty green & gold paper; and Samuel had torn off strips of paper all round the closet as high as he could reach up like this – I could see the marks of his little teeth! Every scrap was taken away.

I wonder what in the world he wanted it for? I think Anna Maria must have been there, with him, to help. And I think she must have wanted to paper her best sitting room!

I only wonder she did not take the paste brush, which was on a shelf in the closet. Perhaps she intended coming back for the brush next night.

If she did, she was disappointed, for I asked John Joiner to make a heavy hard plank of wood, to fit into the opening under the door; and it seems to keep out Mr & Mrs Whiskers.

My fingers are so cold I can't draw!
With love to you & Eveline & Baby from
yrs aff
Beatrix Potter

[To Louie Warne]
[Postmarked: Windermere August 12 1911]

This is a camp of boy scouts – This is my house! & my apple trees, & me in my garden. They arrive in the rain on Saturday. I arrive on Monday morning. I find tents just above my chimnies [sic] and scouts all over everywhere, especially on the walls.

This is me approaching Commander-in-chief. If I give a quantity of *small* apples, will he keep the boys off the big apples. He is most polite, he will send after dinner for the apples.

This is me, expecting 2 boys with a basket! *20* scouts & 1 trumpet.

I take them into my orchard, & point out two aged apple trees, & 3 trees, very very hard pears.

After quarter of an hour, Commander blowing a whistle, to reassemble troop. The 20 scouts have to be pulled out of the pear trees, by the legs.

Specimens of scouts, distended with green fruit inside clothes.

Three cheers for the *old* lady!(!) [Beatrix Potter was forty-five.] The "old lady" has dismissed the scouts with strict injunctions to *cook* the pears, which are stoney.

Ten minutes later a scout reappears, please ma'm may we have a *bucketful* of sugar to cook them with?

I think it prudent to conduct the scout to "Ginger & Pickles", as sugar is cheap.

*Above and right: 'Ginger and Pickles', to which Beatrix directed the scouts, was really the Sawrey village shop owned by Mr John Taylor, used as the setting for* The Tale of Ginger and Pickles *(1909)*

2

This is me approaching Commander-in-chief. If I give a quantity of small apples, will he keep the boys off the big apples. He is most polite. He will sun after dinner for the apples.

This is me, expecting 2 boys with a basket!

20 scouts & 1 trumpet

I take them into my orchard, & point out two aged apple trees & trees, very very hard pears

scouts

3

after quarter of an hour, 20 scouts in trees

Commander blowing a whistle, to remember the The 20 scouts have to be pulled out of the pear trees, by the legs.

pears —pears apples—

Specimens of scouts, distended with green fruit inside clothes.

Three cheers for the old Lady! (!)

"old lady" has dismissed the

4

scouts with strict injunctions to cook the pears, which are stony,

Ten minutes later a scout reappears, please ma'am may we have a bucketful of sugar to cook them with?

I think it prudent to conduct the scout to "Ginger & Pickles", as sugar is cheap.

## DOROTHY ALLEN

Dorothy Allen was ten years old and living in a house called Springfield in Ambleside when she received her letter from Beatrix Potter. *The Pie and The Patty-Pan*, which she had just read, had been published the previous October and Beatrix was now working on *The Story of Miss Moppet*.

Dorothy was the oldest of the four children of William Allen who, for many years, was the doctor for Hawkshead and the surrounding hamlets. When he moved to Ambleside in 1904 Dr Allen was presented with an inscribed gold hunter watch 'by the township of Hawkshead in recognition of long and valuable public services'. He had one of the first motor cars in the Lake District and could often be seen labouring up the Kirkstone Pass or through the Troutbeck Valley in his De Dion Bouton.

When Dorothy grew up she followed her father into medicine, graduating from Glasgow in 1923. She was particularly interested in infant and general medical welfare and worked for a time in Liverpool at Alder Hey, a specialist children's hospital. But whenever she could she helped her father with his practice in Ambleside. She visited her patients by pony and trap for, as she later told her son, 'I could doze in the trap and the pony would take me home by himself. It was very handy after a late call!'

In 1933 Dorothy married a widower, Robert Gibson, who was a teacher of modern languages in the south of England, and their son, John, was born the following year. Dorothy continued her work in medicine, firstly as a Medical Officer of Health in Reigate and Redhill and then as a School Medical Officer for the London County Council, where she had special responsibility for children with mental and physical disabilities. She died in 1966.

During the Second World War Dorothy's son, John, was sent from the bombing in the south to stay with his grandparents in the Lake District. Dr Allen had returned to Hawkshead and was once again the local doctor. He was also the Medical Officer at the Grizedale Prisoner of War

*'Such a dreadful little pickle' – the kitten Beatrix was drawing for* The Story of Miss Moppet *(1906)*

Camp and he held a daily surgery there. His grandson accompanied him on the twenty-mile journey whenever he could and remembers 'the great experience of driving through the Grizedale Forest in Grandad's wonderful Morris 8'.

Both the original letter from Beatrix Potter to Dorothy Allen and its envelope have the wide, black edges that at the time signified the sender was in mourning. July 1906 was almost exactly a year after the death of Beatrix's publisher and fiancé, Norman Warne, and many – but not all – of her letters in those intervening months carried the same sign of mourning.

July 18th 06

Belle Green
Sawrey

My dear Dorothy,

I am glad to hear that you like the Pie and the Patty-pan; I thought it was a funny story when I was making it up in my head; but some people say it is too long, so I am glad to hear that you read right through it!

I am trying to draw a kitten now, it is very pretty but such a dreadful little pickle; it is never still for a minute. I shall not make much of a story about it; it is more like a picture book for babies [*Miss Moppet*].

I have got 2 rabbits called Josephine and Mopsy, they are wild brown rabbits that I caught very young. Josephine is very fond of me & will jump on my knee and on my shoulder; but she is afraid of people that she does not know well. And a few people she quite dislikes; we have an old servant who sometimes feeds the rabbits for me; & when I left the rabbits in London last Easter, Josephine bit the old woman most painfully on the thumb! She does not object to Mrs

Satterthwaite [Beatrix's landlady], it is very funny how animals have likes and dislikes.

Mopsy is very pretty but very stupid, I only keep her because the old rabbit might be dull by herself. I have had rabbits called Peter & Benjamin, they were Belgian rabbits; Peter lived to be 8 years old, he used to lie before the fire on the hearth rug like a cat. He was clever at learning tricks, he used to jump through a hoop, & ring a bell, & play on the tambourine. I saw him once trying to play the tambourine on a straw hat! I wish the rain would stop, I want to go out & make hay.

I remain yrs sincerely
Beatrix Potter

## LOUISA FERGUSON

*Louisa Ferguson aged sixteen months in November 1903*

*In 1910 Beatrix sent Louisa a copy of* The Tale of Samuel Whiskers or The Roly-Poly Pudding *(1908)*

Louisa Ferguson lived in Wellington, New Zealand, and when she was five she received a postcard photograph of a rabbit from England. It was dated 21 November 1907 and it read: 'With best wishes for the New Year to little Louisa Ferguson from Beatrix Potter. This is a portrait of the real old original Mr Benjamin Bunny! Many thanks to Mrs Ferguson for her kind appreciative letter.' Beatrix Potter had sent Louisa one of her photographs of Benjamin (see page 137) in acknowledgement of another fan letter.

Louisa and her brother, fifteen-year-old William, were the children of William and Mary Ferguson, prominent citizens of Wellington. Born in London, William senior had obtained his engineering degrees in the late 1870s from Trinity College, Dublin, where he became assistant professor of engineering in 1880. He sailed from England for New Zealand in 1883 and the following year was appointed engineer-secretary and treasurer to the Wellington Harbour Board. During his twenty-four years' service there William Ferguson witnessed the almost total disappearance of the sailing vessel and the gradual introduction of steam, and under his guidance the port became one of the most efficient and well-equipped in the Southern Hemisphere. In 1890 William married Mary Louisa Moorhouse. She was the daughter of William Sefton Moorhouse, a Yorkshire lawyer who had been one of the early colonists of New Zealand, a much respected Superintendent of the Province of Canterbury and one of the first elected members of the House of Representatives.

In reply to her postcard Mrs Ferguson sent Beatrix a present of a small grass-woven bag, which resulted in Beatrix's letter to Louisa of 26 February 1908 (see page 134) and in an exchange of presents and books between Sawrey and Wellington. From Beatrix there was a copy of *The Roly-Poly Pudding* signed 'New Year 1910', followed by *Ginger and Pickles* signed 'Jan 8th 1910', and with the second book the letter acknowledging the gift of a pen holder.

In August 1910 Beatrix received a letter from Louisa,

together with some photographs, but what she did not know until the following October when she learned the news from another New Zealand friend, Bessie Hadfield (see page 148), was that Louisa Ferguson had died on 14 August, a month after her eighth birthday. Born with a neurological problem that had steadily disabled her, Louisa had been ill for only two weeks and she died as the result of a stroke. In the Karori Crematorium Chapel a stained glass window representing 'Hope' was placed in her memory.

As soon as she learned of Louisa's death Beatrix wrote at once to Mrs Ferguson from Hill Top Farm.

I scarcely know how to write to you in your terrible trouble. One can only hope that you are given strength and patience. Dear child – she has been taken away from a world of troubles – troubles which it is useless to question or try to understand . . . I think I have little friends all over the world, I am glad if my books have given her pleasure. Her little grass bag is hanging up in the house-place here, my house-keeper (the farmer's wife) was so sorry when I told her. We have a handful of children in this house – but not one to spare; and to think that you have lost your one little ewe lamb is dreadful. I hope she did not suffer much. With sincere sympathy for you and your husband.

The following week Beatrix sent Mary Ferguson a copy of the newly-published *Peter Rabbit's Painting Book*. In it she had written, 'For Mrs Ferguson from B.P. with kind remembrance.'

Mary Ferguson was herself not strong and she died twenty years later in 1930. 'In going through the treasures of my late wife' William Ferguson discovered that Mary had kept Beatrix's letters and inscribed books and he presented them to the Alexander Turnbull Library in Wellington, New Zealand.

*Another present for Louisa was* The Tale of Ginger and Pickles *(1909)*

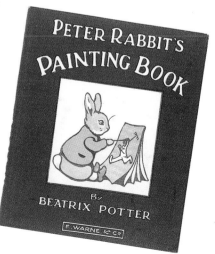

*Beatrix Potter's gift to Mrs Ferguson after she had received the news of Louisa's death*

Feb. 26 1908 c/o Frederick Warne & Co.
Chandos House,
Bedford Street,
Strand,
London.

Dear little Louisa,

It is a dear little bag and a dear little photograph! When I saw the bag I said "This is for Peter Rabbit to carry his pocket handkerchief in!" But when I looked at it carefully I said – it is a great deal too nice for Peter, and he would bite holes in it, as it seems to be made of flax or grass. So I shall keep it for myself, & hang it up on a little brass hook in my parlour, it will look very pretty against the dark wood. I have got a bellows hanging up and a pen wiper and a kettle holder, and some other photographs of little girls that I have never seen! When they send me photographs, I send back a photograph of Peter or Benjamin. I don't write letters to all of them; but you look such a little dear and your Mamma has sent me such a nice present, I am quite pleased.

I hope that you are very well and I remain

with love

yrs aff

Beatrix Potter

c/o

Telegraphic Address: "Warne, London." Telephone No 2208, Gerrard.

Frederick Warne & Co

Chandos House, Bedford Street, Strand.

London. Feb 26 1908

Dear little Louisa,

It is a dear little bag and a dear little photograph! When I saw the bag I said "This is for Peter Rabbit to carry his pocket handkerchief in!"

But when I looked at it carefully I said – it is a great deal too nice for Peter, and he would bite holes in it, as it seems to be made of flax or grass. So I shall keep it for myself, & hang it up on a little brass hook in my parlour, it will look very pretty against the dark wood. I have got a bellows hanging up and a pen wiper and a kettle holder, and some other photographs of little girls that I have never seen!

Polly put the kettle on

When they send me photographs, I send back a photograph of Peter or Benjamin. I don't write letters to all of them; but you look such a little dear and your Mamma has sent me such a nice present, I am quite pleased.

I hope that you are very well and I remain with love yrs aff

Beatrix Potter.

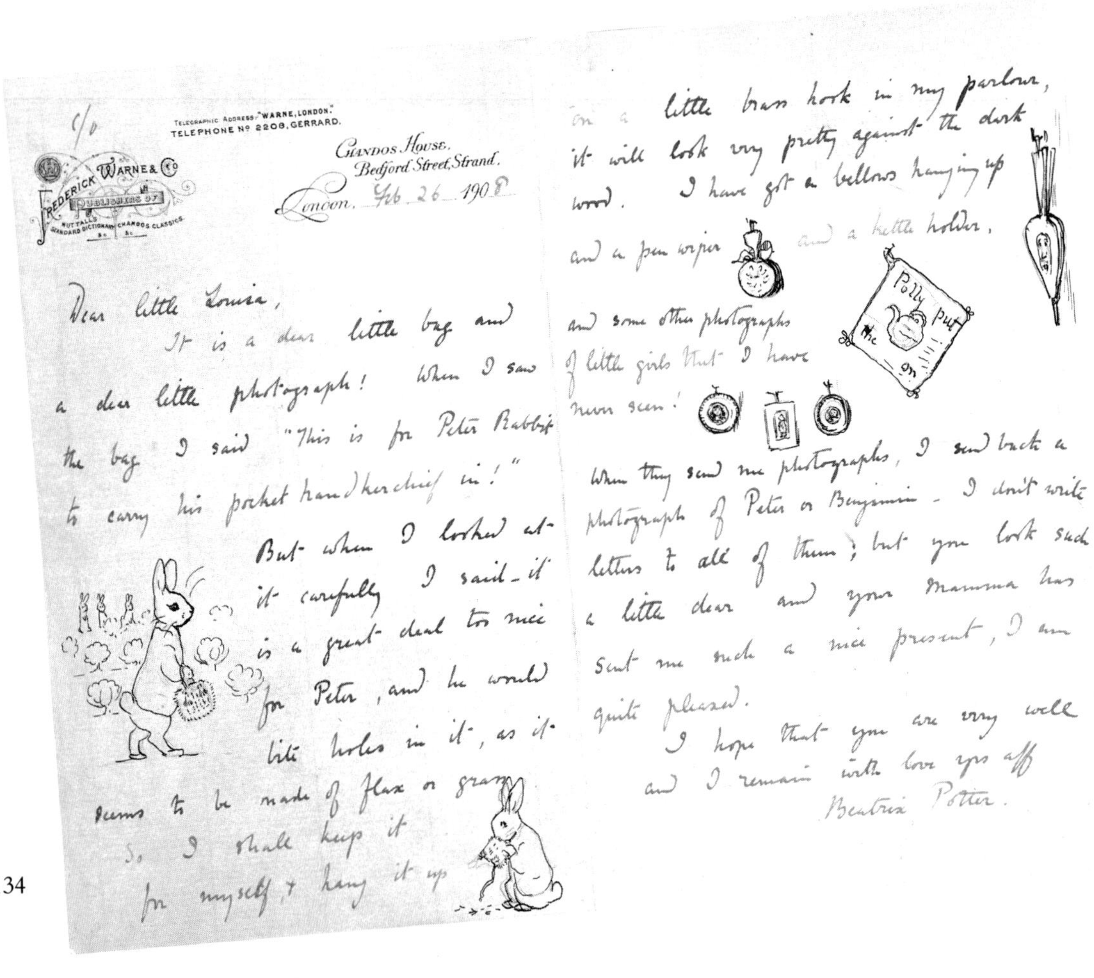

Jan 8. 1910        Sawrey
                Ambleside

Dear Louisa Ferguson

You will think I am *very naughty* – I have never written to thank you for that lovely pen holder. It came just when I was starting on a journey. I think it is beautiful, and such a length. We have greenish agates that are made into brooches but they are only little pebbles.

Now I am sending you a a[sic] new book to make up amends – It was not ready in time for Christmas in New Zealand, so I don't think you have got it [*Ginger and Pickles*].

It was all drawn in the village near my farm house, and the village shop is there.

Only poor old "John Dormouse" is dead – just before the book was finished – I was so sorry I could not give him a copy before he died. He was such a funny old man; I thought he might be offended if I made fun of him, so I said I would only draw his shop & not him.

And then he said I had drawn his son John in another book [*The Roly-Poly Pudding*], with a saw and wagging his tail! and old John felt jealous of young John. So I said how could I draw him if he would not get up? and he considered for several days, and then sent "his respects, and thinks he might pass as a dormouse!" It is considered very like him. Also it is very much like our "Timothy Baker" but he is not quite so well liked, so everybody is laughing. I think I shall put *myself* in the next book, it will be about pigs [*Pigling Bland*]; I shall put in me walking about with my old "Goosey" sow, she is such a pet.

I am so busy over the Election my fingers are quite stiff with drawing "posters" [in support of the Unionist campaign for tariff reform].

                Yr aff friend
                Beatrix Potter

*John Taylor's son, as John Joiner, the handyman dog, in* The Roly-Poly Pudding *(1908)*

135

*It would seem that* The Tale of Benjamin Bunny *(1904) was a favourite with Jack Ripley*

*Beatrix with the real Benjamin on a lead in Scotland in September 1891*

## JOHN (JACK) RIPLEY

It has not been possible to trace Jack Ripley directly but there are two envelopes addressed to him by Beatrix Potter and they have provided a number of clues. The first envelope contains Beatrix's photograph of her pet rabbit, Benjamin, made into a postcard, another copy of the same card that Beatrix sent to Louisa Ferguson three months before (see page 132). This envelope is postmarked February 1908 and is addressed to: 'Master Jack Ripley, Estancia "La Rosita", Canada de Gomez, Argentine Republic, S. America'. The address is accounted for by the discovery that Jack Ripley's father, also John, was a breeder and trainer of polo ponies, many of which come to Britain from the Argentine. Presumably Jack accompanied his father on one of his buying trips. The second envelope is addressed to 'Master Jack Ripley, Siddington Hall, Cirencester'. Siddington Hall is a large, late-Edwardian house in the heart of polo-playing Gloucestershire, now divided into flats and surrounded by a number of smaller houses.

The Ripleys lived in Gloucestershire, in the villages of Siddington, Coates and Ampney Crucis, for a number of years, certainly from 1908 into the 1920s, and their stables resounded to the sound of shoeing of horses and the shouts of the Argentine grooms. Those who remember the family say that Mrs Ripley was 'a very sweet lady', 'a most charming person', but that her husband was of sterner stuff and 'ruled their only child, Jack, with a rod of iron'. 'I remember the Ripleys quite well', came a reply to an appeal for information through the local paper. 'Jack was a very nice boy and everyone liked him. He was very tall and about the same age as my brother who was born in 1904. Jack used to play tennis but he had something wrong with his hands which were rather deformed; he had to have operations on them.'

From the unpublished 'Memoirs of Amy Hill', who was born in January 1896, comes another revealing comment on the Ripleys:

The family who were there [in Siddington Hall] when I was a little girl were Mr and Mrs John Ripley. She was a very sweet lady, but he treated everyone like slaves. He had lived in South Africa with plenty of black servants. He once brought back two zebra which he drove in a dog-cart. They were kept in a field where Bowly Crescent now stands and were a source of great interest to us children.

My mother's cousin, Polly, was a parlourmaid at the Hall at this time, and I can remember how smart she looked in her afternoon dress, a long, black dress with a frilled apron tied at the back in a nice bow with long ends, and a white, frilled cap with long streamers. On Sunday mornings I had to go down to the servants' entrance to get a pound of dripping, price 6d, which was the cook's 'perks'.

*Benjamin with his cousin Peter in* The Tale of Benjamin Bunny

With Benjamin Bunny's love to little Jack Ripley, he has got a very little hand, full of kisses, so he writes very little letters.

Beatrix Potter
Feb 26th 08.

[Postmarked: January 12
1909]

Master J. Ripley
Sidington Hall.

Dear Jackie

   My cousin Peter's
envelopes are a very
inconvenient shape! I have
only got room to say I hope
you are very well, and there
is going to be another book
about me and my family. It
won't be ready till
September, it will be called
(but that is a secret at
present) so no more until
we meet again in
September. I have grown
up since you saw me last!
                    Benjamin Bunny.

[The book was, of course,
*The Flopsy Bunnies*.]

Master J. Ripley
Siddington Hall

Dear Mr Jackie,
   I am obliged to you for
sending me a lovely
calendar like a rose. I have
tasted it and I think it is
made of paper. So I shall
not eat any more of it, I
shall hang it up in my rabbit
hole!
              Love from your friend
                        Peter Rabbit

Master J. Ripley
Siddington Hall

Dear Mr Jackie,
    My son Peter has written
to thank you for the roses,
they will decorate my
rabbit hole most elegantly,
& I was in want of another
calendar.
                Jos. Rabbit
P.S. I had not room to
write my name properly.
            Josephine Rabbit

Master J. Ripley
Siddington Hall

Dear Mr Jackie,
    I have had those there
Rabbits in my garden again!
                yrs respectfully
                Mr McGregor.

Master Benjamin Bunny
The Warren.

Dear Cousin Benjamin
    I have heard that Mr
McGregor is in bed with a
cold, I have heard him
sneezing half a mile off.
Will you meet me at 6 this
evening in the wood
outside the garden gate?
        In haste yr aff cousin
            Peter Rabbit.

*Peter escaping from Mr McGregor in*
The Tale of Peter Rabbit *(1902)*

*Frontispiece illustration for* The Tale of Pigling Bland *(1913)*

*A Randolph Caldecott picture of Anthony Rowley in* A Frog He Would A-Wooing Go

## ANDREW (DREW) FAYLE

All that is known about Andrew Fayle is that in 1909 he wrote to Beatrix Potter from a house called 'Kylemore' in Rathgar, which was at the time a fashionable Dublin suburb. The *Dublin Directory* shows that the house was owned by Edwin Fayle and it gives a second address for him in Greystones, a small sedate village in nearby Co. Wicklow. Edwin Fayle disappears from the Directories in 1921 and the suggestion has been made that perhaps he was an official in the British administration who left Ireland on the establishment of the Irish Free State in 1921.

Sotheby's sale catalogue for October 1950 states that Beatrix's miniature letters to Andrew were written 'in reply to an enquiry as to the matrimonial status of the frog Jeremy Fisher' and it dates them as 1909–10, presumably because the eighth letter in the series is clearly dated 'Jan 22 1910'. However, there is a clue that the correspondence continued for longer than that. In the letter signed by Peter (see opposite) it is clear that Beatrix was working on the illustrations for *The Tale of Pigling Bland*, which we know was not published until 1913. Writing to Harold Warne on 19 April of that year she says: 'I have been drawing pigs, but cannot do much till I see where the plates fall in the letterpress.' She continued drawing for the book throughout the summer of 1913, delivering the final artwork only a few weeks before her wedding in October.

One of the Fayle letters is unique among the miniature letters so far discovered in that it is signed by an animal character that does not come from one of the Potter books. Anthony Rowley (see page 142) first appeared in the early nineteenth-century version of the popular song 'The Love-sick Frog', but Beatrix was familiar with him through Randolph Caldecott's picture book, *A Frog He Would A-Wooing Go*, published in 1883. 'We bought his picture books eagerly, as they came out,' she once wrote to an American friend, and her father, Rupert Potter, had four of Caldecott's original pen and inks for the book in his picture collection. Beatrix's own first drawings for *The Tale of Mr.*

*Jeremy Fisher* had been used in 1896 by the publisher Ernest Nister to illustrate yet another version of the song called 'A Frog he would a-fishing go', although Anthony Rowley was not present on that occasion.

Andrew Fayle's letters were bequeathed to the Victoria and Albert Museum by Enid Linder in 1980.

Master Drew
Kylemore.

Dear Master Drew

I am pleased to hear you like Miss Potter's books. Miss Potter is drawing pigs & mice. She says she has drawn enough rabbits. But I am to be put into one picture at the end of the pig book [*Pigling Bland*].

> yr aff friend
> Peter

Master D Fayle
Kylemore
Co. Dublin.

Dear Master Drew,

In answer to your very kind inquiry, I live alone; I am not married.

When I bought my sprigged waistcoat & my maroon tail-coat I had hopes . . . But I am alone . . . If there were a "Mrs Jeremy Fisher" she might object to snails. It is some satisfaction to be able to have as much water & mud in the house as a person likes.

Thanking you for your touching inquiry,

> yr devoted friend
> Jeremiah Fisher.

The final picture in Pigling Bland *into which Beatrix put Peter Rabbit*

Master D Fayle
Kylemore

Dear Master Drew,

I hear that you think that there ought to be a "Mrs J. Fisher". Our friend is at present taking mud baths at the bottom of the pond, which may be the reason why your letter has not been answered quick by return. I will do my best to advise him, but I fear he remembers the sad fate of his elder brother ['Froggy' in *A Frog He Would A-Wooing Go*] who disobeyed his mother, and he was gobbled up by a lily white duck!

If my friend Jeremy gets married, I will certainly tell you, & send a bit of wedding cake.

One of our friends is going into the next book. He is fatter than Jeremy; & he has shorter legs [Mr. Jackson in *Mrs. Tittlemouse*].

yrs with compliments
Sir Isaac Newton.

*Sir Isaac Newton's friend Mr Jackson from* The Tale of Mrs. Tittlemouse *(1910)*

Master D. Fayle
Kylemore.

Dear Master Drew,

I begin to think it is true? That there are *no* frogs in Ireland, dear Master Drew? Have you never heard the sad story of the Frog & the mouse? And ever since then, all the frogs are *batchelors* [sic] & live by themselves! Hey ho!

says yours truly
Ant[h]ony Rowley.

Master Drew Fayle
Kylemore.

Dear Master Drew,
    I hear that you are interested in the domestic arrangements of our friend Jeremy Fisher. I am of opinion that his dinner parties would be much more agreeable if there were a lady to preside at the table. I do not care for roast grasshoppers. His housekeeping & cookery do not come up to the standard to which I am accustomed at the Mansion House.
        yrs truly
    Alderman Pt. Tortoise.

Master Drew Fayle
Kylemore
Co Dublin

Dear Master Drew,
    If you please Sir, I am a widow; & I think it is very wrong that there is not any Mrs Jeremy Fisher, but *I* would not marry Mr Jeremy not for worlds, the way he does live in that house all slippy sloppy; not any lady would stand it. & not a bit of good starching his cravats.
    yr obedient washerwoman
        Tiggy Winkle.

Master D. Fayle,
Kylemore
Co Dublin

Dear Drew,
    I have got that mixed up with this week's wash! Have *you* got Mrs Flopsy Bunny's shirt or Mr Jeremy Fisher's apron? instead of your pocket handkerchief – I mean to say Mrs Flopsy Bunny's apron Everything is all got mixed up in wrong bundles. I will buy more safety pins.
    yr aff washerwoman
        T. Winkle.

143

Master D. Fayle
Kylemore

Dear Drew,

I hope that your washing is done to please you? I consider that Mrs Tiggy Winkle is particularly good at ironing collars; but she does mix things up at the wash. I have got a shirt marked J.F. instead of an apron. Have you lost a shirt at the wash? It is 3 inches long. My apron is much larger & marked F B.

yrs
Flopsy Bunny.

Mrs Tiggy Winkle
Cat Bells

Mr J. Fisher regrets that he has to complain about the washing. Mrs T. W. has sent home an immense white apron with tapes instead of Mr J F's best new shirt.

The apron is marked "F B".

Jan 22. 1910

*Mrs Tiggy-winkle*

*The Flopsy Bunnies*

*Mr Jeremy Fisher*

Master D. Fayle
Kylemore

Dear Master Fayle

I wish you a Happy New Year rather late! Miss Potter did have to write such a lot of letters. Do you know she gets letters from little girls and boys as far off as New Zealand? and America & Russia. And now somebody wants to give her a Norway kitten! I rather am afraid I shall fight it!

yr aff friend
Tom Kitten.

Master D. Fayle
Kylemore
Dublin.

Dear Drew,
This is love from lots of little mice, sent by

Tom Thumb
& Hunca Munca.

Mrs Tiggy Winkle
Cat Bells

Mr J. Fisher regrets to have to complain again about the washing. Mrs T. Winkle has sent home an enormous handkerchief marked "D. Fayle" instead of the tablecloth marked J.F.

If this continues every week, Mr J. Fisher will have to get married, so as to have the washing done at home.

## DAUNE RASHLEIGH

*Daune Rashleigh*

Daune and Rosamond Rashleigh were the children of Arthur and Edith Rashleigh. Theirs was an old-established family, with roots in Cornwall since the early part of the sixteenth century and a baronetcy created in 1831, but Arthur was a younger son and did not inherit. He lived with his family in Malvern Wells in Worcestershire.

Daune was born in 1900 and her sister three years later. Like Beatrix Potter the children did not go to school; they were taught at home by a German governess. It was a secluded upbringing. Daune was shy and somewhat unworldly and as she grew up she found it increasingly hard to make herself go out at all. She had inherited her mother's artistic talents, excelling at painting miniatures on ivory, at making embroidered pictures and at the now rare art of sculpting wax portraits. She also loved her garden.

Daune belonged to that First World War generation of which so many of the marriageable young men were killed in France, and she never married. When her sister married Sir John Langham in 1930 and went to live in Co. Fermanagh in Northern Ireland, Daune was left alone with her parents to pursue her own quiet life.

Although she had never had any experience of working for her living, Daune responded to the call for women to take men's places in factories and offices in the Second World War, and she offered her artistic skills to the Royal Porcelain Works in the neighbouring town of Worcester. They engaged her to work forty-seven hours a week hand-painting porcelain – at a wage of 29/- (£1.45) a week, plus 10/6 (52½p) war bonus. Daune kept her letter of engagement and it shows that her employers appreciated she was coming from a somewhat unusual situation: 'We are quite willing for you to come in as soon as you can manage it in the mornings, however, we would like to make it quite clear that when the weather etc. improves you would endeavour to make arrangements whereby you would commence work at the proper time.' Daune stayed at the Royal Porcelain Works until the end of the war and it was the only job she ever had.

In 1946 she moved with her parents to Dublin and there, in 1955, her wax miniatures were shown in an exhibition which attracted considerable attention. In 1960 Daune went to live in Fermanagh near her sister until her death in 1988. Her niece remembers that she was still gardening and making pictures: 'Such a gentle, kind person and so bright and cheerful to the end.'

Daune Rashleigh kept her miniature letter attached to the endpaper of a first edition of *The Tale of Benjamin Bunny* which, with the letter in place, was sold at auction in June 1991. The reference to 'Miss Potter is busy drawing Pigs' echoes Beatrix's letter to Drew Fayle on page 141, thus dating it between 1910 and 1913 when Beatrix was working on the illustrations for *The Tale of Pigling Bland*.

Miss Daune Rashleigh
Kaikoura
Malvern Wells

Dear Miss Daune

I am writing for Miss Potter, because Miss Potter is busy drawing Pigs; and she has taken such a long time to answer your nice letter.

It was funny about the 6d on the hills. I would eat your lobelia if I got into your garden! I am Miss Potter's rabbit, I shall be 8 years old next May.

your loving friend
Joseph Rabbit.
'Peter' was before my time!

## KITTY AND HILDA HADFIELD AND

## PETER TUCKEY

*Bessie Hadfield*

Kitty and Hilda were the daughters of New Zealanders Elizabeth (Bessie) and Henry Hadfield. Henry's father had been a much-respected missionary to the Maoris in the 1840s and Bessie and Henry lived in a large property, Lindale Farm, at Paraparaumu, some 45 kilometres north of Wellington. In 1909, when it was diagnosed that Henry was suffering from cancer, he undertook the long journey to London to seek medical help, taking with him his wife and four children – Gordon (aged ten), Kitty (six), Hilda (four) and Selwyn (two).

The Hadfields' first contact with Beatrix Potter had begun, as had that of so many others, as the result of a fan letter which developed into a continuing correspondence. In one of her letters Beatrix asked Bessie Hadfield if by any chance she knew a family in Wellington called Ferguson, from whom she had recently also received an appreciative letter. If Bessie Hadfield had not known the Fergusons personally she certainly knew the family's standing in the community and, as Beatrix told Mrs Ferguson later, 'wrote so pleasantly about you'.

When Beatrix knew that the Hadfields were in London she took the somewhat uncharacteristic step of arranging a meeting; she wanted to send a personal message to Mrs Ferguson and her daughter, Louisa (see page 132). The Hadfields were staying in Blackheath, in south-east London, and it was there that Beatrix visited them. Mrs Hadfield must have shown particular interest in the china depicted in *The Tailor of Gloucester* illustrations, for on 28 September 1910 Beatrix sent her a copy of the 1902 privately-printed edition of the book, drawing her attention in a letter to a colour picture of a cup that had been omitted from the Warne edition and explaining that she had borrowed the china from 'the cobbler's wife at Sawrey'. It must have been Bessie Hadfield's reply to this that Beatrix acknowledged in her miniature letter to Kitty on page 151.

After that first meeting with the Hadfields Beatrix commented: 'I wish I had not had to keep the children at "arms length", I am not generally so severely distant with them! I did enjoy my visit to you, it does one good to see anybody come through a time of trial with faith and courage. I do not know how to talk religion or write it in my books but I can see when faith is there. I hope some day you will write and tell me that you have had a very happy journey home to New Zealand.' But sadly, Henry Hadfield died soon after the family had reached home.

Beatrix kept up her correspondence with the widowed Bessie for many years and sent her a signed copy of each new book as it was published. In June 1918 Bessie added to her family of four her brother's two-year-old son, Peter Tuckey. Peter's father had been killed in France early in that year and then his mother had died from the 'flu she contracted while nursing patients in the epidemic which struck the Paraparaumu area that same year. When Beatrix heard about Peter from Bessie she was deeply touched and when she came to choose the dedication for *Cecily Parsley's Nursery Rhymes* in December 1922 she asked that it should read, 'For Little Peter in New Zealand'.

Only one of Beatrix's letters to Bessie has survived, Bessie's nephew reporting that on her death 'there were several cabin trunks full of her voluminous correspondence at Lindale, most of it mildewed and indecipherable. I regret to say it was all destroyed in a bonfire.' But Beatrix had also sent a series of miniature letters to the girls while they were in London, after first asking which were their favourite characters in the books. The letters to Hilda have disappeared but those to Kitty have been lent by her family to the Dorothy Neal White Collection, which is housed in the National Library of New Zealand in Wellington, together with Bessie's one letter and the early copy of *The Tailor of Gloucester* in which Beatrix had placed markers showing the differences between the privately-printed and the Frederick Warne editions. There is also a copy of *The Fairy Caravan* annotated by Beatrix.

*Kitty and Hilda Hadfield, with their elder brother Gordon*

*Gordon Hadfield with his cousin Peter Tuckey*

*Young Peter Tuckey on the beach at Paraparaumu, New Zealand*

As well as sending them miniature letters, Beatrix promised Kitty and Hilda that one day she would write a story for them and that it would feature 'a little cockleshell fairy who lived on Lancaster Sands'. After Beatrix's death just such a story was found in Castle Cottage, undated and written in the secret code that she had used many years before for her journal, but it is unfinished and even stops in mid-sentence. However, Beatrix did keep her word to them and in about 1911 she wrote in a small notebook a tale called *The Fairy in the Oak*, 'for two New Zealand fairies – by promise'. It was based on a conversation she had had with an old man who was building a wall for her in Sawrey and who had witnessed a series of unexplained accidents when helping to take down an enormous oak tree some years before. In *The Fairy in the Oak* Beatrix attributed all the trouble to the revenge of the displaced and distressed fairy who had lived in the tree. In 1929, with a few alterations, Kitty and Hilda's story was published as the final chapter of *The Fairy Caravan*.

By the early 1930s both the Hadfield sisters were married. Kitty and Edward Cooper went on to have four children, Hilda and Charles Hawkes, two. Kitty died in 1986, Hilda in 1960. Peter Tuckey qualified as a doctor in 1940 and the same year married a teacher of physical education, Pamela Paterson. After serving in the Solomon Islands and Italy in the Second World War Peter established a family practice in Wellington, which he ran for forty years until his retirement in 1986. Peter and Pamela Tuckey have five sons.

Miss Kitty Headfield [sic]
Blackheath
London

              Cat Bells.

My dear Miss Kitty,
    I am flattered to hear I am a favourite, you make me proud, if you please, mam? There is a large wash this week, Tom Kitten has been in the coal cellar and all the people want their blankets washed this week, because it is good drying weather, so no more from yr aff washer woman

              Tiggy Winkle.

Miss K. Headfield
Blackheath
London S.W.
                    The farmyard

My dear Kitty,

   My family have had sad
accidents this spring. I
knew it would happen if I
was not allowed to hatch
my own eggs. There were 9
lovely ducks & they went &
fell into the well, when they
were tiny tinys – and 3 were
drowned and the well was
covered up with a sack, &
somebody took the sack off
& 2 more fell in, and the
cow trod on another – and
only 3 ducklings grew up.
                    yr afflicted friend.
                    Jemima Puddleduck.

Miss Kitty Headfield
Blackheath
London

Dear Miss Kitty,

   Miss Potter has got her
wheelbarrow at present, &
is disobliging, she will not
have me and Samuel on the
place or help us no ways.
And I did overhear she has
told John Joiner to put zinc
on the bottom of the door
& stuff up 2 ventilators
before the corn is carried in.
It is unkind I am disgusted;
when the sparrows say it is
a lovely crop; me & my
family would live on it all
winter in that loft.
                    Anna Maria.

Miss Kitty Headfield
Blackheath
London

My dear Miss Kitty,
   The old Tailor wants to
thank your mother for her
nice letter [see page 148]. It
is not everybody who cares
for my old china. Oh dear
me! how tired Miss Potter
is getting, another funny
book for every Christmas,
and sometimes two. When
you grow a little bigger you
will want a book with more
reading. I think a fairy tale
would be a change, & a rest,
after so many rats and
rabbits.
                    yr aff friend
                    The Tailor.

## CORDELIA, AUGUSTA, ROBERT AND

## FRANCISCA BURN AND BARBARA RUXTON

The four Burn children and Barbara Ruxton were cousins and in August 1911 the two families spent their first holiday in the Lake District. 'That first year we stayed at Lake Bank, Mason's chicken farm near Esthwaite, and then we went deeper into the Lake District to a farm called Deepdale, near Patterdale,' recalls Francisca Burn. 'The Ruxtons were staying nearby and I think they must have arranged for us to go over and meet Beatrix Potter. Certainly three of us went with Barbara – Gussie, Robert and me.'

Robert, usually known to the family as Robin, remembers the visit quite clearly. 'I was not in the least shy of this plump, comfortable woman who reminded me of my mother, and we were all so excited when she introduced us to Tom Kitten and then to Jemima Puddle-duck. We also met her favourite sheepdog, Kep, who was walking across the farmyard, lame on one of his forefeet.'

Robert Burn was nine on that visit and his youngest sister, Hester Francisca, only five. They had two older sisters, Cordelia aged sixteen, and Augusta (Gussie) aged fourteen. All were the children of Andrew and Celia Burn. 'Until 1909 my father had been Rector of Handsworth and then we moved to Halifax,' recounts Francisca. 'We stayed there right through the war until 1920 when he was made Dean of Salisbury. Do you know that when we went to Salisbury it was the first time that I had seen clean flowers in the garden and the only wild flowers I knew were the ones that grew in the Lake District that I had come across on holiday? I had never seen primroses or cowslips. I even thought that swans were grey!

'I don't remember much about that visit to Sawrey. We all knew the books and we knew who we were going to see, and I have always understood that we went for tea. One thing I do remember clearly is standing beside the dresser and thinking, "That dresser is ours!" It was quite a shock to

*Robert (Robin) and Francisca Burn in about 1909*

find that there were two the same. I saw it again, of course, in *The Roly-Poly Pudding* [now *Samuel Whiskers*] in the picture of Anna Maria stealing the dough.

'Miss Potter addressed me as "Double Dutch" in her letter (see page 157) because she could not remember my full name, Hester Francisca. It was also probably because I wore a blue-and-white check dress and had two very small pigtails.'

When she grew up, Francisca, as the youngest daughter, was expected to stay at home to look after her grandmother who lived with the family. Her two older sisters had gone to India, Cordelia as a nurse and a missionary and then as the wife of the Bishop of Madras, Augusta as a mathematics teacher and headmistress of the Anglo-Indian school at Deolali before her marriage to the Archdeacon of Bombay.

*Augusta Burn in her Downe House School uniform*

'Augusta was one of the first two pupils at Downe House School in Darwin's old house, from which the school took its name, and I followed her there soon afterwards. She then went up to Cambridge, to Newnham, in the days before women were allowed degrees. I had to look after my grandmother until she died. I have a wonderful knowledge of the psalms as a result, as she had to have them all read to her every day. My grandmother and father died in the same year, when I was twenty-one, and my mother and I went to India for a year to see my sisters.' On her return Francisca trained as a Froebel teacher and taught for only a short time before she married William Fellowes, whose work for an oil company took them to Mexico for six years.

Robert (Robin) Burn was the scholar of the family, a classicist. He, too, became a teacher, briefly at Berkhamsted and then at his old school, Uppingham, 'where I was so pleased at being taken back as a member of staff'. He was Senior Classical Master there from 1927 until the war. From 1940–41 he was British Council Representative in Greece and then he served in the Intelligence Corps, Middle East, until 1944. Following two years as Second Secretary at the British Embassy in Athens, he became a Senior Lecturer in Ancient History at the University of Glasgow. Together

*Beatrix took Barbara Ruxton's advice in correcting this picture for* The Tale of Pigling Bland *(1913)*

*Opposite: A rare self-portrait of Beatrix in the same book*

with his wife, Mary, Robert has spent a lifetime steeped in Greek history, about which he has written over a dozen books.

Barbara Ruxton was the daughter of Celia Burn's younger sister, Norah Richardson, and her father was a doctor in Newcastle. Although she was a year or two younger than her cousin, Augusta, the two girls were close friends and in the summer of 1913 they stayed with Beatrix Potter at Castle Cottage, the second farm in Sawrey, that Beatrix had bought four years before. Beatrix was working against time to finish the drawings for *Pigling Bland* before her wedding to William Heelis in October, and Barbara reported to the family that she had been able to help in this. Beatrix showed her the drawing of Alexander bidding farewell to the farmyard cockerel and regretted that she would have to do it all over again as she had drawn the bird too high on the page. 'Why don't you put him standing on a plant saucer?' proposed Barbara – a suggestion that Beatrix at once accepted.

Barbara Ruxton's older brother, Billie, was killed in the First World War and when his captain, Ralph Johnson, went to break the sad news to his family, he met and fell in love with Barbara, Billie's very much younger sister. Ralph and Barbara were married and they christened their son Brook, after 'Raja Brooke', the raja of Sarawak, to whom Ralph was distantly related.

Beatrix's letters to Barbara are among the few that survive from the months immediately following her marriage to William Heelis in October 1913. The London address on the letter of 6 November 1913 is explained by a note written to a Mrs Martin only a few days earlier: 'My mother is changing servants. It is rather too soon to have to leave the disconsolate Wm. People are sure to say we have quarrelled!' After their marriage the Heelises decided to live in Castle Cottage rather than in the much smaller Hill Top, but alterations were being made and Castle Cottage would not be ready for them for some months. Writing to her publisher at the end of February 1914 Beatrix told him, 'I have inhabited 3 houses since marriage.'

Dec.13.11

Hill Top Farm
Sawrey
Ambleside

My dear Robert,

Thank you for your letter, which I have been a great while in answering. I had a heap of letters about that time – one of them was a request to make a story about a pet crocodile named Amelia!

That letter is still unanswered, and I am afraid 'Amelia's' story will not get written.

I draw the line at snakes, crocodiles, and monkeys.

I am going to send this letter to Augusta, because you may be away at school – and I think I remember writing your name in a book, so I shall write Augusta's name in T. Tiptoes.

It is wild weather here, such a wind tonight, and the chimney smokes. I came from London yesterday, and I am glad it *was* yesterday, and very smooth & fine. I do not think I could have got across the Ferry tonight; and I could not have come by steamer, because the Lake is too high. They cannot let down the gangway on to the Ferry pier when the steamer is high up on high water. So you see this is a very difficult place in winter times. But I like it in winter better than in summer, provided I am not travelling.

I deeply regret to inform you that there is a beastly fly-swimming-machine [flying boat] on Windermere. There have been two being built; but the other gentleman continually *falls in*. But Mr Wakefield's machine splutters along the water, & then soars at 50 miles an hour. I daresay it is

amusing; I have not seen it yet; they say it makes a fearful buzz *this far off*, nearly 2 miles. It has already caused an accident, frightening a horse. I think motors & motor boats are bad enough.

I have not seen the Mason's [sic] yet, I must call them to ask about a cock.

Now that is all the news!

yrs sincerely
Beatrix Potter

I am afraid others will be built; seriously, I think it is a misfortune.

155

Dec 13th 11             Hill Top Farm
                                    Sawrey
                                    Ambleside

My dear Barbara,

I did not intend to have waited so long before sending you the new book [*Timmy Tiptoes*], I wonder whether you have got it already.

I wrote your address on an envelope that I was collecting flower seeds in – then I put it away with the other seed packets here – and I could not remember, when I was in London.

I came here yesterday for a week, to look after things, and perhaps get a little sketching done – but it is cold for ones fingers at this time of year. I am glad I had a fine day to travel from London yesterday. It is fearfully rough this evening.

I have been writing to Robert and telling him about the flying machine; I may as well tell you, for it is the chief news in Windermere. It has been being built in a large shed half way down towards the lower end of the Lake. Another was built sometime ago at one of the boat builders yards in Bowness. The Bowness gentleman falls in every time he tries, it must be awfully cold in this weather! He fell in between Bowness Bay & the Ferry last Saturday week.

But Mr Wakefield's machine flies successfully. You may be surprised to hear me say – I am *very sorry*! I daresay it is amusing to see it at first; but I am afraid others will be built, and I think they will spoil the lake. This machine makes such a noise, it can be heard *loud* at Sawrey nearly 2 miles distant. It splutters along the top of the water like a motor boat & then jumps into the air, at 50 miles an hour. I think it ought to go on the sea where there is plenty of room, & not so many row-boats.

I wish you a very merry Christmas, and I hope you will like T. Tiptoes.

                      I remain yrs aff
                      Beatrix Potter.

*Above and below: From* The Tale of Timmy Tiptoes *(1911)*

My dear "Double Dutch",
This is a letter from
Tom Kitten. I am a bad
cat; has your dolly told
you, what I did when you
were upstairs in Miss Potter's
room?
I shook hands with Dolly
thing lying in the
mi...
the
nearly grown up now. The
big cat Fluffy is teaching
me to catch mice.
Tibby our old cat has caught
some rats in the barn. They
are stealing the corn, and
nibbling the potatoes.
Now good bye from
Tom Kitten
x x x x x x x

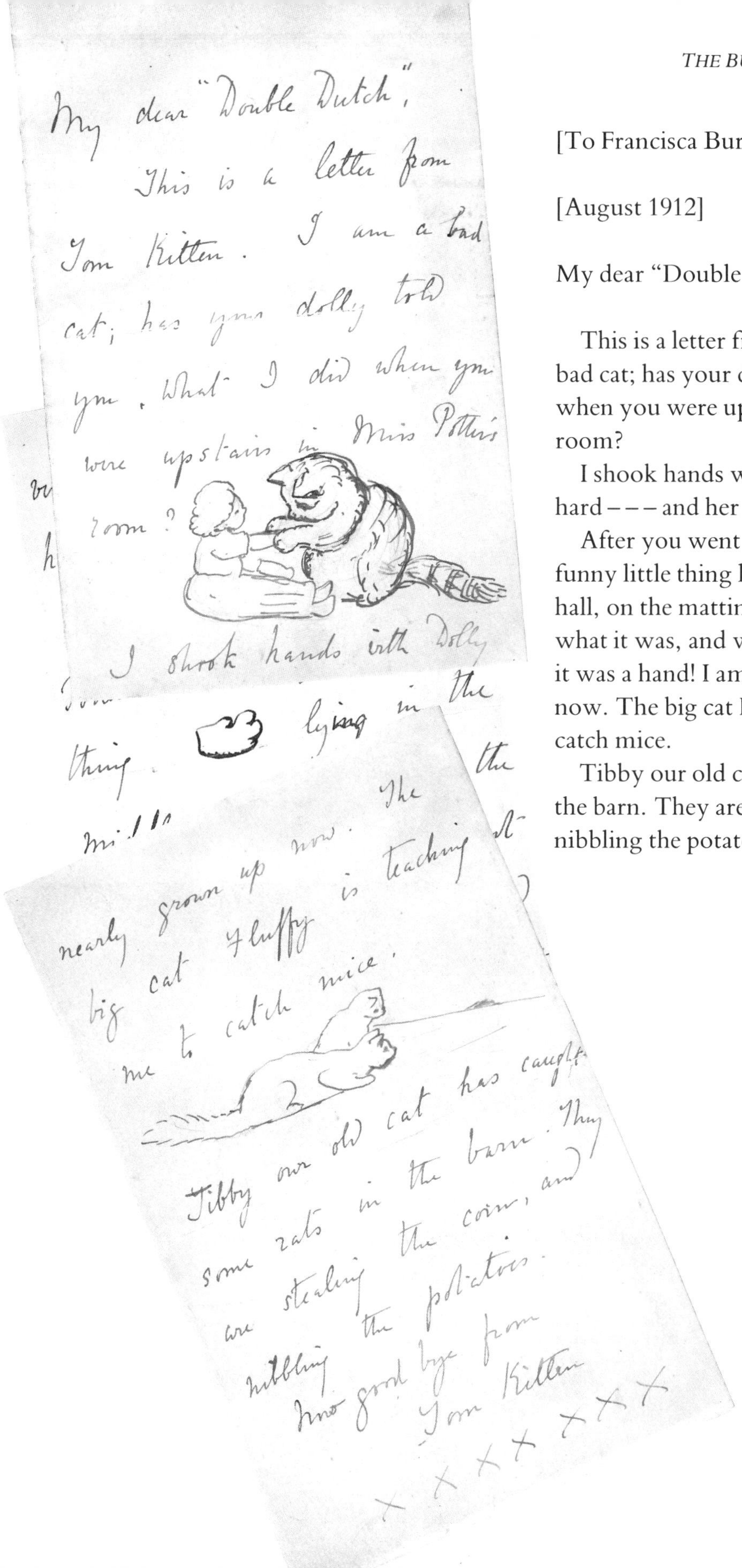

[To Francisca Burn]

[August 1912]

My dear "Double Dutch",

This is a letter from Tom Kitten. I am a bad cat; has your dolly told you what I did when you were upstairs in Miss Potter's room?

I shook hands with Dolly very – very – hard – – – and her hand comed off!

After you went away Miss Potter saw a funny little thing lying in the middle of the hall, on the matting. She could not think what it was, and when she picked it up, it was a hand! I am nearly grown up now. The big cat Fluffy is teaching me to catch mice.

Tibby our old cat has caught some rats in the barn. They are stealing the corn, and nibbling the potatoes.

Now good bye from
Tom Kitten

Aug 25.12                    Broad Leys
                             Windermere

My dear Augusta,

My letter did go on a journey! Mrs Mason had no idea where you were, so she sent it to Halifax, which I might have done myself. Victoria went away a week ago today, it was Saturday 17th I meant – but it was one of the worst of our many wet days, you could never have come. I was much pleased to see Vic so big and strong looking, I had never happened to meet her since they were at Sawrey two years ago, she has grown very much. They only stopped 4 days at the Ferry, which I regretted, as I should have liked to see more of her, she is a dear.

I am afraid I shall *not* be able to see you at all! I generally sleep at this side of the Lake, my parents have had this place for the summer, but it is such hard work toiling backwards and forwards to Sawrey, especially in this terrible weather – that I seem to have little time or energy to go anywhere else. I have been once to Keswick to see a friend who is ill.

I don't remember which is Deepdale Hall, but I do remember how lovely it is at Patterdale, and very peaceful compared to Bowness which is too much a town for my taste. We are 2½ miles south of Bowness near Storrs pier, not bad to get at for you, but I am so constantly out and our time now is so short I am afraid I can't spare to fix a day to ask you over, also for all of us it is dismal weather. We must hope to meet again another summer.

Tell Hester [Francisca] I was looking for some chicken rings and I found her doll's hand put away amongst them in the cupboard. These pictures belong to the next book – "the Tale of Mr Tod"; the fox tying a rope to the tree was crowded out for want of space. I hope he will do for your album.

With love to you & Robert & Hester

yrs aff
Beatrix Potter

Had poor Barbara come all the way from Patterdale when she missed me?

*The unpublished picture for* The Tale of Mr. Tod *(1912),*
*'crowded out for want of space'*

*Above: The cover illustration for* The Tale of Mr. Tod *(1912)*

*Below: The poultry at Hill Top Farm in* The Tale of Jemima Puddle-Duck *(1908)*

Dec 31.12                    2 Bolton Gardens
                             South Kensington
                             SW

My dear Augusta,

Thank you for your card, it is very nicely done, very pretty. I am pleased to send you 'Mr Tod'. I really intended to send him *before* Christmas but I went to Sawrey for 8 days and when I got back to London – all my letters and shopping were in confusion.

I cannot say that I have had a very Merry Christmas! My father has had a bad cold, and when old people are ill they do grumble, even more than necessary.

I am busy already with the chickens. I have 6 nice lively little things here, they are little balls of fluff still, but they are scratching away in the most old fashioned manner in a box with a tray of sand at the bottom – and I have some more eggs in the incubator. It is easier to manage in London, because I have it over a gas jet, & no trouble with an oil lamp. I find chickens are very good travellers – only I sometimes have rows with the LNWR [London North Western Railway]! I generally manage to smuggle them through, but if they are noticed at Euston I have to take a ticket for them. I told the ticket clerk they were infants under age but he said they were "live stock" directly they were hatched – one shilling please!

I hope you will let me know if you come to the Lakes next summer.

I remain with good wishes for the New Year to you & Robert & Hester [Francisca],

yrs aff
Beatrix Potter

Nov 6. 13                    2 Bolton Gardens
                             S.W.
My dear Barbara

I am sending you the new book [*Pigling
Bland*] *now*, instead of writing at Christmas,
because I happen to be in London, & I am
posting my books off instead of carting
them up to Sawrey. I *shall* be glad to get
back on Monday; I had to come up to see
my parents who are very old – so I only had
a fortnight's honeymoon.

It was delightful at the farm, the autumn
colours are lovely.

I haven't got one to spare for Gussie
[Augusta] – hope she won't be jealous! You
must promise to come & see me again some
day – there will be spare bedrooms at one
house or the other.

                             yrs aff
                             "Peter Rabbit"
Nobody remembers to call me Mrs Heelis

Dec 31.13                    Hill Top Farm
                             Sawrey
                             Ambleside
My dear Barbara,

I was delighted with your nice little
basket, it will certainly be useful – and
constantly used. It will just do for holding
card of darning worsted of various colours.
Mr Heelis walks through the toes of his
stockings so it is lucky I like darning!

It is surprising you could do the basket

work so firmly – very creditable altogether.

I have never had time to write, as I went
away to Appleby, to my new relations, for
Christmas, now I am very busy writing
letters & trying to tidy things up before
going back to London to see my parents. I
hope it will be fine tomorrow for the
journey, the roads are very slippy but not
much snow, & bright sun. Taps & pumps
frozen this morning, we have got caught
with no sacking on them.

I am hoping to get settled in the Castle
Cottage soon – it has been in such an *awful
mess*. The new rooms are nothing like built
yet, & the old part has been all upset with
breaking doors in the wall & taking out
partitions.

Those front rooms, where you &
Augusta slept are one long room now & the
staircase is altered, & we are going to have a
bathroom – in the course of time – I think
workmen are very slow.

With love & wishing you a very happy
New Year

                             I remain yrs aff.
                             Beatrix Heelis
Be sure to come & call when you are in the
neighbourhood again, any time of day,
perhaps I am oftenest to be found in the
mornings.

*Cottontail in* The Tale of Mr. Tod *(1912), included because Marjorie Moller 'asked after her'*

## *MARJORIE MOLLER*

Very little is known about Marjorie Moller but Beatrix's letters to her read as though they are answers to an appreciative fan letter. Sold at auction in 1959, Marjorie's letters are now in The Free Library of Philadelphia and with them is an envelope, postmarked 12 March 1912, addressed to Marjorie at 'Caldecote Grange, Biggleswade, Beds'. On the 1901 Ordnance Survey map the house is shown as The Grange, Lower Caldecote, standing next to a public house, The King's Head, just off the main road from Biggleswade going north. Across the road is Manor Farm, bordering the River Ivel with its warning note 'liable to floods', and only a short distance further east, following the line of the road and the river, the Great Northern Railway cuts through the countryside. Caldecote Grange was demolished in the late 1980s, after a life as a transport café with the colourful names of 'OK Café' and 'Tower Café'. The King's Head remains, operating as a free house and, in a tenuous link with the past, the small housing estate built on the site of the big house is called The Grange.

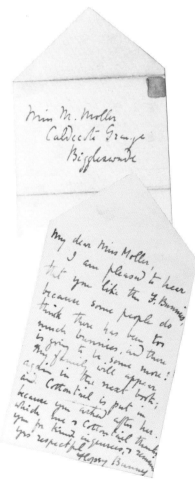

Miss M. Moller
Caldecote Grange
Biggleswade

My dear Miss Moller,
  I am pleased to hear that you like the F. Bunnies, because some people do think there has been too much bunnies, and there is going to be some more! My family will appear again in the next book [*The Tale of Mr. Tod*]; and Cottontail is put in because you asked after her which me & Cottontail thanks you for kind inquiries, & remain

  yrs respectful
  Flopsy Bunny

Miss M. Moller
Caldecote Grange
Biggleswade

Dear Madam

My wife Mrs Flopsy Bunny has replied to your inquiries, because Miss Potter will attend to nothing but hatching spring chickens; there is another hatch chipping this evening. And she is supposed to be doing a Book, about us and the Fox; but she does not get on; neither has she answered all her Xmas letters yet.

yrs
B. Bunny

Miss M. Moller
Caldecote Grange
Biggleswade

Dear Miss Marjorie,

I hope you will like the next book there will be lots of rabbits! but poor Mopsy's story is too melancholy to write, she was killed by a weasel, & buried in the little moss grave under the wall. But there are plenty of rabbits still.

yrs aff.
Squirrel Nutkin

Miss Marjorie
Big –
Beds

Dear Miss Marjorie

I hope this finds you well. I do not like cats.

yrs aff.
Hunca Munca

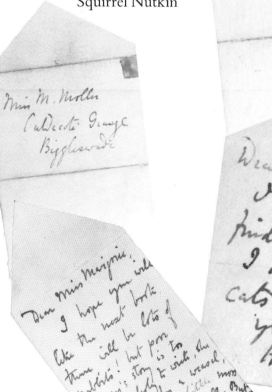

*Above: The 'terrific battle' between Mr Tod and Tommy Brock in* The Tale of Mr. Tod *(1912)*

*Below: Mr Tod discovers 'a deep slow regular snoring grunting noise, coming from his own bed'*

## HAROLD BOTCHERBY

Peter Rabbit and Benjamin Bunny did not wait to hear the outcome of 'the terrific battle' between Mr Tod and Tommy Brock at the end of *The Tale of Mr. Tod*, but six-year-old Harold Botcherby badly wanted to know and he wrote to Beatrix Potter to find out. Born in 1907 at Cookham Dean in Buckinghamshire, Harold and his sister, Sallie, were living in Golders Green in north London when he made his enquiry.

From an early age Harold showed talent as a painter and he studied art at Heatherley's and at the Royal Academy Schools. In 1930 he won the John Crompton Scholarship and two years later was elected to the Royal Society of British Artists. Harold's portraits and still life paintings were exhibited at the Royal Academy, the Royal Society of British Artists, the London Group and at the Brook Street Gallery in London. When he married in 1934 Harold went to live in Danbury in Essex and he had four children, three boys and a girl.

During the Second World War Harold joined the National Fire Service and was tragically killed, when only thirty-six, in an accident during the black-out in October 1943.

Feb.17.13      c/o Messrs F Warne & Co
15 Bedford St Strand

My dear Harold,

I have inquired about Mr Tod & Tommy Brock, & I am sorry to tell you they are still quarrelling. Mr Tod has been living in the willow till he was flooded out; at present he is in the stick house with a bad cold in his head. As for the end of the fight – Mr Tod had nearly half the hair pulled out of his brush ( = tail) and 5 bad bites, especially one ear, which is scrumpled up, (like you sometimes see nasty old Tom Cat's ears) – The only misfortune to Tommy Brock – he had his jacket torn & lost one of his boots. So for a long time he went about with one of his feet bundled up in dirty rags, like an old beggar man. Then he found the boot in the quarry. There was a beetle in the boot and several slugs.

Tommy Brock ate them. He is a nasty person. He will go on living in Mr Tod's comfortable house till spring time – then he will move off into the woods & live out of doors – and Mr Tod will come back very cautiously – & there will need to be a big spring cleaning!

    Love to you & little Sally [sic] & the
Flopsy Bunnies from
yr aff friend Beatrix Potter

*Setting the trap for Tommy Brock
in* The Tale of Mr. Tod *(1912)*

*The Christmas card Beatrix sent to Margaret Hough in 1927*

## MARGARET AND JOHN HOUGH

Efforts to trace Margaret Hough and her brother, John, have ended in repeated disappointment, but from Beatrix's letters to them and from the envelopes that accompany the letters, certain clues emerge.

That Margaret Hough made contact with Beatrix Potter as a fan of the little books there is no doubt, and the first miniature letter refers to her 'nice letter, such *neat* writing'. The letters to both Margaret and John are addressed to a house in Darenth Road, which is in Stamford Hill in north London. The reference in the first two miniature letters to Beatrix's drawings of pigs suggests that they were written between 1910 and 1913 when she was working on *Pigling Bland*, and the letter to Margaret of 4 November 1913 accompanied a copy of that book which had been published the month before. It is apparent from this same letter that Margaret was a regular correspondent and one of the favoured fans to be sent a piece of Beatrix and Willie Heelis's wedding cake. Margaret later recorded in a letter that she was eleven when she wrote to congratulate Beatrix on her marriage.

Beatrix was still in touch with Margaret in 1927, for there is a Christmas card inscribed to her in the museum collection. The card was one in a series which Beatrix designed for the Invalid Children's Aid Association between 1925 and 1941 (see page 206), and that year it featured a version of the *Peter Rabbit* frontispiece picture of Peter being dosed by his mother.

The last clue to Margaret Hough is a letter from her to a Miss Pye concerning an offer from Leslie Linder, the Potter collector and specialist, to buy her miniature letters. Her letter is dated with only the day and month but it was probably written in the 1960s when Leslie Linder was researching for his mammoth study, *The History of the Writings of Beatrix Potter* (Warne, 1971), where John Hough's miniature letters were first published. Linder was continually adding to his Potter collection, which he had resolved to bequeath to a national institution where it would be available for exhibition and research. Margaret Hough accepted Leslie Linder's offer, saying, 'I feel the letters should have a place in a permanent collection, instead of being shut away in the drawer of a private individual.' In 1973 Margaret and John Hough's letters were part of The Leslie Linder Bequest to the Victoria and Albert Museum.

Margaret Hough's acceptance letter was sent from a bungalow called 'Hollyhocks' in Langton Matravers near Swanage in Dorset. A recent occupier of the house reported, 'Miss Hough moved away from Hollyhocks (which incidentally she named) but where to no one can recall. However, it is believed that she has subsequently died.'

Miss M. Hough
88 Darenth Rd
N.W.

Dear Miss Margaret,
    I am writing to tell you that Miss Potter is *pleased* to have that nice photograph of you & John; and what a nice letter, such *neat* writing. She has got your picture with a bag in your hands when you were a very little girl. Miss Potter is drawing Pigs
                    Peter Rabbit

Miss M. Hough
88 Darenth Rd
NW

Dear Miss Hough,
    Miss Potter has been drawing a pigs head on a plate. It had a sweet smile, but it has had to be cooked today because of the weather. She has got real live pigs; but they don't live in London so she had one by post.
                    Benjamin Bunny.

Miss M. Hough
88 Darenth Rd
N.W.

Dear Miss Hough
  If you please 'm a very
Merry Christmas
   These are crackers!
      With love I remain
     Mrs Tiggy winkle

Mrs Tabitha Twitchit
wishes Margaret Hough a
Merry Christmas

Miss Hough
88 Darenth Rd
N.W.

All the little animals and
birds send lots of kisses to
Margaret

Master John Hough,
88 Darenth Road,
N.W.

Dear Master John Hough,
I and my Family (6) are writing to you because Miss Potter has got no stamps left and she has got a cold, we think Miss Potter is lazy. I think you are a *fine big* boy; my children are *small* rabbits at present.

Yrs. respectfully,
Mrs. Flopsy Bunny.

Master John Hough
88 Darenth Rd
N.W.

Dear Master John Hough,
I and my Family
[6] are writing to you
because Miss Potter has
got no stamps left and
she has got a cold, we
think Miss Potter is
lazy. I think you are
a fine big boy; my
children are small rabbits
at present
yrs. respectfully
Mrs Flopsy Bunny.

Master John Hough
88 Darenth Rd
Stamford Hill
N W

Dear Master John Hough
I wish you a Merry
Christmas! I am going
to have an apple for
my Christmas dinner
& some celery tops. The
cabbages are all frosted
but there is lots of hay.
yrs aff
First Flopsy Bunny.
x x x x x x x

Master John Hough
88 Darenth Rd
Stamford Hill
NW

Dear Master John Hough
I wish you a Merry Christmas! I am going to have an apple for my Christmas dinner & some celery tops. The cabbages are all frosted, but there is lots of hay.

yrs aff
First Flopsy Bunny.

Master John Hough
88 Darenth Rd
N.W.

Dear Master John,
I wish you the same as my oldest brother, and I am going to have the same dinner.

yrs aff
2nd Flopsy Bunny

Master John Hough
88 Darenth Rd
N.W.

Dear Master John,
I wish you the
same as my oldest
brother, and I am
going to have the
same dinner.
yrs aff
2nd Flopsy Bunny
x x x x x x x

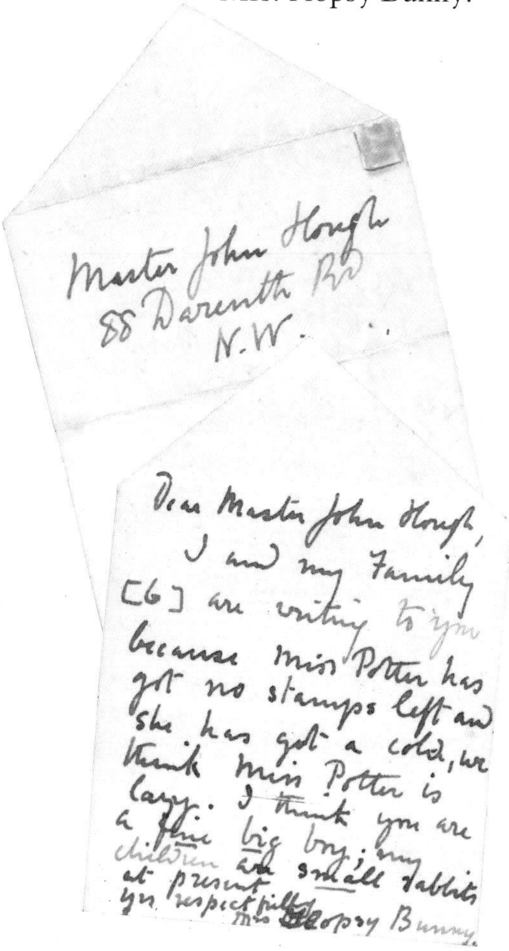

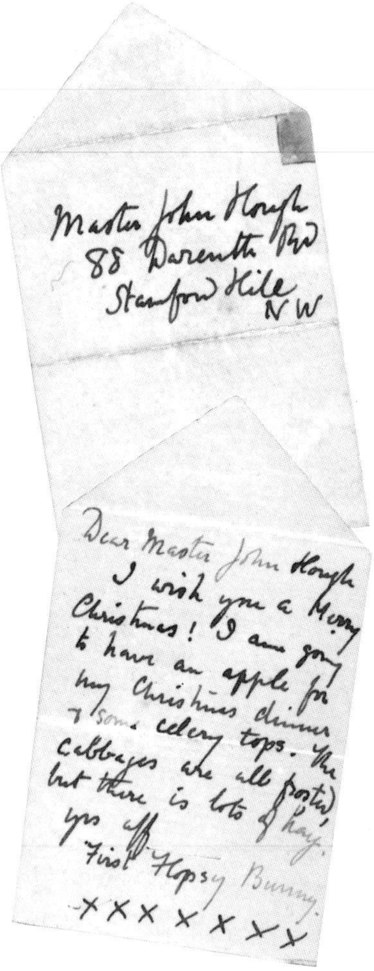

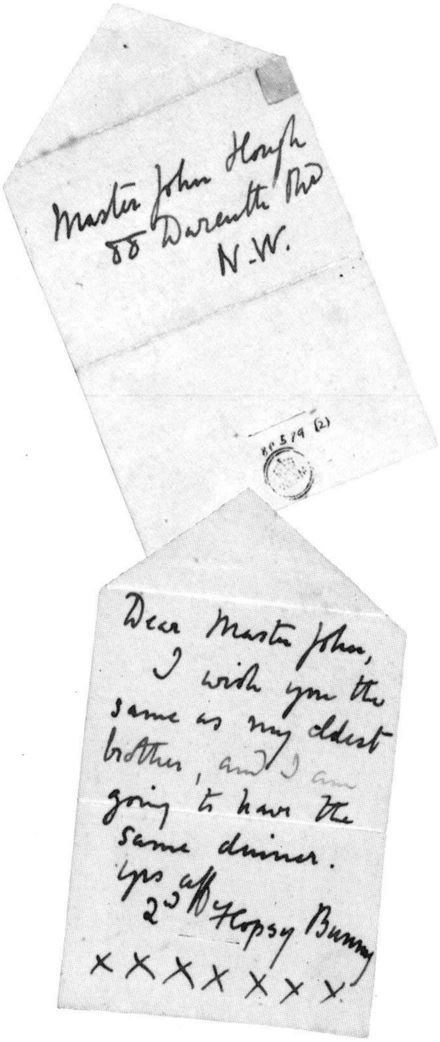

Master J. Hough
88 Darenth Rd
NW

Dear Master Hough,
  I wish you the
compliments of the season.
We have got new fur tippets
for Christmas.

                    yrs aff
        3rd (Miss) F. Bunny

Master J. Hough
88 Darenth Rd
N.W.

Dear Master John
  I have not learned to rite
prop perly.

              Love from
        4th (Miss) F Bunny

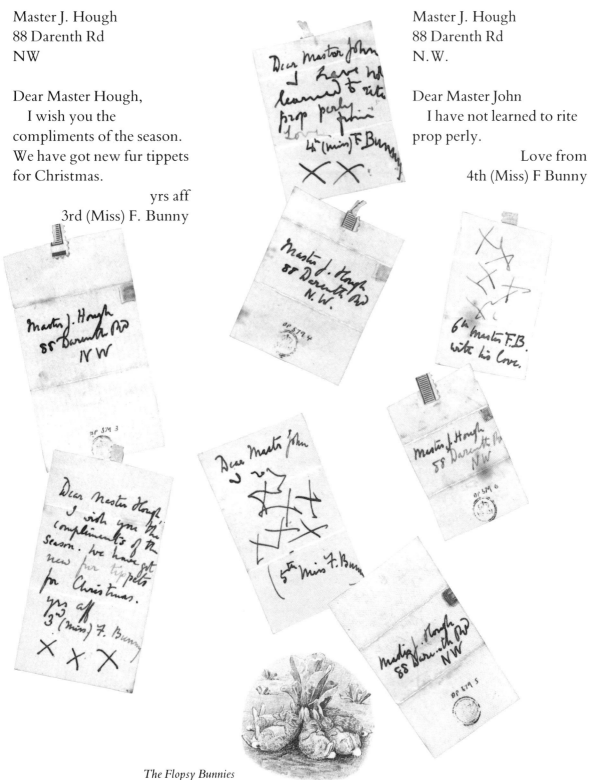

*The Flopsy Bunnies*

*'Not a portrait of me & Mr Heelis . . .'*
*from* The Tale of Pigling Bland
*(1913)*

Nov. 4. 13                    Hill Top Farm
                             Sawrey
                             Ambleside

My dear Margaret,

As I am in London now for a few days, and not likely to be in London at Christmas – I am taking the opportunity of posting off some copies of the new book [*Pigling Bland*] which has just come out. I hope you will like it, I'm afraid it was done in an awful hurry and scramble.

The portrait of two pigs arm in arm – looking at the sun-rise – is *not* a portrait of me & Mr Heelis, though it is a view of where we used to walk on Sunday afternoons! When I want to put William in a book – it will have to be as some very tall thin animal.

Thank you very much for your nice letter of congratulation, I think it was a good idea to send cake to several girls who have written to me – and you have done it regularly. If you ever come up to the Lakes – be sure & let me know, as I should be delighted to see you – I can't do much entertaining at the farm, with farm servants, but we can stand a good farmhouse tea – and I have often packed in little girls for a night or two if their relations were staying in the neighbourhood. I had two [Barbara Ruxton and Augusta Burn, see page 154] for a very jolly picnic last August – so remember the address if you are ever within reach.

With best wishes for the coming Christmas to you & John, believe me,

yrs aff.
Beatrix Heelis

## ESTHER AND NANCY NICHOLSON

When Beatrix married William Heelis in 1913 she became a member of a large new family, for Willie was the youngest of eleven children. Esther and Nancy Nicholson were two of the five children of Willie's youngest sister, Grace, and of her barrister husband, James Nicholson. The family lived in Kirkby Thore in Westmorland.

After a few years Beatrix took on the financial responsibility for Esther's education, and from St Catherine's School in Wantage, Esther went to Somerville College in Oxford. She then became a teacher and in the 1920s she went to New Zealand where she taught English at Amberley House in Christchurch. One of her pupils still remembers her as 'a most excellent teacher'. Esther did not marry and remained in New Zealand, teaching for many years at St John's Girls' School in Invercargill. When she retired she bought half a section of land in Te Anau in the beautiful lake country of Southland. On part of it she built a house and then she gave the rest of the land for the building of a little Anglican church, St Michael's and All Angels. Esther died in the 1980s, leaving her house to the church, of which it is said she was 'the practical founder'.

Nancy was the youngest child of the Nicholson family, seven years younger than her next brother, Christopher, and ten years younger than Esther. She was not only Willie Heelis's niece but she was also his god-daughter. Nancy's first encounter with her new Aunt Beatrix was in 1916 when she was seven and she went with her mother to stay for a night at Castle Cottage. It was a meeting that did not have an auspicious beginning. At Windermere station the Nicholsons were somewhat surprised that there was no one to meet them, but undaunted they set out to make their own way, crossing the lake by the ferry and walking the remaining mile and a half to Near Sawrey. At Castle Cottage they were taken aback to discover that one of Willie's sisters-in-law and her family were already staying in the house and there was certainly no room for two more people. They had come on the wrong day.

*Nancy Nicholson as a young woman*

However, Nancy and her mother were soon found accommodation at the Post Office nearby and after tea the whole party went together up Stoney Lane to Beatrix and Willie's beloved Moss Eccles Tarn. There they planted one red and one white water-lily. Beatrix walked back to the village with Nancy and the two of them formed a bond of friendship that was to last for Beatrix's lifetime. They discovered their mutual love of fairy tales, the small girl confiding in her aunt her particular fascination for imaginary people called Oakmen who lived in trees. Beatrix gave Nancy a baby rabbit and a kitten to take home with her, and in a letter to her mother later in the year commented, 'She is a most amusing little person'.

At Christmas that year the entire Heelis clan gathered for a party at the family home, Battlebarrow House in Appleby, and Beatrix gave Nancy a story she had written about her tree people. It was called *The Oakmen* and featured gnomes with pointed red hats who, when their tree homes were felled by wood cutters, were driven to live in holes in 'a nice dry humpy hillock in the bog overlooking the tarn'. The story was written out in a loose-leaf book and beside the text on each of the six pages there was a watercolour sketch. The following year Beatrix tried to get *The Oakmen* into print, even commissioning another artist, Ernest A. Aris, to do the final colour illustrations as her 'eyes were failing and my hands getting stiff'. But the project came to nothing when it was discovered that perhaps Nancy might have first heard of her tree people from another book and that would have presented copyright risks for Beatrix.

On Nancy's next visit to Castle Cottage she was by herself. She was an active and adventurous child and remembers being cautioned by Beatrix on the danger of running through the heather on the fells without watching out for adders. She was also rebuked for not behaving properly towards Beatrix's housekeeper, Mrs Rogerson. But Nancy loved her aunt and they kept constantly in touch.

When she left school Nancy went to Edinburgh to take a

*Opposite: One of Beatrix's pencil sketches for* The Oakmen *with her instructions for the redrawing in colour by another artist*

*Below: Castle Cottage photographed by Rupert Potter in July 1912 before it was enlarged for Beatrix and Willie*

short domestic science course. Near the college was a
kindergarten nursery and the children there so captivated
her that she went on to train as a Norland nurse, working
very happily for a number of years with various families. In
1956 Nancy married Hugh Hudson who was a farmer in
her home village of Kirkby Thore. He had moved there in
the 1920s from the village of Mardale, which was flooded
when Haweswater became a reservoir for Manchester.

Of the many letters that Beatrix wrote to Nancy over
nearly thirty years only the undated extract from one of
them is available for inclusion here. Beatrix had hoped at
one time to see some of them in print, for in 1924 she wrote
to Fruing Warne: 'I should have liked to have made a book
of some of my "letters to Nancy", they were more fairy
tales; and I see the little men peeping round the mossy
stumps & stones when ever I go up to the wood – but I
cannot draw them.'

Sept. 13. 17                                    Sawrey
                                                Ambleside

My dear Esther,

I was much interested to hear particulars of your exam. You have indeed done well, and I think you will go on well. Don't spoil your eyes or health with too much reading – but you look pretty healthy. We felt quite lost with no visitors – unnecessary porridge bowls & tea cups persevered for several days.

I have bought a cow to distract my thoughts. It kicks most frightfully; your uncle devotes part of his leisure to watching the struggles, at a discreet distance. I don't know when the girls will be able to milk it. We had quite a good day in the corn yesterday – now it is wetter than ever. I can't think what will come of it – bread tickits [sic] I should fear.

I found a bib of Nancy's, so I shall direct this letter to her; and I am not sure whether you are still at home or gone back to school – the time slips away so fast; we seem to have had no summer.

"Dolly" [Beatrix's pony] is right side up, and very lively, so I hope the fall was an accident which won't be repeated for a bit, there will be scarcely any mark. Miss "Becky" wrote the other day with 2 'p s' outside the envelope, the first to the effect that she was offering a reward for a gun metal watch – the second to the effect that she had found it on the place. She said she wished *she* had a niece – poor Miss Becky!

Come again some day – wet or dry.

With love to your Mother & all of you from Uncle Willie & me.

> your aff aunt
> Beatrix Heelis

April 2. 18                                    Sawrey,
                                               Ambleside

My dear Esther,

It is pleasant to have made you happy! I have on several occasions through a sense of duty helped several uninteresting persons; now at last I look forward to the pleasure of pleasing myself as well as you. I hope some day *you* may have equal gratification in starting Nancy. Thank your Father for his kind letter too; and so the subject is happily settled & done with – no there is one thing more – if you get plucked over the Greek . . .??? I wash my hands of you!!

We have arrived quickly after a very cold drive in the rain from Windermere, we were here by 12. The cow has not calved yet, all the rabbits young & old are alive; poultry ditto – but I rather suspect a turkey is laying in the garden, which is a nuisance. Your Uncle Willie has gone to Hd. [Hawkshead] after lunch, very sleepy. I wonder if he will ever remember to call on the butcher & try for some meat! We have brought back 4 trout & there are plenty of eggs so we shall not starve before Saturday. Now I must go to the farm & decide who is to do without butter – Bother that cow!

> I remain with love yr aff
> Aunt Beatrix

July 16.18                    Sawrey,
                              Ambleside

My dear Esther,

What a catastrophe! But I was joking when I said I would wash my hands of you, if you failed again. You should certainly have another try – or two – as Miss Penrose encourages it. But do not try with insufficient preparation, as I cannot think that repeated rebuffs are very good for you. You do not strike me as one of those insufferable young persons who require sitting upon. If you fail again you may lose confidence.

I know so little about exams I felt afraid of meddling at all last Easter; but I am rather surprised now to hear that you tried to prepare yourself for Greek *in such a short time*, without help. I asked your Uncle Willie what you would be likely to do, & he said perhaps "someone at the Grammar school may coach her" – or "perhaps Lelis will do it by post", I thought no more about it. If you had gone to Oxford to be coached there I should have accepted the position placidly as part of your Oxford career; I wish you to have every advantage. Now you say your Uncle Arthur [William Heelis's older brother] offers to coach you. Your Uncle Wm. (who I understand kept a ferret in his desk at school) – your Uncle Wm. says that your Uncle Arthur is competent. And from what I have seen of the Revd gentleman I am quite disposed to believe he is, – apart from the testimonial, but has he time – or (what shall I say to explain what I mean?) has he a separate piece of mind to give up to your Greek, if

he is absorbed with farming? I *know*; because I have a horrible book in hand that should have been done in June [*Johnny Town-Mouse*]; and I have also a large interesting farm, no servant, and an epidemic of measles; some anxiety about my poor old mother, who has had a great shock in losing my brother [Bertram Potter had died suddenly in June]; and now these butter rations. We are churning today, & what with the bother of 5 oz which is no standard weight & the customers all in a muddle about their ration books registered at shops, on accnt of lard etc etc. I shall have to break off this letter & go down to the Food Control at Windermere; we are really under Ulverston, *16* miles off!

We have no hay out just now, so perhaps the measles will recover as soon as the weather. Will you please show this letter to your Uncle, I haven't time to write to him, as I had intended.

I am clear about one thing, it isn't advisable for you to fail again so soon as Oct. either get well up in it then, or wait longer. You are fully young, & it is a great thing to learn to cook!

How in the world have you got a *joint*? Has the Revd been killing a sheep on the sly?

Love to you both, from yr aff Aunt
Beatrix Heelis

*Opposite: Beatrix was working on the pictures for* The Tale of Johnny Town-Mouse *(1918) during April and May of this year*

[?1918]

My dear Nancy,

I am very sleepy. I have been cross cutting firewood from a large broken oaktree with Ethel Green A little robin has been watching us all day, hopping on the logs. He was so tame he nearly touched us – He had very bright little beady eyes, and a very red cap – no, not a cap, a red waistcoat. I did not feel quite sure whether he was a real robin, till he found a worm in some rotten bark . . . I do not feel quite sure. He kept flying round behind the tree, to speak to some one, & coming back. He came back dozens of times and I had nothing for him – except a bit of apple. He went home before we did on accnt of chilblains on his toes. I believe he lives with the Oakmen. At all events he had supper with them. He sat on a chair with his feet in hot water and ate pickled caterpillars out of a pie dish!

[unsigned]

*This illustration of the robin with Peter Rabbit's shoe was never used*

## DENYS LOWSON

It is not absolutely certain whether Denys Lowson ever visited Hill Top, but there is no doubt at all that he was often the subject of conversation there between Beatrix Potter and her helper and friend, Louie Choyce ['Choicey']. Miss Choyce first went to Hill Top in 1916, during the First World War, when most of the men from the farms had been called up to fight. Beatrix had complained in a letter to *The Times* that it was difficult to persuade women to take the men's places when munitions factories were offering wages with which farmers could not compete. Louie Choyce was forty years old; she had been Denys Lowson's governess until it was time for him to go to school, and now she answered Beatrix's letter offering her services.

Louie Choyce stayed at Hill Top until the end of the war and over the years she and Beatrix Potter became firm friends. She returned as a summer visitor between the wars whenever her other appointments allowed, and in 1941 she again answered Beatrix's call for help, this time bringing her brother, Tom. For Christmas 1942 Beatrix gave her an illustrated story, *The Chinese Umbrella*, in which she featured (see page 232).

*Denys Lowson aged 9*

Louie Choyce's pupil, Denys Lowson, had been born in 1906, the youngest of three children. He was educated at Winchester and then read History and Law at Christ Church, Oxford. While he was at university Denys was a member of the shooting team and shot for Oxford against Cambridge, Harvard and Yale. He was called to the Bar in 1930. In 1936 he married Patricia, the youngest daughter of Lord Strathcarron. Although Beatrix Potter was invited to the wedding she was unable to go, but one of the Lowsons' wedding presents was a signed set of her little books.

Denys Lowson was a successful financier in the world of unit trusts and in the 1940s he began a long record of service to the City of London, which culminated in his election as Lord Mayor of London for 1950–51, the year of the Festival of Britain. In 1951 he was created a baronet. The Lowsons had three children, a son and two daughters.

*The Hill Top garden and house from*
The Tale of Tom Kitten *(1907).*
*Beatrix often referred to Hill Top as*
*'Tom Kitten's house'*

*The Hill Top landing from* The Tale
of Samuel Whiskers *(1908)*

Oct. 3.16

My dear Denys,

Your letter was a pleasing surprise! I perceive that "Choicey" has taught you to write good round hand; and to be a polite little gentleman, which is still more important! I wonder how many tiresome unknown children have bothered me with birthday books, and letters wanting answers etc and – would you believe it – not more than one in twenty ever writes again to say "thank you".

That awful big beast at the museum is like a bad dream; I once did dream about it; it was coming downstairs on crutches into the big hall of the museum, and I was unable to run away. I am glad there are none of them left alive in the world now. Probably they did last long enough for the earliest men to see, and that was the beginning of the tales about dragons. There was an enormous bird, much bigger than an ostrich which lived in New Zealand until quite recent times. And that odd looking bird called the Dodo really lived till 16??. (Choicey says she taught you dates, I have forgotten mine – except William The Conqueror 1066)

She will have a great deal to tell you about Tom Kittens house, and all our rabbits, and potatoes, & cats, & cows. I think you ought to come and see them some day when she is here again. I have heard so much about you, we would feel quite like old friends to start with.

I remain yours affectionately
Beatrix Heelis

## THOMAS (TOM) HARDING

The envelope that is with Tom Harding's letter in the Free Library of Philadelphia, addressed to 'Master Tom Harding, Histon Manor, Cambridge', has provided a lead to some details of the Harding family but little is known about Tom himself. *The Hardings at Madingley* (Extra Mural Studies Board, Madingley Hall, 1988) has a chapter about his grandfather, Colonel Thomas Walter Harding, by Edmund M. Butler and it tells us that Tom was born in 1906, christened Thomas John, and that he had a sister, Rosamond, who was eight years his senior. Tom was therefore eleven years old when he wrote to Beatrix Potter in 1917.

The Hardings' home, Histon Manor, was a handsome mansion with an extensive garden in the picturesque village of Histon, three miles north-west of Cambridge, a village noted at the time for its large jam factory. Chivers and Sons could produce over a hundred tons of jam a day there from the company's surrounding fruit gardens.

Tom's father, Walter Ambrose Heath Harding, had bought Histon Manor in 1899, bringing his family south from his home county of Yorkshire. Ambrose Harding was a zoologist, a Fellow of the Linnean Society and of the Zoological Society, and he spent much of his time travelling the world engaged in zoological research, returning to Histon to prepare papers for scientific journals. To the children's delight he frequently brought back with him a new addition to his private zoo, which was housed in a brick and thatch snake house in the garden.

Tom's mother, Ethel Adela Hirst, was also from Yorkshire and she was the author of two books, *The Dominant Chord* and *A Daughter of Debate*; his sister, Rosamond, was already on her way to a distinguished career as a music historian. So, about Tom's family it has been possible to discover a certain amount. About Thomas Harding all else that is known is that he died in 1975 at the age of sixty-nine.

*The Puddle-ducks and hens at Hill Top Farm, in* The Tale of Tom Kitten. *Beatrix describes the real Hill Top animals in her letter to Tom Harding overleaf*

Dec 21. 17                    Hill Top Farm
                             Sawrey
                             Ambleside

Dear Tom Harding,

"Better late than never!" You must have thought no answer was ever coming. When I tidied my desk today – or to be exact when I had a long *untidy* search for a letter about sheep – I found yours. I get so many letters from boys and girls all over the world – especially from Australia & N. Zealand – that I put them in a bundle & answer if I can. As it happens *I* am partly indoors with a cold today, so I have a little time for writing.

I have a big farm and a very great deal to do, since the war, for my men left me, and now I have an old shepherd, 2 boys & 2 girls, which requires more looking after. Old "Kep" is dead. I have a black white dog, she is called "Fleet" – and I have a pony called Dolly, such a useful good little thing, my husband saw her in a gypsy cart and bought her for me to go about the farm, & she will carry sacks on her back, & cart turnips in the tub or sticks or anything. Then there are 3 horses, Diamond, Lady & Gipsy and I hope next spring Gipsy will have a nice foal. There are 14 cows, a lot of calves & young cattle, and 80 ewes & 40 young sheep & some pigs & 25 hens & 5 ducks, & there *were* 13 turkeys. But I am thankful to say they are killed except the hens. I do everything for the turkeys myself & I have had so much anxiety about foxes – a great big turkey was killed at the next farm last week, & in August a fox took 9 chickens & their mother hen, just outside the garden, I was vexed. The Drake – Mr Puddleduck is very handsome, he is brown fawn, Jemima & Rebeccah are white, Semolina is a comical little Indian runner. She made a very deep nest under a nut bush & sat on 11 eggs. She came running back to the house twice a day & running back to her nest in such a hurry after being fed, she came quacking into the kitchen if not fed at once. But alas – Semolina never turned her eggs. The bottom eggs were always stony cold, only the top ones hatched. I called the two children Tapioca & Sago. We have eaten Sago. It was rather dreadful & the stuffing disagreed with my conscience, but he & his father had begun to fight. I have lots of rabbits, Belgians – Old Benjamin & Cottontail are pets, but I'm afraid we do have rabbit pies of the young ones. Our cat is "Judy", there have been lots of Tom Kittens. Have you seen my new little book Appley Dapply? I must send you a copy if you have not got it. The pictures were done a long time ago – I have little time for painting now, & I have to wear spectacles.

With love & best wishes for Christmas
              from your affectionate friend
              "Beatrix Potter" (Mrs W Heelis)

## 'DULCIE'

Dulcie is one of the most intriguing of 'Beatrix's children', probably because there is no clue at all to her identity. There is a hint in the letter of 29 July 1924 that she lived in London. She and Beatrix obviously enjoyed exchanging anecdotes about their pets and Beatrix's letters to Dulcie are particularly warm. The collecting card mentioned in the letter of 18 April 1925 was a scheme to raise money for the Invalid Children's Aid Association (see page 206).

*Dulcie sent Beatrix her own version of this picture from* The Tale of Jemima Puddle-Duck *(1908)*

Oct 18. 18                                  Hill Top Farm

My dear Dulcie,

How very nicely you have painted it! I like Mrs Tiggy with the clothes line, and Jemima walking with Mr Tod is lovely! Indeed they are all well done. I have 4 ducks, they are called Jemima & Rebecca, and a funny little brown runner duck is called Semolina. She made a nest, very deep – shape of a flower pot in some rubbish under a nut bush, it was comical to see her come running for breakfast & supper as fast as she could trot, and away back to her nest. But alas! Semolina was as incapable as Jemima; she didn't change her eggs, so the bottom eggs never got warm & only the top eggs hatched. There were two children reared – Tapioca & Sago. We ate Sago as he proved to be a drake; Tapioca is very tame, I can pick her up & stroke her. I have lots of cows & pigs & sheep. It is a job to feed them now, for all the corn is lost & the straw is rotten. Thank you for the nice book.

your aff. friend
"Beatrix Potter"

Nov. 16. 23          Sawrey
                       nr Ambleside

My dear Dulcie,

I was tidying my desk and I found your letter, received as long ago as March, and not answered! It was very naughty of me. I have had so much to do, I have not always answered letters directly they come, and then other letters get put on the top of them and they are forgotten. I did like to hear about "Puff", because I once had a dear white rat called Sammy; and there are not many people who like rats except you and me. Sammy was a dear; but he was a bit of a thief like Puff. I used to find all sorts of things hidden in his box. Once I found a stick of red sealing wax & some matches, just as if he had intended to write a letter to Puff, and seal it carefully. Have you ever given Puff a hard boiled egg? I used to give one to Sammy, as a very great treat when eggs were cheap. I used to give it to him a long way off at the other end of the passage away from his cage and he used to push the egg in front of him rolling it over & over. I think Sammy was rather old when I bought him, he grew very very fat and sleepy, I was sorry when he died. Our cat Tommy has 2 very pretty kittens just now, most of her kittens are black, but these are tabby, very nicely marked. There has been a nest of young owls in our barn this summer, they are very funny when they are waiting for the old owl to bring mice, they sit on a board outside a narrow ventilator high up in the gable; when the old owl comes there is such a scramble & a squaking [sic] then the owlet that has got the mouse turns his back on the other two and spreads his wings & tail like an umbrella to keep his brothers away from the mouse while he gobles [sic] it up. I am so sorry to hear you have not been well again, I hope you are feeling better. Thank you for the pretty card, it is very nicely done.

I hope you & Puff will have a Merry Christmas next month.

From your aff. friend
Beatrix Potter
(Mrs W Heelis)

July 29. 24                    Sawrey
                               Nr Ambleside

My dear Dulcie,

I am going to answer your letter right away. It was naughty of me not to write. I really was sorry about poor dear "Puff". I am afraid white rats don't live long. Now I have got a white guinea pig. I call him 'Tuppenny', he is rather like a rat without a tail, he has the same kind of little pink hands and feet. He is a very talkative friendly person – only he *won't* let me touch him. He is in a small rabbit hutch with wire netting on the bottom and he nibbles the grass off short. Directly he hears my footsteps he begins to twitter like a little bird, but if I try to touch him – he rushes about his box. Perhaps he will get tame in time. I used to know 2 guinea pigs called Titwillow and the Sultan of Zanzibar, they belonged to a friend of mine and we used to pick them up & stroke them. Titwillow was a dear person and drank tea; the Sultan used to bite. I am disappointed with Tuppenny. Still it shows nice feelings to recognize my footstep! He knows who gives him bread & milk.

It is funny that you ask about a painting book! I have just finished a Jemima painting book, it has some of the old pictures in, and some new ones, I have drawn one of my sheep & her lambs in one picture. I really ought to do a sheep book or a guinea pig book, should not I?

I have got a new pair of spectacles, and I can see better again. First we must get in the hay & corn, it is such a horrid wet summer up here, all the time you had hot weather in London, we were in the mist, it comes from

'I have just finished a Jemima painting book.' It was published in 1925

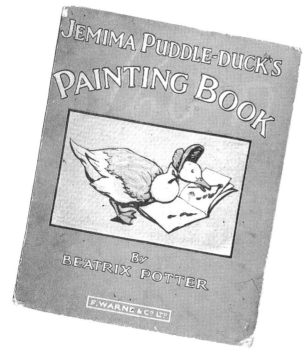

183

the mountains & the sea. Yes I have lots of flowers, I am very fond of my garden, it is a regular old fashioned farm garden, with a box hedge round the flower bed, and moss roses and pansies and black currants & strawberries and peas – and big sage bushes for Jemima, but onions always do badly. I have tall white bell flowers I am fond of, they are just going over, next there will be phlox; and last come the michaelmas daisies & chrysanthemums. Then soon after Christmas we have snowdrops, they grow wild and come up all over the garden & orchard, and in some of the woods.

I hope you will enjoy Wembley [the British Empire Exhibition], I don't think I am likely to see it – not this year anyway – The next entertainment up here will be the agricultural shows which is always great fun – you would never guess what I am going to show, a white bull, with a ring in his nose – What a bad drawing, I have drawn him like a sheep. I shall also show some lambs and a cow.

These old cards are not much good if you collect sets, I found them just now in my desk.

Yours aff.
Beatrix Potter

*Beatrix's 'old fashioned farm garden' at Hill Top in* The Tale of Jemima Puddle-Duck *(1908)*

Dec 29th 24            Hill Top Farm
                         Sawrey
                         Nr Ambleside

My dear Dulcie,

I was just wondering – is your letter coming? and here it comes tonight! but I wish you were not feeling ill; you seem very often to be not quite well, poor Dulcie.

Thank you for the wonderful card, now I think I ought to be lucky, with a horse shoe, and *another* black cat! I must tell you about the first one that came, he was on the doorstep on Christmas morning, a very large fat black cat, with a round big head, a thick coat and a stumpy tail.

I cannot find out who he belongs to, some days he is here, and some days he stays with Miss Mills next door, when I went to see her this morning he was asleep on a cushion before the dining room fire and Miss Mills' little dog Kiltie was watching him, quite good friends. Kiltie understands what is said to him – She said "Kiltie, shall we go for a walk; and where is your collar?"

He tore away up the staircase and brought her *shoe*, and she said "not shoes – *Collar*"! and off he went again, racing upstairs along the landing and came back with the collar in his mouth! My dog always wears her collar; but she understands "walking stick" and "gun" – especially gun, she is wild on going shooting with Mr Heelis. The queer thing is that she is quite annoyed if she hears our neighbours shooting on the next farm, she seems to know the noise of different guns going off. Her name is Fleet she is a big dog, with no tail at all.

My guinea pig Tuppenny is quite well, I shall have to bring his box into the house if the weather turns cold. There is a lot of snow on the hills. Flopsy and the black rabbit are quite well, they had hay and apples and a carrot for Christmas dinner. I have got a new turkey cock, I see I shall have to give him a whipping to teach him who is master, he is too tame; he knocks the corn tin out of my hand when I feed the fowls. The young turkeys are killed and one of the pigs; so there is not so much to do in the way of mixing buckets of pig meal and toiling about in the mud. It has been so dirty in the fields it nearly pulls my big boots off do you know I walked across a field up that high in water on Saturday! such a flood.

I have heard of a most polite cat; he goes out and catches small rabbits. Instead of eating them himself he gives them to a Mrs Tabbitha Cat – at least he allows her to take them from him, and she skins them and eats them! The horses, the cows, the calves, the sheep, the farm dogs, the ducks and the hens – are all very well thank you; except a brown duck called Tapioca, who has rheumatism; and a hen with a sore toe who had a cow tread on her foot, and I have her in a basket till it is better. Now I wish you a very happy New Year, and many thanks for the card, I like it best of any I have had –

yrs aff friend<br>Beatrix Potter

---

April 18. 25          Sawrey<br>Nr Ambleside

My dear Dulcie,

No more bunny books! I never seem to have time, and I cannot paint very well, with being obliged to wear strong spectacles. I drew a picture of Peter and Cottontail for the "Invalid Children", I would like you to have a copy of it, so I am sending you a collecting card, with the stamps stuck on ready. Will you put your name & address, and post it, and I hope they will send you the last year's Christmas card. I am not quite sure whether all the collectors get it, I think you will get one, in return for this many postage stamps.

Your Easter egg is very funny! No, I don't think it would have hatched any chickens! I have 3 hens sitting, and 2 turkeys on nests. The chickens will be rather late, but it has been such a cold spring it is better to wait for warm weather, there was a lot of snow on the hills yesterday. Today it is wet and cloudy, I hope it will turn warmer – we have 51 lambs. One sheep has 3, she is very proud of them. They look comical, there is a big one, a middle sized one, and a little teeny weeny that is always crying. I think it will have to have milk out of a bottle, as its big brothers get all its share as well as their own.

Tuppenny is quite well; but much annoyed by rats. His bread & milk disappeared so quickly, I wondered he did [not] bust up! one saucer after another. But it was not poor Tuppenny, it was a rat stealing it through a hole under the hutch. I have put wire netting now, and Tuppenny's

appetite is quite reasonable & moderate.
But the rats are nibbling the boards below
the wire netting, they get any bread & milk
that slops over. I have not got a big pig just
now, I shall get one at the beginning of

May, a neighbour has got a pig family
coming on. Our cat has 2 kittens, striped &
black.

Now I must stop & go out in a
waterproof to feed hens. No I don't collect
stamps, but I have kept some cigarette cards
for you – somebody does smoke too many!
It is not me; and it isn't Tuppenny. Old Mr
Benjamin Bunny smoked rabbit tobacco,
but he smoked a pipe.

I am sending you a Jemima painting
book, it is the only new book for some time
past.

I remain yr affectionate friend
'Beatrix Potter'

Oct 27.25                               Sawrey

My dear Dulcie

    Yes – I have been frightfully busy, and I am still! But I must spare a minute, especially if you are laid up with mumps. How horrid! The little bird and cherries is quite good. It is rather a funny nest, how does it stick to the branch? We had lots of nests in the garden this year, and a brood of young owls in the barn, they don't build a nest, the eggs are just laid on some boards high up in the loft. They are very comical while they are fluffy; just like aged – aged – old men with fluffy white hair & hooked noses. "Tommy" has no kittens just now. The guinea pig is very chirpy, he twitters loudly when he wants dinner. I have 2 rabbits still, but the brown one – Flopsy – is getting very old & stiff. There was lovely weather at the beginning of October, now there is rain wind & thunder, blowing the leaves away.

    Sorry I haven't time to write more, I have a lot of letters waiting.

        Love from the animals & yr aff friend
                      Beatrix Potter

Dec 18.25                               Sawrey
                             nr Ambleside

My dear Dulcie,

    I do not know whether you got this card or not when you sent up the stamps to the Children's aid, I am sending it to you now, as its better to have 2 copies than none at all! Also some more "badges", and very many Merry Christmas wishes to you from the various little animals.

    The snow has not been deep here, but the frost has been pretty; skating on the lakes & bright sunshine.

    It has been a hungry time for the birds, there have been crowds of birds coming to be fed in the garden. The animals are all well; only Flopsy is looking very old, and getting stiff in her legs.

    Now there is a nice mess! since the thaw our big water tank up the hill has run empty, there is a pipe burst somewhere – no more baths till we find the leak. I expect it is in the yard, not far off.

    Merry Christmas & Happy New Year to you

                  from your aff friend
                      "Beatrix Potter"

*The front of the 1924 Invalid Children's Aid Association Collecting Card which Beatrix sent to Dulcie*

Nov 18.27                    Sawrey
                            Nr Ambleside

My dear Dulcie,

I am indeed grieved to hear of all the sad trouble that your mother and you have had to bear, it is terrible when one trouble comes after another. And nothing but time and patient resolution can deaden the painful memory of that great loss.

I'm sorry you bothered about the collecting card too! You should have sent it to me or to the secretary explaining that you couldn't finish it, of course you had to do something with it when people had given part of the stamps. I should think there are a lot of cards that don't get filled. It was not *my* idea; I always thought it had drawbacks, as a means of collecting.

Now I do hope you will keep warm and get strong again, there is so much illness with this bad weather. We have not had snow here, like there has been in Yorkshire & Scotland, which is fortunate as all farmers are very short of hay, and much of it is spoilt. It has been a wet summer, and the fine autumn came too late for haymaking.

My old guinea pig Tuppenny is dead, I should think from old age, he just got sleepy and eating less, and one morning I found him curled up in his hay bed – gone to sleep for good and all. Soon after that I had some American visitors to tea [the Coolidges, see page 210], and the young boy was very keen to give me 2 new guinea pigs – he said from Boston U.S.A.! – but fortunately he got them at Harrods which was a shorter journey. They are two lady pigs this time; Mrs Tuppenny who is lemon

& white, exactly like the last one; and the other is a most peculiar colour, black with a yellow patch on its nose. It has to be called "Henry P." by special request. Mrs Tuppenny is *not* kind to Henry P. She had scratched a lot of hair off its back where it ought to have a tail; that was in the travelling box. I don't hear them fighting now; but Mrs Tuppenny has grown twice the size of the black one, so I think she steals its food, but it is warmer for them two in a cage.

Talking of tails, I saw a most curious sight the other day after heavy rain the hill sides are slippery, and I saw a neighbour's cow tobogganing as if she had been shot out of a gun – she *flew* down hill sitting on her tail. If she had not kept all her legs in front of her, she would have broken her neck, but she finished on a flat piece of grass, sitting down like a cat, just before she reached the river. I had a calf drowned in one of the floods, but that was with trying to wade across.

Our cat has reared a mischievous little black kitten in the barn, a regular little pickle, I have given it away. There are no puppies at present. Only calves and pigs; the lambs are grown up, and most of them sold at the fair.

Now I hope you will get quite strong again before Christmas comes.

Love from the guinea pigs and
your aff. friend
Beatrix Potter

*Beatrix had always liked guinea pigs and included an 'amiable' one in* Appley Dapply's Nursery Rhymes *(1917)*

## EILEEN AND NEVILLE ROWSON

The letters to the Rowson children were first published in *Signal: Approaches to Children's Books* (May 1972). Neville was eight and Eileen fourteen when they wrote to Beatrix saying how much they enjoyed her books. Eileen 'had drawn on her letter a group of Potter animals and had coloured them in'.

The original of Beatrix's reply to Neville has vanished but her letter to Eileen is in a private collection in Canada, addressed to 'Miss Eileen Rowson, Newlyn, Frodsham', a small town in Cheshire. Enquiries in the district produced the photograph of Eileen as Rose Queen of Frodsham, and the information that she was a keen sportswoman. She became Mrs Layton, had a daughter called Gillian and died in the early 1980s. Neville was killed while serving as an airman in the Second World War.

*Eileen Rowson*

March 6.19            Hill Top Farm

My dear Eileen Rowson,

How nicely you have copied the little animals – (I was going to say anim*u*les, like my niece Nancy – bad habits are catching!) – I thought for a minute that the group was printed. My publishers had a plan to bring out a set of paper & envelopes for children; but everything has been delayed & thrown out of order by the war – dolls, china and all. You do seem to understand and enjoy the books!

Yes! it was the same policeman, a nasty German doll! The real Mrs Tiggy was a dear. I caught her & her brother Pricklepin when they were tiny little things; I let the little boy hedgehog run away in the autumn, but Mrs Tig lived in the house a long time. She was not a bit prickly with me, she used to lay her prickles flat back to be stroked. I seem able to tame any sort of animal; it is sometimes rather awkward on a farm, we cannot keep them out of the house, especially the Puddleducks, & turkeys. I am always afraid Sarah [her pet pig] will get upstairs someday, she got into the dining room one day & nearly smashed the window with running her nose against it, while we were turning her out. She hates stopping in the pig stye! Chippy Hackee belonged to a cousin, I drew the bear at the Zoo [characters from *Timmy Tiptoes*] – now no more.

love from yr aff friend
Beatrix Potter

March 6.19            Hill Top Farm

Dear Neville Rowson,

I must find time to thank you for your dear little letter – do you know I had 3 by that post? I'm afraid I don't find time to answer them all – I have so much to do – for I have a big farm and not so much help as before the war. I have cows and sheep and horses, and poultry – I look after the poultry & rabbits and pony and my own particular pet pig. She is called Sally [Sarah], she follows me about the farm like a dog, through gates and along the road, and if she gets left behind, I call Sally! Sally! and she gallops. I am very fond of rabbits. I have big brown Belgian rabbits, and silver gray; and one rabbit is chocolate colour. I rather like spiders too, they are useful catching flies. I won't have them brushed away in summer, only when we do the spring whitewashing we have to sweep down their webs.

I am glad you saw the bunny family, popping in and out of their hole. Did you ever grunt to them?! Try saying umph! umph! in a very small voice; sometimes I have coaxed wild rabbits to answer me.

With love from yr aff friend
"Beatrix Potter"

*Neville told Beatrix about seeing a bunny family 'popping in and out of their hole'. This is from* The Tale of Peter Rabbit *(1902)*

## JUNE STEEL

June Steel was nearly thirteen when she met Beatrix Potter in 1936, although she had been receiving letters from her for as long as she could remember. It was June's mother, Ivy Hunt, who had first known 'Miss Potter'. Together with her younger brother, Jack, young Ivy had delivered hats in the early 1900s to the Potters at No. 2 Bolton Gardens from their mother's millinery shop in Sloane Square. Ivy and Jack also delivered hats to Beatrix's neighbour at 28 Bolton Gardens, Miss Paget, who kept twenty-eight guinea pigs and for whom the Hunts' friend, 'Aunt' Jessie, worked as lady's maid.

When Ivy was nine her mother died of consumption and she was sent to live with relatives. Aunt Jessie retained her link with the child, sending signed copies of Beatrix's books as they came out, and Beatrix herself wrote to Ivy, though none of those early letters have survived.

In 1920 Ivy emigrated to Canada to join her sister, Beatrice, who had gone there some years before, and Beatrix recorded that she had received 'a happy letter' from Ivy soon after her arrival in Galt, Ontario. In time Ivy Hunt married Jack Steel, who had come to Canada from Dundee in Scotland, and the couple moved to the United States of America. Their daughter, June, was born in Brooklyn, New York, in September 1923.

June Steel's first communications from Beatrix came in the form of drawings of rabbits exchanging kisses and of Peter and Tuppenny sending kisses at the end of the letters to her mother. She also received a toy rabbit from Beatrix in 1924 in her Christmas stocking. But times were hard for the Steels in New York and in 1925 they moved north to Buffalo where Jack was at last able to find employment.

Beatrix's letters to Ivy were increasingly full of stories for June, usually concerning the animals in the village and on the farm.

[November 13 1926] . . . I must tell June about my very little lamb called Dumple. He had a mother, but

*Beatrix's first communication to June Steel was sent with a letter to her mother in November 1924*

he got lost when he was only a month old – His mother was a careless old sheep – she went off to the high hills with the rest of the sheep and lambs and poor Dumple was left behind calling baa! baa! baa! The shepherd found him all alone; but the shepherd could not tell which was Dumple's mother, because she was not calling baa, baa! she had forgotten all about him. So he just walked about by himself all summer, and ate grass like an old sheep, and he has strong straight legs, like June; and as lively as can be; but he is hardly any bigger than a pussy cat!

I never saw such a comical little sheep. I thought he would be safest near the house in winter, so I carried him home in my arms, and put him in the field behind the house. But he was not satisfied with the other sheep's company. It came on to rain in the evening, and Master Dumple went into the stable with the great big cart horse! I was afraid Captain would tread on him, so we put him out of the stable. In about five minutes I met Dumple coming by himself up to the back door, he is so small he can get through any railing. At present he is in the barn, eating hay very comfortably. I shall have to be careful he does not get into the pig stye, the big pig might hurt him.
With lots of kisses for June.

In August the following year, when June was nearly four, Beatrix started to enclose a separate letter for her in the envelope for Ivy and so began a correspondence that lasted for the next ten years. By October that year the Steels were back in New York and Beatrix urged Ivy to take June to Fordham Branch of the New York Library on Bainbridge Avenue to meet the children's librarian, Mary Haugh, who had recently accompanied Anne Carroll Moore, the Superintendent of Children's Work at the New York Public Library (see page 222), on a brief visit to Beatrix in Sawrey. The Steels and Mary Haugh became firm friends and in her letters Beatrix would send messages between them. June Steel recalls those far-off days in New York. 'I well remember Mary Haugh and Anne Carroll Moore, as Mother and I often visited the libraries. Mother allowed the letters and our books to be put on exhibit on a couple of occasions.'

As the Depression took hold, the Steels found themselves in more trouble. Jack Steel was plagued with bad health and he was repeatedly unable to work. Once again the family moved out of New York City. To offer some relief Beatrix conceived the idea of inviting Ivy and June to Britain for a holiday. They would collect Aunt Jessie in London, visit Ivy's brother, Jack, and his family in Surrey, and then travel up to Sawrey. Beatrix would pay for everything, including the cost of their Atlantic crossing. She recommended that they travel tourist class on one of the smaller Cunard ships rather than on the *Queen Mary*, 'these very grand ships with swimming pools and extremely quick passages are the last word in luxury; but surely an 8 days passage in a not-the-very-fashionablest would be alright, provided it were tourist class.' They took her advice on the way over, sailing on the *Britannic* in June 1936, but it was on the *Queen Mary* that they returned the following October.

*June Steel at Hill Top Farm in 1936*

Beatrix also sent the money for their return train fare – £2.3.6. each. 'We travelled to Windermere on the *Flying Scotsman*, which was once the fastest train in the world,' writes June. 'I remember how amazed I was that the countryside changed so much in such a short trip. Beatrix Potter sent her chauffeur to meet us at the station and he drove us to Castle Cottage, where we had tea. Then Beatrix took us to Hill Top, which is where we were to stay. It was a great surprise to me to find that everything there was just like all the stories and drawings in her letters and her books.'

The visit was an undoubted success. Beatrix reported on it to American friends in September:

I have had a good many American visitors . . . a young woman, a Londoner, who went out as a young girl and married. I had not seen her for twenty years. She came over to see her brother bringing her own child. I was very relieved to find I liked "Ivy" as much as when she was a young girl, and I was interested in her girl. I suppose you have no classes in America?! Anyhow Ivy's husband is in the telephones and her child goes to what would be equivalent to board school = council school here. It was the first time I had ever heard the native accent of Bronx. I am tempted to say I hope I may never hear that accent again. She was a dear child. When one got over the accent she compared favourably with the average English child of the same class; obedient, intelligent and natural manners without forwardness. But the accent was a caution; on her father's side descended from Glasgow Scotch which is even worse.

*By the time the Steels visited Beatrix Potter in August 1936 she was well established as a prize-winning sheep farmer*

Over fifty years later June still remembers the visit very clearly. 'I particularly remember the collie, Lassie. Every morning and evening the farmer stood at the barn and sent Lassie out to herd the cows from a hillside, by whistle commands only. To me this was amazing. The Pekes, Tzusee and Chuleh, were everywhere and such a joy to me. I had had to leave my dog, Ginger, at home with my father and I missed her so much.

'Beatrix Potter had a colt in a field next to her house and while Mother and Beatrix were busy I used to go out, with the Pekes, to the field and feed the colt caramel candies. It was so funny to me to see a horse chewing the candy like gum. Every time I went by the field he would trot over to the fence to greet me. This went on for a week and then my mother and Beatrix saw me in the field with the colt. Beatrix became really excited and anxious, telling me to get back over the fence very slowly. Apparently the colt was very unruly and was kept in the field because he had smashed down his stall in the barn. When I told her that I had been visiting him every day and feeding him caramels, she broke out laughing. She told me that none of the hands on the farm had been able to approach him and here a child had been doing it every day!' Beatrix kept June up-to-date with news of 'her' colt after her return home (see her letter of 2 August 1937) and in December she reported that the horse had been sold to a farmer at the Kendal horse fair for £35.10, 'which was a good price . . . I hope he will have a good home and enough work ploughing to keep him quiet!'

June also has happy memories of Beatrix Potter herself. 'She seemed to me to be very fond of children. All her letters to me show this. I remember her including me in the conversations and she would always answer my questions. I have very fond memories of our trip and of her kindness.'

On their return to the United States the correspondence between Beatrix and the Steels resumed. The last known letter to June is dated 11 October 1939 but those to Ivy continue until September 1943. From her first marriage June had three children, a daughter and two sons. For twenty-five years she worked in banking; she is now retired and remarried, to Bill Vargo, who also has three children. Ivy died in 1987.

Beatrix's letters to the Steels were bought by the Toronto Public Library in 1976. Permission has been given for the inclusion of only a selection of June's letters here, but the entire collection can be found in *Dear Ivy, Dear June*, published by the Friends of the Osborne and Lillian H. Smith Collections in 1977.

*Beatrix's sketches of her sheepdogs*

Aug 15th 27

My dear June

I think you are big enough to have a letter all to you. I am writing in the farm house parlour The men are dipping the sheep such a wet job! They are put into a big cement bath with carbolic "soap", they do splash and kick, if it gets into their eyes and mouths. When I came round the corner of the stable what should I see but little dog Sandy, standing on a box on the tips of her toes, she could just reach into the bucket of meal that had been hung up to keep it safe from puppies!

Sandy is a sheep dog puppy. There is a hound puppy called Brilly, it is a little thief too! It stole a fried egg off the plate on the kitchen fender. And there is a very funny pet – a young fox. He has a collar and chain. I doubt if he will ever get quite tame. He was too old when he was caught, he was sitting in the sun with another brother – or sister – and the shepherds chased him into a rabbit hole, they fetched a spade and dug him out. They call him "Vic". He is very pretty and he can be stroked, but he is always looking out to snap and run away. It has not had a chance to bite *me*. I don't touch it unless somebody is holding it. There are ever so many sheep dogs, my favourite is "Nip".

The only animal I do not like is the white Bull He has a ring in his nose, like a pig. He runs after people they get over walls in a hurry. He is going to be made into roast beef as soon as he is fat.

I like cows and calves, but I do not like bulls. Tuppenny [her guinea pig] is getting very very old, he sleeps a great deal he sends his love xxxxx to June.

yrs aff
"Beatrix Potter"

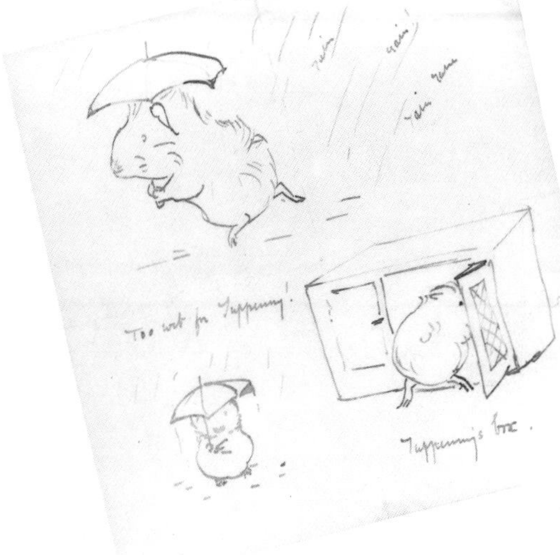

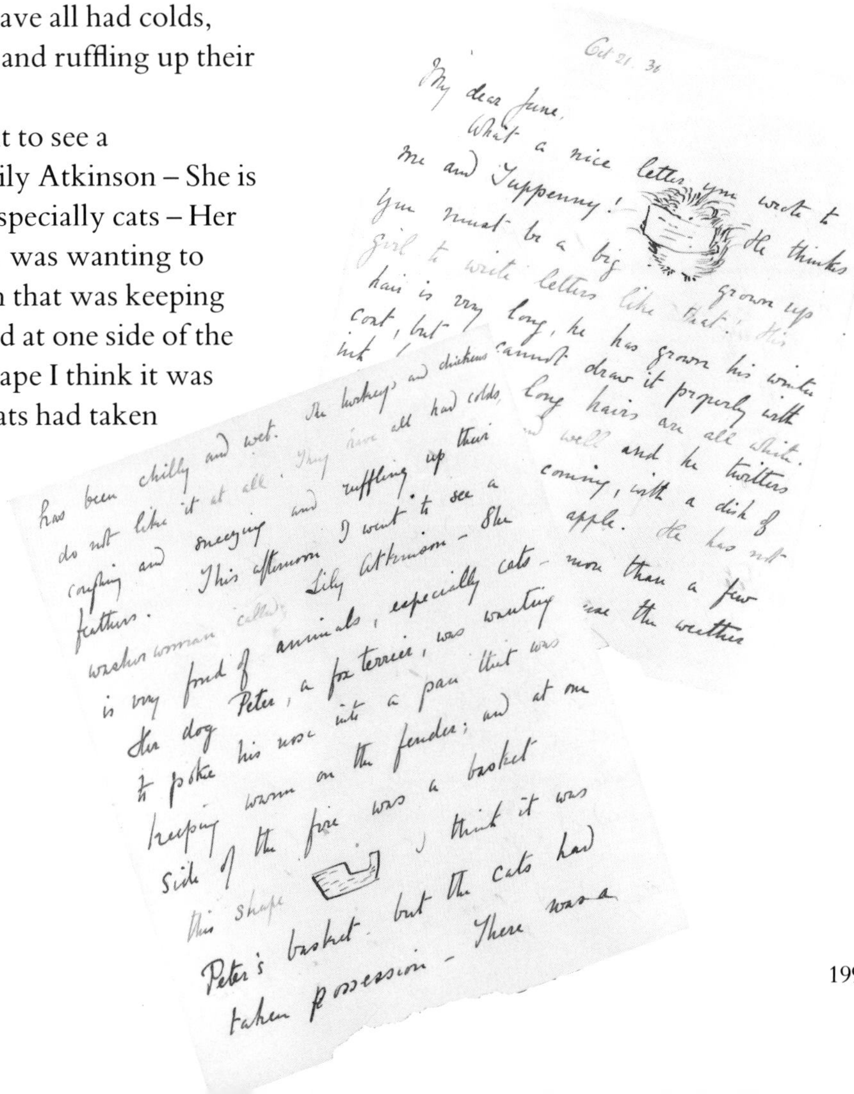

Oct 21.30

My dear June,

What a nice letter you wrote to me and Tuppenny! He thinks you must be a big grown up girl to write letters like that! His hair is very long, he has grown his winter coat, but I cannot draw it properly with ink because the long hairs are all white. He is very fat and well and he twitters when he sees me coming, with a dish of bread and milk and an apple. He has not been out of doors for more than a few days this summer, because the weather has been chilly and wet. The turkeys and chickens do not like it at all. They have all had colds, coughing and sneezing and ruffling up their feathers.

This afternoon I went to see a washerwoman called Lily Atkinson – She is very fond of animals, especially cats – Her dog Peter, a fox terrier, was wanting to poke his nose into a pan that was keeping warm on the fender; and at one side of the fire was a basket this shape I think it was Peter's basket but the cats had taken possession – There was a white cat and a tortoiseshell, and a little black kitten in it. The old cats were washing each others faces.

Lily wanted to give me the kitten but I have 2 cats of my own, that is enough.

Tuppenny and I send you lots of xxx

xxxx

xx

yr aff. friend
'Beatrix Potter'

May 8.33

Castle Cottage
Sawrey
nr Ambleside

My dear June,

Thank you for your nice little letter – I am glad to hear you are getting on well at school. I will write to you while I remember a pleasant walk I took this afternoon in Mr Todd's [sic] big wood. But first I must tell you I heard a noise just now like somebody talking in the kitchen – there was Mr Drake Puddleduck and 6 Mrs Ducks *sitting* on the *mat* before the *kitchen fire*!! Our servant had gone out and left the back door open and it was raining very hard. But that is no excuse for ducks, they like rain. Had it been hens, or turkeys, I should not have been surprised. I said "Whatever are you doing here Mr Puddleduck?" And out they waddled in a hurry, Mrs Possy duck always last; she is quite blind of one eye She runs against apple trees etc, but she seems as fat as any, so I suppose she can find worms & corn to eat.

The woods are lovely now, wild cherry trees covered with blossom as white as snow, and violets and primroses and blue bells amongst the nut bushes. The deer have been making a noise at nights, they make a curious gruff barking noise like a dog that is very hoarse. I wanted to see them. It is a time of year when the stags have no horns. It is very strange their horns fall off in spring, and grow again.

First I saw lots of rabbits, big old rabbits, and tiny baby rabbits of all sizes. One was peeping out from the root of a big fir tree. I saw nothing of Tommy Brock or Mr Todd. I was looking out for Mr Todd because something carried off one of my young lambs into the wood. We were afraid others might be taken so I hung up an old jacket for a scarecrow – at least I did not hang it up, I folded it and put it down as if someone had taken their coat off while at work, and I moved it every few days to a fresh place, & Mr Todd kept away afterwards. I saw footmarks of deer. I saw Mr Todd's old house, long deserted; the walls made of sticks & bits of wood have gone; only the chimny [sic] stack is standing. A wood pigeon has a nest in a holly tree near the door way. I went on and I saw the stump and the fallen tree where Mr Todd sat and read the newspaper. I was getting tired and very warm and thought I would turn back, only I could hear a cock pheasant calling cuck! cuck! Cuck!! very excited and cross, so I knew there was something stirring. I saw two light coloured patches that moved beyond the nut bushes – light brown ends of deer. I wonder why they have a light patch at the tail end. They were reaching up, eating the young leaves on the ash and oak saplings. I stood quite still and watched them for a time then I climbed up a little hill in the wood and got a view sideways, looking down. The biggest deer were in front, five very big animals, taller than donkys [sic]. They are rather like donkies (how do you spell donkys at school?) only they are red brown and they have awfully thin legs. One of the young bucks had knobs about an inch long on his head that was the horns growing. He looked dirty, in fact I saw him splashing about in a bog, they often roll in the mud to get away from flies and midges.

I watched them for some time keeping behind them. When the stags have horns it is not safe to go near them as they sometimes run at people like a bull. They seem to think the woods belong to them. They wander about for miles and miles. I only saw 10, but sometimes there is a drove of 40. They can do a lot of mischief if they come out onto the turnips and potato crops. It was a pretty sight to see the herd of deer moving away slowly. They never took any notice of me.

I hope you are very well. It is sad times in the big world but we must learn our lessons and hope for better days to come. There are nice showers of rain here, plenty of grass for the lambs.

With much love to you and your Mother
yrs aff
Beatrix Potter

Dec 12.34

Castle Cottage
Sawrey
nr Ambleside

My dear June,

Its a long time since I heard any news of you and I am afraid it is my fault and you have had no answer to your nice letter of July 26th. You are getting on! Fifth grade!! And a Girl Scout!!! In this country we call them Boy Scouts, and girl Guides. It is all the same. There were 3 companies of girls camping here in August and a fourth company on a distant part of the farm. They had bad weather, rain and wind. They took no harm (except one girl had tooth ache) but there was a lot of wet bedding, one tent blew down, I had some blankets to lend to them. They seemed to think it was fun, they stuck to their tents although there was a barn. Some of them don't like barns because they think there are rats. The guides did not swim. Some cousins who came here for a holiday were swimming every day. It was very very hot till the end of July. Then it was cold and wet all the time, we got our hay just right before the rain began. It has been bad weather – there was 4 inches of rain last week – no frost, and just one fall of snow, in October. I have been interested to hear about a cat. It was taken to London from Kendal – a town 10 miles from here, and it walked home 200 miles from London to Kendal. Poor cat, what a journey on foot! I have known dogs go a long way, but nothing to compare. One of our collys [sic] went by train to a market 25 miles away and got lost while the shepherd was selling the sheep. It came

*Beatrix with a group of Girl Guides who were camping on her land*

home in less than a week; and I remember a Scotch dog that run away from a farm 30 miles south of here. The funny thing was we caught the dog and sent it home to the man – his name was on the collar – and two months afterwards the same dog passed through again, going north. We did not get hold of it the second time, so I do not know the end of the story. I have sheep at another farm 10 miles away, and the dogs sometimes remove. A colly called Fly who is very fond of me, worked for a week on the other farm last spring. I went to see how the lambs were getting on, and Fly wanted to come home with me in the car. So next night she ran away. She wanted to come across Windermere ferry – but she had no money to buy a ticket! so she set off to go round the lake. Somebody caught her and sent word. Fly knows where she likes to live. I hope your mother and you are very well.

Yrs aff.
Beatrix Potter

Aug 2.37

Ashyburn
Ancrum
Scotland

My dear June

I have owed you and your Mother letters – oh such a time! Now I am trying to get a lot written while we are on holiday. We are going home tomorrow after a pleasant weekend with my sister-in-law [Mary, Bertram Potter's widow]. I am sure the little Pekes will be glad to see us back; they had an invitation to come with us, but they are awful fidgets in a car, and we stopped one night at an hotel on the way north, so I thought best to leave them with Miss Mills and their brother Yummy. There is a serious grave fox terrier here, called Peter, a dull dog, but better behaved than ours. He does not take stockings and socks etc into the garden and hide them. Tsu-zee has been very mischievous lately; she has been pulling such a lot of bits out of the doormats, I do not know why she takes these fits of mischief. She and Judy [Chuleh] caught a rat one day but they could not hold it, it got away down a drain. They have caught some mice in the house. Your friend the colt has gone away for the summer to stay at a farm on the marshes, south of Kendal where the farmer takes young horses for the summer months. While the fields are in hay grass we had no room for him. The mare has been very well behaved in the hay making; some mares object to being separated from a little foal. The foal is called Betty after Queen Elizabeth as it was born Coronation time. [King George VI and Queen Elizabeth had been crowned on 12 May]. I am glad the hay making is finished at Sawrey. It has been a wet cold spring, and thundery showery summer. It is real hot weather now, lovely. We go for long drives with my sister-in-law and her niece [Hetty Douglas] – this is a pleasant place to stay – And all the district is History – real history – not dull. Don't you find English history more real since you have been to England? Here on the Border of Scotland it is all history of the old wars between the English and the Scots. Small wars where they fought with bows and arrows and hand to hand with swords. The battle of Flodden was fought not far from here, on land that is now corn fields. There are old roofless Abbeys, Melrose, Dryburgh, Jedburgh near by, and memories of Mary Queen of Scots – We went on Saturday to see an old strong town, such a curious old strong house, and the family who owned it had been there since 1450, and they had belongings kept through all those centuries, different bits of armour and old swords and pikes and spears. Mary Haugh [the American librarian] ought to have seen it; she could have made up fine stories to tell the children. She walked in – Sunday week – with her husband Mr Zipprich, they were staying at Windermere and came to tea at Sawrey – She was just the same, very merry and pleasant. I wonder if you are on pic nic near a lake this summer. It was very nice seeing you and your mother and Aunt Jessie – Now I must stop, it is getting dark.

Much love from yours aff.
Beatrix Potter Heelis

Ap.14.38

Castle Cottage
Sawrey
Ambleside

My dear June,

Thank you for your nice letter – We are sharing your weather! It is lovely; only a bit dry for the lambs. Very bright hot sunshine in the daytime, and a little ground frost at nights. I am afraid some blossom is spoilt but there are buds still closed up warm. The trees in this garden are as white as snow, and lots of daffodils and other spring flowers. The blue bells are not up yet.

I am writing rather punctually to tell you about Tsuzee's great doings. She killed two rats on Tuesday without getting bitten, both large rats, and one of them a monster like the old man rat who frightened Tom Kitten. I had left the pantry-cellar door open while I was sorting apples and weeding in the orchard. I suppose it was open for an hour. Later on I went into the china storeroom, behind the dining room and saw a big rat on the stone shelf near a basin of pickled pork. I shut the door, shut myself in with the rat, and put all the best china into the cupboard & other things on shelves. The rat was quiet, hiding, then I let in the Pekes – you never heard such a row! Chuleh *sang*, she bayed like a pack of hounds – [T]Suzee did more barking which is not proper with fox hounds. The rat bounced about & got behind things chased by the Pekes, then Mrs Rogerson came with a broom & a shovel & screeched, & I tried to kill the rat in the window with a stick. Then Mrs Rogerson fetched Tom with a stick. They said the rat was in the dark spot behind the dining room. I could not understand how it had got out of the cellar, but she said it had. Suzee caught it cleverly and chewed it up. It was smaller than I expected; and very shiny. About 9 o'clock the dogs jumped up & wished to get into the back cellars again; they sniffed and pointed to some boards which I moved cautiously and there was the big rat hiding. I don't know how Suzee catches them without being bitten. She seems to pounce like a cat, and punch them on the back of the head till they are dead. Judy [Chuleh] is just as keen, but Suzee is sharper & gets the rat first. Fancy that bold bad mouse stealing Ginger's Christmas stocking! Where was Ginger I wonder?

We are very well here and glad to hear you are well too.

There are over 60 lambs, and more expected. No foal this year, which is a pity; the year-old filly is a beauty. Love to you & your Mother

Yrs aff
Beatrix Heelis

Nov 26.38　　　　　　　　Castle Cottage
　　　　　　　　　　　　　Sawrey
　　　　　　　　　　　　　Ambleside

My dear June,

What a pretty 'snap' of you and your friend and the horses! I hope they did not 'snap' your fingers? Their teeth can nip! I am sure you and your Mother will be enjoying a move into the country. I hope you have a warm house – if it is colder than here, as is likely. There has been snow on the hills since Monday, and down here in Sawrey there is one hail shower after another – Its been miserable weather ever since last spring – We did not finish hay until Sept 19th, instead of in July or early August. It spoilt the season; so unsettling and always getting wet when it was just about ready to carry to the barn. I have not been very well since September, I got a chill and sciatica and one cold after another. I have been away to stay with a friend near Liverpool for ten days and it has done me good [she had really been in hospital] – but there won't be much satisfaction till Spring comes. The fear of war is a worry – and the shame of being bullied by Hitler is worse, we do not know how it will end. We have no gas masks here. Aeroplanes do not like coming amongst the hills and valleys. But if war comes we will be crowded with refugees from the towns – And there are such rough people in Barrow! We will gladly help them, but its a funny prospect! I think *you* are lucky to live the other side of the ocean. Susie [Tzusee] and Chuleh are very well and lively, just as sporting as can be. All for going out with the gun. Chuleh got herself caught in a steel rat trap, but strange to say she was not lamed. She sat still and howled until Mr Heelis came and released her paw from the trap. The next time she was out – she went back to hunt the same place. There was another animal 'trapped' in a funny way; 'Betty' the year old foal – She was nibbling leaves off a tree that blew down, and she pushed in amongst the branches till she could not turn round. Tom Storey noticed old Lofty always tramping round and round the tree, then he found that Lofty's young companion had been fast for two days! Lofty had worn quite a footpath round about. The foal must have been thirsty, but it took no harm. It is a pretty foal, not so big as the first one. I think we will not sell it, as one of the horses is getting very old and stiff – old 'Dolly' at the Coniston farm, you don't know her. The lambs are sold, the corn is threshed, and things are quiet for the winter. I hope you and your mother are very well – its a long time since I heard from Auntie Jessie.

　　　　　　　　With love yrs aff.
　　　　　　　　Beatrix 'Potter' Heelis
The garden flowers were spoilt with rain & wind, and there are scarcely any apples – Better luck next year!

*Opposite: Beatrix with her two Pekes, Chuleh and Tsuzee, photographed in 1936*

*Above and below: Beatrix's preliminary sketches for the drawings in her ICCA letter*

## INVALID CHILDREN'S AID ASSOCIATION

In January 1924 Beatrix was approached by Sir Alfred Fripp for permission to associate Peter Rabbit with a special appeal to the 'better-off children' for 'pennies'. It was for the ICAA, whose stated aims were 'to help, to supervise, and if possible to cure the seriously-invalided and crippled children of the poor by obtaining for them the best medical treatment and continued after-care, and finding for them when possible a means of earning a livelihood in the future'.

Collecting cards were issued with room on them for sixteen stamps to be bought from the Post Office which would be 'worth much more' when redeemed by the charity. The money was to go to the ICAA Home at West Wickham where, it was stated on the cards, there were already 'four Peter Rabbit beds called after him'. The scheme proved difficult to administer, and as many children were unable to complete the cards they were soon discontinued, but the inauguration of the project was the start of Beatrix's special connection with the charity which continued until her death in December 1943. Beatrix wrote the following letters which were printed and sent to the children who did manage to complete their cards.

My dear

Peter Rabbit is so pleased about the stamps, he thinks it is just splendid! He was busy in the garden when the postman came. Not a big post MAN, oh no! Peter's post-rabbit has a tail as well as a letter bag. His bag is stuffed full of the funniest little letters. Some are from the birds to the mice, and some are for the squirrels and the rabbits. There was one for Timmy-Willie-mouse— "Dear Timothy, Plum cake for supper on Wednesday, yours Johnny Town Mouse." But Timmy Willie answered "Dear Johnny, no thank you, I am previously engaged to dine with Jeremy Fisher." And there was a letter written by Squirrel Nutkin, commencing "Honoured Sir, I feel the want of my Tail now the cold weather has come. Sir, Mr. Brown, please, please post me my Tail; the Tailor has promised to sew it on again, and I will post you three bags of nuts by return. Yours respectfully, S. Nutkin." And somehow, Mr. Brown's reply had come by the same post—"Master Nutkin, you do not deserve it; but as a reward for Respect, I enclose Tail herewith. O.B." There was also a letter from Jemima Puddle-Duck to Sally Henny Penny about rearing ducklings, and several addressed to Messrs. Ginger & Pickles, Grocers. And two addressed to Mrs. Tiggy Winkle about things that had been lost at the wash. It seems as though things are often lost at Little Town. Lucie, who lost her 'hankins, had been losing her gloves, and Mrs. Tittle-mouse had found them when she went round with a mop. So Mrs. Tittle-mouse posted them back to Lucie, in a piece-of-poetry letter; not good poetry but rather pretty—

"I found a tiny pair of gloves, when Lucie came to tea,
They were the dearest little gloves, I thought they'd do for me!
I tried them—quite inside them, they were <u>much</u> too big for me!
I wear gloves with one button hole when <u>I</u> go out to tea.
I'll put them in an envelope with sealing wax above,
And send them back to Lucie; I'll send them with my love."

But the sweetest letters of all were from the little Invalid Children thanking Peter Rabbit's little friends for all they have done to make Christmas happier. And one of those letters told Peter Rabbit a great secret. Before another Christmas we hope there will be enough stamps collected for a Peter Rabbit Bed; a hospital bed where many little invalid children will get well again.

yours sincerely
Beatrix Potter

My dear little friend [name of child]

Cousin Benjamin and I do not often write letters, but I do want to thank you for all that you have done for the little Invalid children; it is splendid!

Today Benjamin Bunny and I have been choosing our Christmas tree. We went to a wood where there are nut bushes and cherry trees and oak coppice; and in a cleared space amongst the oaks we found a plantation of young fir trees. We chose a lovely little tree 4 feet high. Said Benjamin, standing on his hind legs – "I'm afraid it is too big, Peter; we could not reach the top to tie on apples and nuts and fairy candles." But I said – "It is just right Benjamin; Twinkleberry will climb up and help us; not Nutkin, he would crack the nuts."

You know we do not move our tree; we leave it growing in the wood. When Christmas-tide is over, it looks like any other little fir tree. But you should see it on Christmas Eve! All aglow with fairy lights, and hung with hips and haws and holly berries, & nutcrackers and mouse toffee in silver paper, and nutcrackers, and garlanded with chains of sparkling icicles. Then all of us little animals dance round, around, around, while Cock Robin sings overhead and Pricklepin plays the bagpipes. And we shout and sing so loud that you may hear us through the dark, wishing you all a Merry Christmas and a Happy New Year!

from your [sic] affectionately
Peter Rabbit (and Beatrix Potter)

*Beatrix's drawing of the animals'*
*Christmas tree was used on the ICCA*
*Christmas cards for 1932 and 1941*

# JOHN WOOLVERTON

John Woolverton is another of Beatrix's child correspondents it has not been possible to trace and it is only assumed that John was a child because Beatrix would be unlikely to illustrate a letter to an adult. Her reference to his returning to fish another day when the tittlebats had grown suggests that he might have been a local child, but enquiries in Sawrey have failed to uncover a Woolverton family. Perhaps John was one of the many summer visitors or possibly one of the Boy Scouts who regularly camped on Beatrix's land? What is certain is that he was asking for permission to fish in Moss Eccles Tarn, the only stretch of water owned by Beatrix. She had bought the small lake perched on the hill overlooking the village in 1909, at the time she had acquired Castle Farm and Castle Cottage, and it had become a favourite place of retreat for her and Willie after a hard day's work. They planted the tarn with water lilies, stocked it with fish and put a boat in the boathouse. After a short walk up the bridlepath from Castle Cottage the two of them spent many a happy summer evening there.

June 14.28                                   Sawrey

Dear John Woolverton

   Yes, certainly! As long as you don't trample hay grass or leave gates open; and Mr Heelis says put back the very little tittlebats so that you can catch them another day when they have grown into this size. I saw some nice fish on Monday after the rain, they will be running up. I hope you have a good catch if you are out on Saturday.

Yrs sincerely
H.B. Heelis

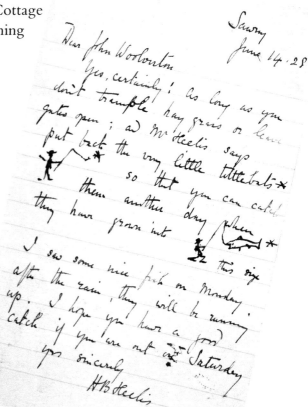

*Henry P. Coolidge with his bantam chicks*

## HENRY P. COOLIDGE

Henry Parsons Coolidge, always known by the family as Henry P., was born in Portsmouth, New Hampshire, in 1914, the elder of the two sons of Mary-Abigail (Gail) and John Templeman Coolidge. His father was an excellent portrait painter, a collector and one of the prime movers in the establishing of The Boston Museum of Fine Arts.

In 1927 the family spent the summer in England, staying at Fawe Park, a large house on the shore of Derwentwater, not far from Lingholm. What they did not know then was that it was the same house that the Potter family had rented for their holiday twenty-four years earlier and that in the garden there Beatrix had made the sketches for her sequel to *Peter Rabbit, The Tale of Benjamin Bunny.*

Mr Coolidge's stay at Fawe Park was frequently interrupted, for he journeyed backwards and forwards to Boston where he was concerned with the installation of his eighteenth-century ship models in the museum, but his wife and two sons, Henry P. and Usher, had a long and enjoyable holiday in the Lake District. Like a number of other American families from New England they were intent on meeting the author whose books they so loved. In turn Beatrix enjoyed the American overt appreciation of her work, something she felt was lacking from readers in her own country, and she welcomed visitors from across the Atlantic, as long as they gave her warning so that she could ensure she was not busy with farm work. In answer to Gail Coolidge's enquiry as to whether she could bring Henry P. to Sawrey she wrote: 'I shall be very glad to see your boy . . . I am always pleased to see Americans, I don't know what to think about you as a nation (with a big N!) but the individuals who have looked for Peter Rabbit have all been delightful.'

Henry P. was then thirteen.

I had a maudlin passion for animals. While my brother and most of my friends constructed model steam-engines, polished guns, and tinkered with

*An illustration from* The Tale of Benjamin Bunny *(1904) showing the garden at Fawe Park where the Coolidges stayed in 1927*

automobiles, I raised rabbits, guinea-pigs, mice, cross-bred bantams, flew pigeons and showed dogs. Of course the works of Beatrix Potter had been from my earliest recollection like unto the books that make up the bible. I knew every creature, every place, every conversation.

So, leaving Usher behind with his latest model steam engine, Mrs Coolidge and Henry P. drove to Sawrey.

Over sixty years later Henry Coolidge writes about that visit.

*Henry P. Coolidge (left) with his father John Templeman Coolidge and his brother Usher*

As I look back, Mrs Heelis seemed fairly aged – twelve years older than my mother – plump, and rather bent, with rosy cheeks and firm blue eyes in a weather-beaten face. Her somewhat untidy grey hair was carelessly drawn back in a bun. On the whole, I thought she had the familiar air of a shrewd, battered, independent Maine fisherman's wife. Though not very aware of clothes, even I was conscious that she was dowdy. My composite impression, made over several years, would be of some baggy wool skirt drooping toward the ground, an old brown sweater, perhaps, pulled over a shirtwaist and clumsily bunched at the neck with a cameo brooch. She wore, I believe always, stout, clumsy boots for trudging through the muddy barnyard outside her little house. I also remember her always jamming on a squashed flat hat to go outside to show us a rooster, the calves, or a pet collie. Perhaps women always wore hats outside in those days. Certainly my mother, as a visitor, had on something towering, black, and Bostonian. Aside from this, I don't recall much for the constant excitement of recognizing views and buildings as she took us on an expedition through the little town [Sawrey] – scene after scene, page after page. After buying some post cards from *Ginger and Pickles'* shop and crossing the small field from *Pigling Bland*, we were at the gate to Hill Top farm. Here Mrs Heelis produced an

*A detail from 'Blind Man's Buff', one of the six pictures that make up* The Rabbits' Christmas. *Beatrix's pencil corrections to the outlines of the rabbit's legs can just be seen*

enormous key and let us into *Tom Kitten*'s home which is kept as a little museum unchanged forever from the time of the books.

Henry P. and his mother were taken back to Castle Cottage for a hearty tea and a long discussion about Beatrix's work. They then went upstairs to Beatrix's study where she kept her numerous unused pictures and sketches.

This was a room entirely filled with portfolios of her work. A series of long, deep, baseboard cupboards ran the whole length of one wall, and, when she opened one of these to take out two pictures, I saw they were stacked with more portfolios still. The pictures were the middle two in the delightful set of six comprising *The Rabbits' Christmas Party* – early work for which she professes some scorn. 'You can see how poor my anatomy was,' she said, and, seizing a blunt pencil, she bent forward and made a couple of swift curves, doubling the size of the leading rabbit's paws.

When they left to return to Fawe Park Henry P. was the proud possessor of a number of Beatrix's pictures, including the two from *The Rabbits' Christmas Party*.

A few days later the Coolidges received a summons from Castle Cottage. 'They weren't autographed. So you must come again, to get my precious signature.' This time Henry's father was included in the party but once again Usher stayed with his steam engines. Gail Coolidge and Beatrix Potter warmed to each other immediately. Mrs Coolidge contributed to Beatrix's fund to save some land from developers (see page 215), and Beatrix was delighted with Henry P., writing:

Everyone is happy and satisfied. Henry P. is pleased, and so am I – pleased to have given pleasure and drawings to such an appreciative friend of Peter Rabbit's, and such a very charming boy . . . I can quite believe that when Henry P. was a very very small white headed baby he may have been acquainted with fairies, like I was, if there are fairies in New England.

While at Castle Cottage the Coolidges had been distressed to discover that, only a few weeks before, Beatrix's much-loved long-haired guinea pig, Tuppenny, had died of old age. On their way home through London Mrs Coolidge arranged for two new guinea pigs to be sent from Harrods, and although both guinea pigs turned out to be female, one of them had to be called Henry P. 'by special request' (see Beatrix's letter to Dulcie on page 189), while the other naturally assumed the name Mrs Tuppenny.

The Coolidges' visit, their enthusiasm for Beatrix's books and their keen interest in her surroundings and way of life – coupled with a coincidental approach from an American publisher – were directly responsible for the first new Beatrix Potter story for eleven years.

For some time Beatrix had been writing short pieces about the animals on the farm at Hill Top and about her pets for her own amusement. She had been recording her thoughts and fantasies as she journeyed between Sawrey and her newest farm Troutbeck to oversee work, and the previous winter she had been developing a story about a long-haired guinea pig which she had first written in 1903. Although she had considered the possibility of putting all the material together for publication, Beatrix was reluctant to see the stories in print in England, feeling that they were too autobiographical, too sentimental and too revealing. Publishing them in America, however, was something she could countenance.

In June 1928 Henry P. received a copy of the revised version of *The Tale of Tuppenny*, the 1903 guinea pig story which was now retitled *Over the Hills and Far Away*. It would appear the following February in *The Horn Book*, an American magazine devoted to children's books and reading, and it was to be the first chapter of a new book, *The Fairy Caravan*, for publication in October 1929 by David McKay of Philadelphia. The book is dedicated 'To Henry P.' and there has been speculation about whether the

*This early sketch of an ailing guinea pig was redrawn by Beatrix for* The Tale of Tuppenny

*Beatrix and Henry P. both loved old oak furniture. This is a detail of a sketch by Beatrix of a traditional Lakeland room*

dedication was to the guinea pig or to the boy. Henry P. himself writes engagingly on the subject: 'It is perhaps presumptuous of me to feel I share the honor of dedication with that little animal – but then the author did write on 27 October 1929, "Dear Henry P., I hope by this time you have received your copy of *Our* Book!"'

Henry P. did not return to Sawrey until 1936 but both he and his mother had kept up a regular correspondence with Beatrix and she had followed his education progress with interest. This time his brother, Usher, was with him when he returned. 'We had been to Venice beforehand where I bought two little ivory goats and I gave one to Beatrix Potter.' Again, in 1938, the young men toured Europe together by car. 'I was in graduate school at Harvard and my brother was an undergraduate there. In England, as well as collecting some prize Lakeland terriers and some ornamental bantams, we of course visited Beatrix Potter for what turned out to be a farewell visit.' Although Beatrix was in her early seventies and slowed by arthritis, she was as busy as ever, keeping a close eye on her farms and attending local sales to rescue good furniture, about which her knowledge was considerable. Writing to a friend about Henry P.'s last visit Beatrix said, 'He looked over my old oak with renewed interest'.

In 1950 Henry Coolidge married Alice Crawford and they have four daughters. After a lifetime of 'teaching various literature courses at Harvard and Tufts Universities' Henry P. retired in 1987 at the age of seventy-two.

In her first letter to Henry P. Beatrix 'hopes that the bantam hen did her duty'. Henry P. had recently acquired some bantam chicks which, as he recalls over sixty years later, 'were new pets for me that year and the start of a life-long hobby which led to much grander varieties which I cross-bred and showed for years. My speciality was Japanese bantams which we produced in about twenty different colours. I haven't had the energy for some years now to carry on all this single-handed, but I still collect carvings and prints of the "Chabo". It has been a pleasant monomania.'

June 28.28                    Sawrey
                              nr Ambleside
                              Westmorland

Dear Henry P. Coolidge,

I have taken such a long time to answer
your two letters that I am almost ashamed
to write! I hope the bantam hen did her duty
more conscientiously than Jemima
Puddleduck, and hatched her eggs
successfully. Things have "hatched" badly
here this spring; which is in part my excuse
for not writing sooner. There are seasons
when things go wrong; and they just have
to be lived through; like the old inscription
"Good times and bad times; all times get
over". It is strange where all the rain comes
from, after such a wet winter of rain &
sleaty [sic] snow we *did* hope for a fine
summer.

All my spare time last winter I was
working at the guinea pig story. I became
so much interested in it – it grew longer and
longer, and I kept re-writing earlier
chapters. In spring, before lambing time I
came in sight of a halt (or convenient pause)
in the tale; but before I could finish off the
series of stories up to that point – the spring
work outside commenced – and various
disappointments and annoyances; so that I
had no time to "finish" the adventures of
the caravan. Besides being out of tune and
cross. The wanderings of the circus
company go on and on without end or
"finis"; next winter I hope to write out
carefully a sufficient number of varied tales
up to a point that is a convenient breaking-
off-place. I could have finished it after a
fashion; but I like to do my work carefully.

The yellow-and-white Mrs Tuppenny-
guinea-pig is such a beauty, she looks twice
the size now. The little dark one died in the
cold weather, I do not think it was the cold
though. It was rather badly treated by the
other, and always seemed scared and thin.
Nip my favourite colley [sic] has a
promising puppy, a blue gray coloured
dog. I have not started to break it in yet for
sheep work.

I was very much pleased with the way
you wrote about your visit here; it was well
done in every way, no word too much nor
anything one could dislike; and it made me
understand so well the sort of interest that
readers of the books feel when they see the
real place. A very pleasant account of the
old house. I wonder what you had for tea –
was it pear jam? I forget! This cottage is
nearly smothered with roses, the rain has
weighed them down over the porch and
door. There was a spell of fine weather
early in the spring between Easter &
Whitsuntide. Tell your mother it was
pleasant to see the holiday makers sitting on
the grass on the new recreation ground; the
walk beside Windermere lake is much
appreciated. [Mrs Coolidge had contributed
to a fund to save a strip of foreshore near
Windermere Ferry from extensive building
development.] We had a jolly camping
party of girl guides at the farm. They
brought 5 tents.

I will send you a copy of the first chapter
of "Over the hills & far away"; but you
must understand there is not so much
exclusively guinea pig in the other later
chapters after Tuppenny joins the caravan. I
don't know what Miss Mahony [the editor

of *The Horn Book*] is thinking of my delays
– but I *can not* write if I am out of humour. I
hope you have been well, as we have – With
very kind regards to your mother & you,
and thanks for the Horn book which I will
always keep.

yrs sincerely
Beatrix Heelis

Yes, it has been a lovely spring of blossoms.
The hawthorn bushes were like snow, and
the bluebells like a bit of sky come down.

June 29.28

Dear Henry P.

Keep this if you like [the handwritten
revised version of *The Tale of Tuppenny*], as
I have another copy. I have written perhaps
six pieces of this length, but there are
connecting pieces that I am not satisfied
with yet; and I want another fairytale
(partly invented) to round off this
collection. And I do not wish to include one
or two that I sent to your mother last
autumn; because they belong to Cherry tree
camp. You see – you and I take our fiction
*very seriously*. The circus did *not* get as far as
cherry tree camp during this first part of
their wanderings. They only had 4 camps
(I) in the stone quarry, (2) at the Ellers Ford,
(where they met with the flock of sheep)
(3) Codlin Croft farm where Paddy Pig was
seriously unwell, (4) after a journey
through the woods, to a camp on the moor
where they met the Plopfoots. They were
hearing & telling stories all the way, so their
progress (and mine!) is slow.

yours sincerely,
Beatrix Potter

*Paddy Pig arriving, 'seriously unwell',
at Codlin Croft farm, from* The Fairy
Caravan *(1929)*

Oct 27th 29

Castle Cottage
Sawrey
nr Ambleside

Dear Henry P.

I hope by this time you have received your copy of Our Book [*The Fairy Caravan*]! I have got my English copies bound in gray paper backs; it looks well. I am already in trouble – I cannot give the correct name and ownership of the horse waiting at the smithy. It is obviously not really "Maggret", because she was a pony, belonging to Joe Taylor, and Maggret and her master have been dead for many years. If it is a white horse it would be Ambrose Martindale's. But to the best of my recollection the animal was brown, when I sketched the smithy – so it's either John Kirkbride's or William Postlethwaite's. William is quite enough in the book being owner of Fan, and Dick, Duke, Sally; but he wishes to claim that horse. Sally was white in old age; a grand wagon mare but a kicker. In fact it was always suspected 'Sally' had 'done something' in her youth; William bought her so cheap, it was suspicious. I did not intend to draw a white horse. I left it light to try and look as if its hind quarters were in the sun.

I hope you and your mother are very well. This year has been hard work, (apart from the drawings). I shall be glad of a quiet winter when the last of the fairs are over. We are selling 300 sheep at Ambleside on Tuesday; and same day my stirks [yearling bullocks or heifers] go to a Scotch sale at Newcastleton. Prices have been good up to now, and we had a grand haytime & harvest.

The weather has been wild and rough. Today is glorious, after a white hoar frost. The autumn colours are still splendid. After dinner Mr Heelis & I are going to Coniston. There is a lovely stretch of mountain and valley to sell there and the National Trust are trying to buy it [Monk Coniston Estate]. Did you drive that way when you came here I wonder – past Tilberthwaite and Yewdale. I am very interested because my great grandfather had land there and I have always longed to buy it back and give it to the Trust in remembrance. I was very much attached to my grandmother Jessy Crompton and said to be very like her, "only not so good looking!!" according to old folks. Perhaps I will be able to help out of this book – it would be like a fairy tale, would it not? I would be glad to hear from you and your mother how it is received. Mr McKay seems quite satisfied with the advance sales.

I have 52 copies bound here with the English title page and copyright notice.

I remain with kind regards to you and your mother

yrs sincerely
Beatrix Heelis

Tuppenny is flourishing – Charles [the cockerel] is having a severe moult; but I hope to nurse him through. He is very old, but still fighting. I had to hold a young cockerell [sic] this morning and let Charles give it a good kicking. He will get killed someday I am afraid.

217

Jan.1.1930

Castle Cottage
Sawrey
nr Ambleside
England

Dear Henry P.

I am glad to hear that the dedication has given you pleasure; and you show discriminating appreciation (as Louisa Pussycat might say) in your choice of favourite pictures. I was perplexed what to do with the hair brushing picture till I had a sudden inspiration about pig tails. But do you not notice it should have been Xarifa who '*brushed* behind"? And on p 183 [p 154 of the current edition of *The Fairy Caravan*] Jenny Ferret should have worn spectacles.

The coloured plate of the blue bell wood is bound into a wrong chapter; pony Billy is without the caravan; I intended it for the chapter where he goes back alone to look for Paddy Pig, and hears a faint tingle ringle of laughing from the thousands of blue bells in the wood.

Now for the old words – *sneck* is the sort of door latch that lifts/opens by pressing a flat thumb piece.

All our cats from generation to generation learn the trick; Tamsine jumps up and opens the door into the kitchen. She tries the house door if she is left loose at nights; it is rather weird and troublesome, but I usually shut her in the granary. I had a dog, old Fleet, who "went one better". She used to open a similar latch in the iron garden gate, and what's more she (standing on her hind legs) holding the latch used to step backwards pulling the gate open towards herself. I could never teach her to close it; I have heard of a fox-terrier which would shut the door obediently. *Midden stead*, a 'stead' or place where farm-yard manure is heaped. *Clothes swill* Swills are flatish [sic] baskets woven out of interlaced thin broad parings of oak wood. *Uveco* a cattle food, yellow flakey rolled indian corn, from which the oil has been extracted. It is a waste product and comparatively cheap. *Lish,* active supple energetic; an expressive adjective; an old man who has preserved his youth and worn well is said to be "as lish as a lad". *Coppy* stools, three legged stools such as are used for milking. "*Shippon*" a stable-like building containing stalls – or 'boosts' – for tying up cattle. *Ring widdie* the double ring, with a swivel between the rings which slides loosely up & down on the rett-stake to which the cow is haltered. It would be possible for a ring

widdie to "clink" on the stone floor of the bruist [rough bed or shelter]; but "clink" is *not* the right word for a very pleasing sound. When anyone opens the shippon door, there is a sort of scraping noise of the rings, usually followed by a gentle 'moo', if it is feeding time. There are new fangled ways of tying up cows; but I prefer the ring-widdies. '*Keshes*', wild parsnip, tall coarse plants – does not Shakspeare [sic] speak of "rude kecksies-burrs"; burrs doubtless were burr docks = teazles. Wither [or] "widdershins", contrary way – there is an old verse "The stars shall gae wither shins Ere I will leave thee" *Demerara* sugar. A soft sugar not much refined. I suppose in old times it came from Demerara. What would you guess if I had put in the puzzling numerals of the old sheep counting,

"Yan tyan tethera methera pimp

  1    2    3    4    5

(is it 'pimp' or dick?) 'bumfit' is 15.

Very interesting words they are, for they are supposed to be one of the few remains of the old Celtic language. Sheep have been kept in this district from early times. A fragment of woolen [sic] cloth was found in a "barrow" or ancient burial mound with a funeral urn, and bronze implements. I guess the stone men who set up 'Long Meg' and the stone circles had sheep. Now I wish you and your Mother a very Happy Year. Tuppenny is still flourishing; and we are all pleased with the success of the book.

yours sincerely<br>Beatrix Heelis

*Opposite: Xarifa the dormouse and Tuppenny the long-haired guinea pig in* The Fairy Caravan *(1929)*

Dec 15.31                    Castle Cottage
                             Sawrey
                             nr Ambleside

Dear Henry P.

How is the algebra? Still troublesome? or have you mastered it? I have got along fairly well in the world without ever having acquired the art of doing sums! Never by any chance did they come right. What is the old rhyme?

> "Multiplication is vexation,
> Division is as bad.
> The Rule of Three it puzzles me,
> And Fractions drive me mad!"

But I fear *you* will have to learn to understand Euclid – bother him!

I am struggling with another volume of the Caravan. I think of calling it "Cherry Tree Camp". [It was never published.] There are a number of stories that were not used for the other book – though I do now think I was rather extravagant in using up all the prettiest in one volume. This collection does not wander up amongst the hills, it is in a sunny pasture, surrounded by woods. As a matter of fact the site is where the Girl Guides camp in summer, and the Scouts. We had such a number for the August holidays, over 80. And one troop arrived in such a downpour that they could not get their tents up so there were 30 sleeping in the barn and cooking in our small kitchen, for 2 hours.

The country is very lonely and deserted now, in winter. Last week one of the shepherds, searching for stray sheep, found the bones of a poor man who had been missing for many months.

The sheep sales have been bad this autumn, disastrous prices. I am fortunate in not having to pay rent, as I farm my own land. The tenant farmers are having a severe struggle; if things don't improve next year many of them will have to give up. There has been a sprinkling of snow twice on the top of the fells, but none in the valleys, and it is very mild and muggy weather. We are quite well here (amongst measles and influenza epidemics!) I hope you and you mother are well, and with all good wishes for Christmas and New Year,

> I remain yrs aff
> Beatrix Heelis

I hope we will meet again in more prosperous times. Very few Americans have been to the Lakes this season.

I wish someone would tell me how to address the friends in U.S.A.! Do you put Esq or Mr on the envelope? I am always puzzled if I write to Mr McKay.

*Rescuing sheep on the fells in* The Fairy Caravan *(1929)*

Dec. 14.33                    Castle Cottage
                              Sawrey

Dear Henry P.

This comes to wish you and your Mother a Merry Christmas and Happy new year. I had a most interesting letter from her last Christmas, about your studies and interests. I liked the cutting that she enclosed, it was well written and interesting – something to say is the first point; and the manner of saying it is the second.

I have very little to say now! except that I have been poorly after a chill six weeks ago – a great waste of time in ones [sic] old age, although the doctor says lumbago is of no consequence.

Last winter my mother's illness & death interrupted my Christmas letters. She was very very old, and fretful, she had lived her time [Helen Potter had died in December 1932 at the age of ninety-three].

We have had a most lovely summer & autumn, and no snow until last week in this part of the country. It is not deep but the roads are very slippery which is awkward on steep hills.

There have been rather more American visitors this summer – though they all complain of the bad times.

Over here things are decidedly on the mend especially in farming – our lamb sales were about £200 better than last year's sales. But it seems as though your country has much to struggle through yet.

My kindest remembrance to your mother. I hope someday in better times you may visit the Lakes again.

yrs sincerely
Beatrix Heelis

*Footprints in the snow, Near Sawrey,*
*painted by Beatrix in March 1909*

*Above: Nancy Dean*

*Below: Nancy with her grandmother,
Bertha Mahony Miller*

## NANCY DEAN

Among the Americans Beatrix enjoyed seeing and writing to most were those who worked with children's books and with a number of them she made deep and lasting friendships. The first to visit Castle Cottage was the Superintendent of Children's Work at the New York Public Library, Anne Carroll Moore. On her way back from France in 1921, where she had been visiting children's libraries on behalf of the American Committee for Devastated France, Miss Moore's tentative approach to Beatrix was answered with a warm invitation to lunch. The meeting was such a success, the exchange of ideas so stimulating for both of them, that lunch extended to tea and then to the visitor staying the night.

The editor of children's books for J.B. Lippincott in New York, Helen Dean Fish, was invited to Castle Cottage for tea in 1930 and her initial letter from Beatrix encouraged further approaches: 'Most welcome! I always tell nice Americans to send other nice Americans along. Perhaps "understanding Americans" would be a better adjective than "nice". You come because you understand the books, and love the same old tales that I do – not from any impertinent curiosity.'

But not everyone was able to travel the long distance between America and the Lake District and much of Beatrix's contact with Americans took place solely through letters. Nancy Dean never met Beatrix but she was only a child of seven when she received her first letter from the author of her favourite book and only eleven when Beatrix died. Nancy's contact with Beatrix came through her grandmother.

Bertha Mahony was the founder of The Bookshop for Boys and Girls in Boston and the co-founder and first editor in 1924 of *The Horn Book*. She had approached Beatrix in 1925 asking for some personal details and for an account of how she came to write her books, all of which she would publish in the magazine. Beatrix was reluctant to supply them, commenting to Anne Carroll Moore, 'I have a most intense dislike to advertisement. (And I have got on quite well without it.) On the other hand, a mystery is silly, and it invites curiosity.' But Beatrix liked the copies of *The Horn Book* that had accompanied Miss Mahony's letter and she eventually supplied a short note, following it a few months later with fifty copies of four of the illustrations for *Peter Rabbit*. These she asked to be sold at one guinea each to help the National Trust to save the strip of the foreshore of Windermere from developers. It was the start of a long and enduring correspondence between the two women.

During the summer of 1939 Mrs Bertha Mahony Miller (as she had now become) read *The Fairy Caravan* to the youngest of her husband's grandchildren, Nancy Dean, who so took the book to her heart that she was seen later patting it and saying, 'Oh, lovely *Fairy Caravan*, if only there were ten of you.' Mrs Miller recounted the story to Beatrix, whose response was to write the letter that follows directly to Nancy. From then onwards Nancy was mentioned frequently in the exchanges between Beatrix and Mrs Miller, and Beatrix later told Anne Carroll Moore that, 'I have a weakness for the name of Nancy.'

In November 1940 Beatrix assured Mrs Miller that she would 'write out Nancy's Christmas story before the scribbly fit passes' and a few months earlier she had promised 'to copy out an old story for Nancy', but there is no record of what that story was. The following year, in response to a request from Nancy for news of the animals in *The Fairy Caravan*, Beatrix wrote out two of the stories from the material she was collecting together for a possible sequel and sent them to Mrs Miller. *The Solitary Mouse* featured a shy brown mouse, called Joseph Moscrop after Beatrix's faithful Scottish shepherd; *Wag-by-Wall* was a tale about poor Sally Benson and the clock that stood by the wall in her house. Mrs Miller's response was to ask if she could publish them in *The Horn Book*, a suggestion that at first surprised the author and then, once she had got used to it, delighted her. She asked, however, to be allowed to work on the stories before publication and first she cut them considerably in length. *The Solitary Mouse* was then

Wag-by-Wall *was published in book form in America in 1944*

223

completely rewritten and appeared in the May 1942 issue of *The Horn Book* as *The Lonely Hills*, with only three paragraphs of the original story left. Publication of *Wag-by-Wall* was held over so it would feature in the twentieth-anniversary number of *The Horn Book*, due in May 1944, but Beatrix was never to see it in print for she died on 22 December 1943.

Nancy Dean inherited her grandmother's love of children's books. In 1953, after receiving a Bachelor of Arts from Wellesley College, she worked as a library assistant in the Fitchburg Youth Library in Fitchburg, Mass. for nine months. The children's department was in a very new, very modern addition to the nineteenth-century public library building. It was airy and bright and filled with one of the best collections of children's books in the United States. 'It was heaven. Every morning when I walked into the building my spirits lifted.' In 1954, Nancy married William Kingman – who was then a naval officer, now an investment adviser. They have two children, a son and a daughter, and a young granddaughter, Martha. Nancy writes:

> After my grandmother died in 1969, I lost touch with the children's book world. My children were in their teens, and my interests were developing in other directions, primarily horticultural. At present, as an amateur horticulturist, my love of books is still obvious in a good sized collection of volumes on natural history, gardens and gardening.

Bill and I haven't yet visited Sawrey. Our only trip to England was spent in the south, but next time we plan to explore the Lake District. It will be fun to tell Martha about Peter Rabbit's countryside. I've started to buy books for her, and soon shall show her my watercolor of the curtseying mouse from *Tailor of Gloucester*. It is one of the copies of illustrations Beatrix Potter sent to this country to raise money for the land conservation. When Martha is older, we will read *The Fairy Caravan* together.

*The curtseying mouse from* The Tailor of Gloucester *as she appears in the book (1903)*

July 30.40                                Castle Cottage
                                          Sawrey
                                          Ambleside

My dear Nancy

So you would like news of the Fairy Caravan? Where is it camping? or whither is it wandering? I wonder if I can tell you! When we grow old and wear spectacles, our eyes are not bright like children's eyes, nor our ears so quick, to see and hear the fairies. Just a glimpse I catch sometimes through the trees, and I hear a tinkling tinkle tinkling of little pots and pans & cans. I seemed to know last week that they were in Clogger Meadow. I saw something white through the trees; I looked hard – and alas it was a cow! Two wood cutters were working in the wood. Until the underwood of nut bushes grows up again – Sandy and Pony William will not stay more than a night or two in the lovely green meadow that lies hidden amongst woods. And they did not go to Cherry tree camp where I *know* they have always camped in May, when the cherry blossom & hawthorns are in flower. And now in August the Girl Guides cannot camp there either because there is a footpath leading to another sort of camp.

So the Guides are camping in a little larch wood near our cottage, and their tents are dyed green. Where can the circus have wandered to? I believe I know!

Right away amongst the fells – the green & blue hills above my sheep farm in Troutbeck. Such a lonely place, miles along a lovely green road. That was where I first saw the mark of little horse shoes. There is an old barn there that we call High Buildings – it is never used except sometimes by the shepherds; and when I was younger and used to take long walks I used to eat my bread & cheese at High Buildings, or shelter from the rain. That was where the Caravan sheltered in a very wild rainstorm, and Xarifa made acquaintance with the melancholy Mouse. There was a story about that place and that very wet night – but it was so silly I really could not print it. Besides it might have offended my friend Joseph, who is not really a mouse. He is a shepherd. Every spring Joseph Moscrop has come to help with the lambs; for 14 springs he has come from Scotland with his dogs and fed the weak lambs and the twins with his milk bottle. And in very cold springs Joseph has a little gin in a little bottle and last March Joseph told me "the corrk had coom oot" in his pocket!! There was a smell of gin; but Joseph is a total abstainer – what Americans call "dry". He does not like being laughed at, especially on Sundays. He is wonderful with lambs and dogs; we all love Joseph. I do not think he would approve of me calling a mouse "Joseph Mouse-trap", perhaps the censor would not tell him? If I copied out that very silly story? There was one about Cherry tree camp – but it was long and tiresome.

Good night Nancy, I am going to bed.

Yours aff
Beatrix Potter

225

## ALISON HART

In April 1940 Reginald Hart, a keen collector of children's books, received a letter from Beatrix Potter confirming that the illustrations for *Johnny Town-Mouse* had indeed been sketched in Hawkshead. He was tracing the origin of each of the little books for a private record, *A Lakeland Enquiry*, and he was coming to take photographs in the neighbourhood at Easter with his wife, Betty, and their daughter, Alison. After photographing in and around the villages of Hawkshead and Sawrey, the Harts called at Hill Top, only to discover that the house had been lent by Beatrix to her cousin, Sir William Hyde-Parker, and his family while he recovered from an accident. Reginald Hart was refused permission to photograph either the house or the farm and he was forced to return to Blackpool with his project unfinished. Undeterred, the family made plans to repeat their journey to Sawrey in October when they would make a direct approach to Beatrix.

This time they stayed at High Green Gate with Mary Postlethwaite, who was the daughter of 'Farmer Potatoes' in *The Roly-Poly Pudding*. The house was almost opposite Castle Cottage and when they called on Mrs Heelis, three-year-old Alison was clutching her copy of *The Pie and The Patty-Pan* for Beatrix to sign. Reginald Hart later recorded his impressions:

> Seventy odd years may have bowed her and a failing eyesight may have made the steel rimmed spectacles necessary but her complexion remained rosy and there was a deal of shrewdness behind those glasses. She was wearing a grey tweed skirt, a white blouse and a grey cardigan, with a little lace edged cap over her grey hair. Yes, she would write in Alison's book and would we come in.

After inscribing the book 'With love' Beatrix then turned her attention to Reginald Hart's *Lakeland Enquiry*. An assurance that it was not for publication secured permission

*Alison Hart, aged 5, with one of Beatrix's Pekes at Castle Cottage*

to photograph at Hill Top but there was the reservation, 'I cannot show you the inside as it has evacuees.' The conversation then turned to the work of Randolph Caldecott and the Harts were taken upstairs to see the set of his original drawings for *The Mad Dog*, bought many years before by Beatrix's father, Rupert Potter. On leaving Castle Cottage Reginald Hart was presented with a signed copy of the privately-printed *Tailor of Gloucester*; for Alison there was a kiss and a request for her photograph. Reginald Hart was then able to continue his trail of the little books and *A Lakeland Enquiry Part II* has photographs of Hill Top house and farm, of Jemima Puddle-Duck's hillside and wood, and of Tom Kitten's gate and garden path.

For the next two years the Harts returned to Sawrey for their holidays, each time calling on Beatrix. Reginald Hart was an architect by profession and had been sent to Blackpool from London by the Ministry of Works, where part of his job was concerned with the granting of permits for building and for the allocation of materials. He was able to give Beatrix some valuable advice in both respects and he helped to ensure that her applications for permission to repair her property went to the right desk. He also shared many of Beatrix's enthusiasms and they had long discussions about early pottery, slipware, antique furniture and children's book illustration.

*Alison with Beatrix in 1942*

On their visit to Castle Cottage in the summer of 1942, when Alison was five, she was rather more interested in Beatrix's pekinese dogs, Tzusee and Chuleh, than in their seventy-six-year-old mistress. She was handed precious pieces of rationed chocolate with which to feed the dogs, and she posed with them in the photographs her father took in the garden. Beatrix was so pleased with the pictures that she asked for copies to send to America: 'I am quite delighted with the photographs of the little dogs – and *Alison* is even more delightful!'

It was in November 1942 that Beatrix ended one of her letters to Reginald Hart, 'Tell Alison – I may – just – possibly – address to her a Christmas letter – from Chuleh.' The Christmas letter duly arrived. It was the story of *The*

*Beatrix gave Reginald Hart a signed copy of her privately printed* Tailor of Gloucester *(1902). The Warne edition (1903) includes the pictures (above and below) of one of their shared interests – beautiful china*

*Chinese Umbrella*, dated 19 December 1942. A few days later, on 23 December, Beatrix sent the same story to her friend Louie Choyce (see page 177). She had made a few changes to the text, added a bit more colour and another small drawing. Both versions are reproduced here for comparison; neither of them has been published before.

Early in 1943 the Harts informed Beatrix that they planned to return to Sawrey in the early summer but by the middle of August they had not arrived and Beatrix was missing them. 'Summer has not lasted long – and no Alison has come to see the pekes and the old body.' It was September before the Harts managed to get there and they found that Beatrix was ill in bed with bronchitis. Even so she welcomed them to Castle Cottage and they were able to be of assistance to her – as she reported to an American friend: 'Reg. S. Hart . . . is an immensely tall thin man, with lengthy limbs . . . a gibbon monkey. He hung up some plates – old blue delph – opposite my bed last time he and his family were on holiday, it was comical to see him reach up to the picture rail without the stepladder. Mrs Hart is short & shy, Alison is a little dear.'

Alison had brought news of a new family cat, a Seal-Point Siamese christened Simpkin but which they usually called Buzzy. Beatrix remembered the cat when she wrote to Reginald Hart in November, 'Chuleh and Suzie [Tzusee] send most kind regards to the new Siamese kitten, but they would bark at it unless properly introduced. It may be rather the same colour as Chuleh.' Beatrix also brought Reginald Hart up-to-date with her health. 'I have not quite got rid of the doctor, but I hope as the weather improves I may get back to my usual health – or nearly so – one must expect to lose a little ground as one gets older.'

But by mid-December Beatrix was back in bed and she died at Castle Cottage on 22 December.

The Harts left Blackpool in 1943 to live in Cambridge, where Alison continued her schooling. In 1955 she started training to be a doctor at the Middlesex Hospital in London. She married a surgeon, Brian Duff, in 1965 and they have two children, a boy and a girl.

## THE CHINESE UMBRELLA

I do not hear many new stories now-a-days, but I have heard a tale about an umbrella; an umbrella with a duck's head handle.

Umbrellas get lost. Nobody can tell me where that umbrella has gone to?

Pekes know all about umbrellas, because the first umbrella came from China. The Emperor of China had an umbrella and he had 8 little Pekes to carry his train when he went for a walk.

This story begins with a biscuit. Our Mrs Rogerson in the kitchen gave ½ a dog biscuit to TzuZee and ½ to Chuleh.

Tzuzee ate her ½ biscuit, but Chuleh buried her ½ biscuit in the garden.

At night it rained and rained. Pekes do not like getting wet. But that evening TzsuZee and Chuleh stopped outside in the rain for an hour. They would not come in until they had dug up the biscuit, and agreed who would eat it. At last they came indoors, just as sopping wet as a wet sponge.

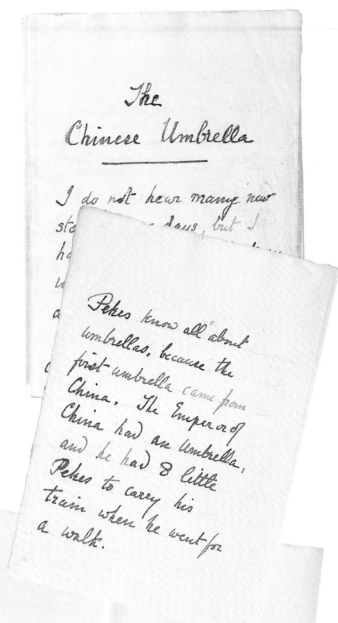

I said to Chuleh "What do you mean by this? do you expect to sleep on my bed, like a watering can? *Where is your umbrella*? You naughty naughty wet dog!"

Chuleh made no answer. I rubbed and rubbed and dried her with a towel before the fire until she was dry enough for a footwarmer. I told her she must really get an umbrella. Waterproofs require coupons. Umbrellas do not require coupons. [By this time in the Second World War clothes were rationed and could be bought only on the surrender of personal clothing coupons.] "Go and get an umbrella for yourself – you naughty wet dog,!"

Miss Louie Choyce is living in Tom Kitten's house with her brother Tom Choyce. She wanted an umbrella. So she bought a Jemima Umbrella.

I never saw one before!

This morning before I got up Miss Louie Choyce came to say "Good morning Mrs Heelis! Good morning Suzee and Chuleh.

Chuleh did not say anything she was curled up at my feet, like a footwarmer.

Then Miss Choyce said "Such a funny thing happened about an umbrella – an umbrella with a duck's head – its gone!"

I looked at Chuleh: but Chuleh said nothing. "Explain yourself?" said I to Miss Louie Choyce.

"I wanted an umbrella, so I bought a Jemima Puddleduck umbrella at Lizzie May Coward's shop in Hawkshead while I waited for the Ambleside bus – but the Rebecca Umbrella is gone! gone!"

"Have you lost your umbrella?" said I to Miss Choyce. (Chuleh opened her one eye, but said nothing) [She had lost an eye in January 1942 while out for a walk.] 'No, said Miss Choyce 'I have it hanging on a loop at my wrist. Its Rebecca has gone." "This is a confused story?"

So Miss Choyce said "I ran to Lizzie May's shop, between buses, she has sold all the Peter Rabbit jugs and tea cups, but she has two Puddle duck umbrellas, so I bought Jemima. And when I got to Brathay Hall – (where Miss Choyce dishwashes for the Waifs and Strays [evacuees]) all the ladies who dishwash Chuleh seemed to be listening: she dishwashes too said "What a lovely umbrella! We all want duck umbrellas! And Mrs Thompson who is champion dishwasher, gave Miss Choyce 15/ and said "run to the shop while you wait for the Sawrey bus! buy me Rebecca!"

So Miss Choyce ran to the shop – she runs fast. Lizzie May burst out laughing and said – "How many people in the Ambleside bus did you show Jemima Umbrella to? There has been 1–2–3 ladies out of the 10 o'clock bus and 3–4–5 out of the 1 o'clock bus! Rebecca Umbrella is gone! No, I don't know *who* bought it; the shop was full of customers – ladies and little Dogs – wanting duck umbrellas."

"Where can it have gone to?" said Miss Choyce –

"I don't know!"

We might ask Chuleh?

Where is Rebecca Umbrella?
Love and a Merry Christmas to Alison from Tzuzee and Chuleh and 'Beatrix Potter' Dec 19th 42

231

[The version of *The Chinese Umbrella* that
Beatrix sent to her friend, Louie Choyce]

The
Chinese Umbrella—

I do not often hea[r]
tale now-a-days. I [
rather a funny one [
umbrella. Um[
—missing. Nobod[y]
has become of th[

Pekes know all a[
because the first [
came from China [
The Emperor of Ch[ina]
an umbrella, and n[
8 little Pekinese dogs
carry his train when [he]
went for a walk.

This story begins with a biscuit.
Our Mrs Rogerson in the kitchen
gave ½ a dog biscuit to Tzu zee,
and ½ a biscuit to Chu Leh.
[     ] ate her ½ biscuit [
[                      ] in

Love and a Merry Christmas —

Beatrix Potter
Dec 26° 42

They hate rain
they stopped
the biscuit and
in sopping w[...]
— I said to Ch[...]
meaning [...]
sleep on my [...]
. Where is y[...]
naughty [...]

her and rubbed her
with a bath towel
until she was
dry enough for a
foot warmer.

Next morning Miss Louisa Cho[...]
who is li[...] in Tom Kitten's [...]
[...] before I go[...]
[...] morning [...]
[...]u ze[...]
Umbrella

'I must tell you such a funny thing
has happened about an umbrella,
with a duck's head. It is gone!
Gone I don't know where?"
I looked at Chuleh.
She pretended to be
asleep.
"Have you lost your
umbrella?" I asked Miss Choyce.
"No, said she, I h[...]
Umbrella

hanging on my wrist with a loop
but Rebecca Umbrella
is gone!" "Pray ex-
plain?" So Miss
Choyce continued —
[...] umbrella so I ra[...]

When Miss Choyce arrived at Brathay
Hall where she dis wash[...] [...]

buses! Buy me Rebecca Umbrella!" So Miss Choyce ran nimbly to
the shop.         But when she opened the door of the shop Lizzie May
Coward burst out laughing and asked—"How many people in the bus did
you show Jemima Umbrella to? Here has been 1.2.3 ladies out
of the 10 o'clock bus, and 4.5.6 out of the 12 o'clock bus and they
all wanted Puddle duck umbrellas! Rebecca Puddleduck is gone!"
"Gone! Gone? Where has she gone?" asked Miss Louisa Choyce.
"I do not know. I don't know who bought it! The shop was full of
customers— little dogs and ladies, all wanting Puddle duck Umbrellas."
Gone! Gone!! Where has Rebecca Puddleduck gone to?
Suppose we ask Chuleh?

233

## LETTER ACKNOWLEDGEMENTS

The author and publishers are grateful to the following for their kind permission to reproduce the letters in this book, which appear on the pages listed below.

Felicity Barker, 158, 159; John E. Benson, 191; Dr Robert Burn, 155; Lucie Carr, 109–12; Henry P. Coolidge, 215–21; Free Library of Philadelphia, Rare Book Department, 76, 77 (*left*), 161–2, 180; Doris Frohnsdorff, 181–2, 188 (*both*); Joan Frost, 122–3, 126–7; John Gibson, 131; Alan Gill, 175; Betty S. Hart, 120–1, 229–31; Judy Hough, 174 (*left*); Houghton Library, Harvard University, Department of Printing and Graphic Arts, 42–3, 47–51, 54, 61–2, 64–5, 69–70, 77–8; Urling Sibley Iselin Collection, 78–9; Nancy Kingman, 225; Lady Marian Langham, 147; The National Trust, 36, 81–3, 208; The Pierpont Morgan Library, New York, *MA 2009*, 21–2, 28–35, 38–40, 44–6, 52–4, 58, 66–7; Private Collections, 98, 123–6, 128, 178, 232–3; Robin Rogerson, 150–1; Toronto Public Library (the Osborne Collection of Early Children's Books), 198–205; Alexander Turnbull Library, National Library of New Zealand, 134–5; National Art Library, Victoria and Albert Museum, 26, 56–7, 60–1, 63, 68–9, 71–6, 80, 84–9, 100, 104–5, 141–5, 156–7, 166–70, 176, 207; Frederick Warne Archive, 23–4, 164, 183–7, 189–90, 209; John Wilson Catalogue, 174 (*right*); Collection of Mary K. Young, 102, 137–9, 160 (*both*)

Despite every effort to trace them, the owners of the miniature letters on pages 90–3 and of the letter to Neville Rowson on page 192 are still unknown.


## ILLUSTRATION ACKNOWLEDGEMENTS

Where an illustration is part of a letter it has no separate acknowledgement. The majority of the additional illustrations are taken from Beatrix Potter's books, published by Frederick Warne. Other photographs and illustrations are reproduced by courtesy of the following.

Beatrix Potter Society, 7; Trustees of the Linder Collection, Book Trust, 9, 101, 165, 176; Museum of Fine Arts, Boston, 212; Frederick Warne Archive, 3 (*left*), 66, 91 (*left*), 197, 208; Private Collections, 3 (*right*), 6, 7, 11, 12, 13, 14, 15, 16, 17, 18, 19 (*above*), 20 (*below*), 94, 95, 96, 97, 100, 106, 108, 114, 117, 119, 132, 136, 146, 148, 149, 150, 152, 153, 157, 171, 177, 191, 194, 195, 202, 204, 210, 211, 222, 226, 227; Toronto Public Library (the Osborne Collection of Early Children's Books), 193; National Art Library, Victoria and Albert Museum, 19 (*below*), 20 (*above*), 49, 105, 107, 115, 140, 172, 173, 188, 206, 213, 214, 221

## SOME FURTHER READING

*Beatrix Potter's Art* Anne Stevenson Hobbs, Frederick
  Warne, 1989

*Beatrix Potter: The V & A Collection* Anne Stevenson Hobbs
  and Joyce Irene Whalley, Frederick Warne/The Victoria
  and Albert Museum, 1985

*The Tale of Beatrix Potter* Margaret Lane, revised edition,
  Penguin, 1986

*A History of the Writings of Beatrix Potter* Leslie Linder,
  revised edition, Frederick Warne, 1987

*The Journal of Beatrix Potter* Leslie Linder, revised edition,
  Frederick Warne, 1989

*Dear Ivy, Dear June: Letters from Beatrix Potter* Margaret
  Crawford Maloney, Toronto Public Library, 1977

*Beatrix Potter's Americans: Selected Letters* Jane Crowell
  Morse, The Horn Book, 1982

*Beatrix Potter, A Bibliographical Check List* Jane Quinby, Ian
  Hodgkins, 1983

*Beatrix Potter: Artist, Storyteller and Countrywoman* Judy
  Taylor, Frederick Warne, 1986

*Beatrix Potter's Letters: A Selection* Judy Taylor, Frederick
  Warne, 1989

*Beatrix Potter 1866–1943: The Artist and Her World* Judy
  Taylor, Joyce Irene Whalley, Anne Stevenson Hobbs and
  Elizabeth M. Battrick, Frederick Warne/The National
  Trust, 1987

*Yours Affectionately, Peter Rabbit* Frederick Warne, 1983

All the Little Books are currently in print with Frederick
Warne, as is *The Fairy Caravan*.

# INDEX

Figures in italics refer to illustrations.